FIRST LADIES OF THE REPUBLIC

First Ladies of the Republic

MARTHA WASHINGTON, ABIGAIL ADAMS, DOLLEY MADISON, *and the* CREATION *of an* ICONIC AMERICAN ROLE

Jeanne E. Abrams

NEW YORK UNIVERSITY PRESS

New York

NEW YORK UNIVERSITY PRESS
New York
www.nyupress.org
© 2018 by New York University
All rights reserved

Book designed and typeset by Charles B. Hames

References to Internet websites (URLs) were accurate at the time
of writing. Neither the author nor New York University Press is
responsible for URLs that may have expired or changed
since the manuscript was prepared.

Library of Congress Cataloging-in-Publication Data
Names: Abrams, Jeanne E., 1951– author.
Title: First ladies of the republic : Martha Washington, Abigail Adams, Dolley Madison,
and the creation of an iconic American role / Jeanne E. Abrams.
Description: New York : New York University Press, 2018. |
Includes bibliographical references and index.
Identifiers: LCCN 2017034128 | ISBN 9781479886531 (cl : alk. paper)
Subjects: LCSH: Presidents' spouses—United States—Biography. | Washington, Martha,
1731–1802. | Adams, Abigail, 1744–1818. | Madison, Dolley, 1768–1849.
Classification: LCC E176.2 .A27 2018 | DDC 973.09/9 [B] —dc23
LC record available at https://lccn.loc.gov/2017034128

New York University Press books are printed on acid-free paper, and
their binding materials are chosen for strength and durability. We
strive to use environmentally responsible suppliers and materials
to the greatest extent possible in publishing our books.

Manufactured in the United States of America

10 9 8 7 6 5 4 3 2 1

Also available as an ebook

CONTENTS

Prologue

When George Washington was inaugurated as the first president of the United States on April 30, 1789, King George III and Queen Charlotte occupied the throne in Great Britain. Queen Charlotte had been raised as a princess in a small German duchy, and the proposed royal union was cemented only after intense secret negotiations. Charlotte met her future husband just hours before their evening wedding at the Chapel Royal in St. James's Palace in London on September 8, 1761, and she spoke no English at the time. The English-born George was the heir to the Hanoverian royal line and ascended to the throne in 1760 at the age of twenty-two. Yet, despite their exceedingly short acquaintance prior to their marriage, by all accounts they shared many mutual interests, led a relatively simple lifestyle compared to earlier British monarchs, and before the development of George's mental illness, their amiable and long union resulted in fifteen children, thirteen of whom survived to adulthood.[1]

For their official coronation at London's Westminster Abbey, just two weeks after their marriage, the English royal couple were decked out in elaborate costumes, and the event followed intricate ceremonial rituals that had been developed over centuries. The coronation reflected the pomp, splendor, and opulence that had long characterized the investiture of European crowned heads of state, and it was witnessed by a crowd made up of members of the British royalty and the aristocracy in resplendent dress. The new queen Charlotte wore a lavishly decorated ermine-trimmed, silver-and-gold embroidered gown, which was studded with diamonds, pearls "as big as Cherrys"[2] and other priceless gems, and on her head rested a "Circlet of Gold adorned with Jewels." The train of her dress was supported by a royal princess, and sixteen barons held a canopy over her head.[3]

In contrast, Washington's wife Martha was still in Virginia at their Mount Vernon plantation home at the time of his far less ostentatious first-term inauguration, when he took the oath of office on the balcony of Federal Hall on April 30, 1789, in New York City. It was witnessed by members of Congress, marked by the ringing of church bells, and then cheered enthusiastically by a crowd of ordinary citizens, who had stood respectfully outside the building. George wore a simple but well-made brown suit of American broadcloth woven at the Hartford Woolen Mill in Connecticut. The buttons on the suit featured carved eagles, the symbol of the fledgling republic.[4] Washington's choice of dress was consciously made to reflect that he was a man of the people.[5] And when they had wed over thirty years earlier in 1759 in a modest ceremony attended by family and friends at her home, Martha and George Washington entered into the marriage by mutual consent without the need for the outside official negotiations that characterized royal marriages.

Although the Washingtons had never traveled to England, in his earlier years one of George's highest aspirations had been to become a respected Englishman, one who reflected British values and displayed unwavering loyalty to the crown. Washington had always been an avid reader, and as a young man, he had undoubtedly read popular newspaper and magazine accounts about King George's coronation, so he was likely familiar with the rituals surrounding European royalty. And after his election as president, Washington had two close advisers at his side, both of whom had firsthand experience at the European courts. John Adams, the new vice president, had served as a United States emissary first to France and then later to the English Court of St. James, and Thomas Jefferson, appointed the first secretary of state, had returned to America from Paris at the end of 1789, after having spent five years as the minister to France then under the reign of Louis XVI.

When Martha later joined the newly elected president during May 1789 in the young nation's first capital of New York City, she arrived in an elegantly simple gown sewn from material made in America rather than a more fashionable European import. It was clearly a symbolic gesture made to convey the egalitarian underpinnings of the newly minted nation. As the *Gazette*, the local Federalist newspaper, approvingly noted, "She was clothed in the manufacture of our Country."[6] The glittering canopy at Queen Charlotte's coronation was sewn of cloth of gold. As the original First Lady of the United States, as the position would later become known, Martha Washington had to create her new quasi-official role from whole cloth.

Despite the fact that the role of First Lady was not an elected position, Martha and her two successors, First Ladies Abigail Adams and Dolley Madison, would all come to symbolize the heart and character of their husbands' administrations. Never officially authorized, nevertheless, the position of First Lady became a highly influential role in American history. These three women were responsible for essentially creating the role of First Lady without having a roadmap to follow. To do so, they often had to walk a social and political tightrope. None of the three could simply imitate the role of European queens; instead, they each had to construct a unique and distinctively American style as the partner of the young nation's leading political figure, the president.

Introduction

FORGING THE ROLE OF FIRST LADY

I have lived to witness changes, such as
I could never have imagined.

ABIGAIL ADAMS

to Catherine Nuth Johnson, August 20, 1800

Martha Washington, Abigail Adams, and Dolley Madison, the inaugural First Ladies of the United States of America, created a role that was uniquely American in both its style and substance. Each of them shaped the role of First Lady by placing their own imprint upon the position, but at the same time they learned from one another as they sought a path that would blend their roles as women, wives, mothers, and public figures. With no precedent to follow, Martha, Abigail, and Dolley began to construct the position of the president's spouse, often consciously working to make it distinct from that of consorts in European courts and aligning it more closely with emerging republican ideals and standards for presidential behavior.

In the American imagination, at the time Europe was viewed as the site of monarchial and aristocratic displays of power. That perception played an overarching role in the quest to define the roles that the wives and daughters of significant male political figures would play in the new American political culture, especially First Ladies. Use of the word "Europe" often became a code word for everything that needed to be eradicated in the new republican undertaking—from issues about rank, status, elaborate ceremonies, excessive luxury, corruption, and ostentatious fashions and lifestyles to the perceived "excessive influence of women on public life."[1] That is one reason that small gestures in the quasi "courts" surrounding the Washingtons and Adamses, such as sometimes serving lemonade instead of fine wine, took on such significance.

To this day, the role of First Lady has no official mandate, and while in practice it was and is ofttimes a very constraining and conservative position, it continues to hold the potential for significant power, for it reflects informal but still critical political responsibilities that affect matters of state.[2] The three initial First Ladies directly or indirectly influenced one another in developing the parameters of that semi-official "office." Few of their successors played as public and active a role as these exceptional women, who were among the most highly visible females among the early political social elite in the United States. To examine their political involvement demands that we view their endeavors against the backdrop of their times and not with a presentist lens.

This book examines the marital partnerships of America's first three presidential couples, but it especially focuses on the prominent roles of Martha Washington, Abigail Adams, and Dolley Madison in their years as the nation's earliest First Ladies. Martha Jefferson died at the young age of twenty-seven and never stood beside her husband as First Lady. Thomas Jefferson's daughter Martha Jefferson Randolph sometimes supported her father as a substitute, but it was really Dolley Madison who experienced an "internship" as First Lady, so to speak, during Jefferson's two terms in office.

The stories of America's first three presidential spouses have received attention in countless volumes since the days in which they occupied their pioneering positions. However, we now have the opportunity to reassess their roles and ask new questions about their levels of political impact, and we can ask what Martha, Abigail, and Dolley—and other early elite American women who were related to significant political figures—might have done similarly or differently from one another as well as from their counterparts in Europe. After all, Europe, especially England and France, was the primary point of reference for early Americans. For example, female royal figures and French female *salonnières* have achieved perhaps a mythical status in the American imagination, but were they indeed as influential as first thought?

Moreover, it might be more fruitful to look at the key players in the new American political order after the American Revolution as a *family unit* rather than as individuals. Certainly, in the case of the Washingtons, the Adamses, and the Madisons, they operated more visibly as a partnership than as a male/female binary divide. Martha, Abigail, and Dolley viewed themselves as wives of prominent leaders of the new American governing class with an important part to play, and they understood that it was through their traditional domestic roles that they acquired access to the public sphere as members of the political social elite. In other words, the three First Ladies stood at the center of America's political world through their husbands. That was the reality of their times, but it does not follow that they therefore did not possess significant influence.[3]

The term "First Lady" was probably not commonly used in print until the 1860s when Mary Todd Lincoln occupied the position, although President Zachary Taylor is reputed to have earlier referred to Dolley Madison as the "first lady of the land," and it may have first been formally applied to President James Buchanan's niece, who served as his White House hostess in the late 1850s. But in retrospect we can surely apply the title to the initial "First Ladies" examined in this book, who were all extremely capable, strong women. For the most part, they operated in the accepted contemporary boundaries of women's sphere, personally content overall with what they considered their primary roles as dutiful, loving, and nurturing wives and mothers. But because women, unlike men, at the time were considered to be disinterested parties "above" politics, in reality they were given a wider berth in exercising some level of political power behind the scenes.

Since the time that Martha Washington became the original First Lady, not only Abigail Adams and Dolley Madison but also all those who followed have struggled with the proper manner in which to carry out the role, one that conferred celebrity, public scrutiny, and, at the least, close access to political power. This earliest trio was often involved in real-life politicking through patronage activities, interacting regularly with other political figures and their family members, as well as serving as unofficial advisers to their presidential spouses. At the beginning of her tenure as First Lady, Martha reported to her niece that she often visited with other female acquaintances—women like the "Vice President's Lady," Abigail Adams—who were an integral part of the contemporary "political circle," as Martha described it.[4]

Probably influenced by a combination of her own personal preferences and her new good friend Abigail Adams, as well as her desire to deflect criticism away from her husband George, who increasingly came under attack from the Republican press for allegedly mimicking kingly behavior, Martha Washington adopted a more austere style than had been exhibited at the royal courts of the Old World. It was a style that attempted to reflect the dignity of those courts melded with the new republican ideals that had fostered the nascent American nation. In other words, elite women like Martha and Abigail, who had access to cultural power in the early republic, helped mold a ceremonial protocol that appropriated select European court manners "for republican elite purposes."[5]

When Abigail later became the second First Lady, she expanded the model created by Martha to bolster and support her own husband John's administration. Abigail had witnessed the British royal version firsthand while she was in England in 1785, when John served as minister to Great Britain on behalf of the United States. She had met both George III and Queen Charlotte at the Court of St. James and had found the two monarchs polite and civil but uninspiring and decidedly lacking in what she considered superior American virtues.

Moreover, Abigail had looked with disdain upon the drawn-out intricate rituals that surrounded the London court, where visitors at the queen's carefully orchestrated drawing rooms often had to wait for hours before the royal couple briefly greeted guests and exchanged social small talk. Abigail described her first visit to the court to her sister back in America, noting that, after meeting the king, "it was more than two hours after this before it came to my turn to be presented to the Queen. The circle was so large the company were four hours standing. The manner, in which they make their tour round the room, is, first, the Queen, the lady in waiting behind her, holding up her train; next to her, the Princess Royal, after her, Princess Augusta, and their lady in waiting behind them." The princesses were elaborately "both dressed in black and silver silk," while "the Queen was in purple and silver."[6] Clearly, through their dress, the royal family exuded their privileged status. Back in America, over a decade later and as the wife of the second president of the United States, Abigail unsurprisingly and often consciously sought to distance her own "court" style from its European counterparts.

As the historian Catherine Allgor so succinctly put it, the initial two First Ladies of the United States, Martha Washington and Abigail Adams, "both strove to create personae that contrasted with a queenly one, using a dignified, formal style that could command respect without a crown or a throne."[7] Still, both Martha and Abigail incorporated their own distinct elements of proscribed ceremonial protocol at the events they hosted, and the functions were aimed at decidedly elite participants. Ironically, and often to their chagrin, although both the first two presidential couples, first George and Martha Washington and later John and Abigail Adams, intentionally tried to strike a "proper" balance between an open ceremonial style and one that reflected the status, gravitas, and dignity of the new government and displayed the authority of the new executive position, detractors accused them of trying to bring back monarchical practices that would threaten the fragile democratic republic.

Dolley Madison was certainly aware—at times as a firsthand observer or often through newspaper reports and correspondence with family and friends—of the significant public efforts undertaken by the two First Ladies of the United States while they resided in Philadelphia during their husbands' terms in office. Dolley lived in the city during Washington's presidency when Philadelphia served as the temporary capital, and she became centrally involved in its political life after her second marriage to Congressman James Madison in 1794. The Madisons remained in Philadelphia until James temporarily retired from politics in 1797, when they returned to the Madison Montpelier family estate in Virginia. James later served as secretary of state under Thomas Jefferson, the young nation's third president, and it was during that period that Dolley actively began building her own robust public social and political power base at their welcoming Washington City home on F Street.

Dolley likely appreciated Martha's and Abigail's earlier efforts to shape their respective "courts" through their hosting of drawing rooms and salons, for both women had understood the power of those social institutions to inform public manners and to display their presidential husbands' characters and agendas in the best possible light, thereby even influencing the direction of politics. Although on one level the social occasions operated as a venue for sociability and entertainment, they were fundamentally political in a practical manner, for many alliances were built or broken there, and the events also helped to smooth over regional and personal fissures that emerged. Yet Dolley undoubtedly found her predecessors' events to have been overly formal, elitist, and much too limited in reach. After her husband's election as president, Dolley would later adopt her own more accessible and flamboyant style as First Lady, even welcoming the sobriquet of "Queen Dolley," as she was dubbed, a title both Martha and Abigail would have very likely disdained.

But Dolley Madison did not create her political public persona as First Lady in a vacuum; she built her enlarged presence as a "republican Queen" on the foundations that Martha and Abigail had initiated. Dolley retained some of their practices and discarded others that she found were not useful in her concerted campaign to build unity in a nascent republic that had not yet developed a path for working with fragmented, competing political parties and interests. Dolley did not originate the position of First Lady, nor, as some writers have suggested, did she introduce the popular custom of hosting drawing rooms or even serving ice cream at those successful and highly crowded "squeezes," as her events were nicknamed.

Martha Washington pioneered the role of presidential wife, followed quite capably by Abigail Adams. And although the serving of a frozen dessert may seem to have been a rather inconsequential custom, it symbolically reflected republican simplicity over the excesses in cuisine of the European courts. We know from Abigail's letters to her sister Mary Cranch that Martha certainly served ice cream at *her* drawing rooms long before Dolley made the refreshment popular. From Dolley's correspondence written while she resided at Montpelier, we learn that she sought information about Abigail's drawing rooms from her own friends among Philadelphia's elite society women.[8]

Arguably, however, Dolley Madison went on to enthusiastically *expand* the position of First Lady in a manner that was at once more visible, intentional, and more "democratic." It was a role that ultimately earned her the admiration of many of her contemporaries and future generations as one of the most popular, well known, and acclaimed of the nation's First Ladies. For Mrs. Madison moved well beyond cultivating merely a select group of the nation's early elite to include male and female guests from virtually all classes at her social gatherings, although everyone realized that most real power was in the hands of the governing elite. Her efforts not only aided in promoting national unity in a highly contentious political environment but also helped the United States move forward as a budding democratic republic.[9]

First Ladies of the Republic embarks on an unusual path by examining as a group the three "First Ladies" of the American republic, Martha Washington, Abigail Adams, and Dolley Madison, whose lives intersected and who influenced one another during the nation's formative years. Indeed, shortly before Abigail stepped into the role of presidential wife and First Lady, she wrote to "her most amiable predecessor" Martha for advice and guidance.[10] Although they exhibited vastly different personalities and came from varied backgrounds, the three women were among the most influential females in the history of the United States, part of the early inner elite political and social circle, and they created a distinctly American quasi-political role. The role of First

Lady was not an elected position, and none of three became policy makers, but they still were able to exercise considerable influence and even some measure of power through what today we would consider unconventional means.[11]

When Martha supported the needs of Revolutionary War veterans she became the first presidential wife to take on a public cause. Abigail Adams was the first to voice her strong personal opinions on critical public issues, and Dolley Madison became an effective behind-the-scenes lobbyist. All three wielded at least some degree of the power of patronage, which even in the new republic proved a useful tool for building presidential authority. Without any roadmap to guide them, they crafted and shaped the unique position of First Lady and played a part in defining the tone and style of their husbands' administrations. Moreover, as leading American women, Martha, Abigail, and Dolley forged important social and political networks that helped influence the country's development during the early republic and national periods as it moved in small increments toward a more unified federal nation.

In an age when women were not allowed active political voices as either voters or elected politicians, Martha Washington, Abigail Adams, and Dolley Madison also had to learn how to negotiate their female roles to accommodate their new public responsibilities. All three women considered the eighteenth-century normative domestic role as primary and personally held it in great esteem. Yet we also need to reexamine some of our long-held views about an artificial "binary" division between the private and public spheres during their era.[12] For all three, and many other elite women in the early republic, the two areas were often connected, interrelated, and operated simultaneously. Their hosting of dinners, levees, and similar salon-like social events while they served as First Ladies not only called on their traditional robust domestic skills but also allowed them to help shape public opinion and the social and political parameters of the emerging republic, at times through what has become known as the "Republican Court." That paradoxical institution, which at first glance appears to be an oxymoron, was first launched by the Washingtons in 1789 in New York, when that burgeoning urban center served as the seat of the new government.

Moreover, the salon-type events that Martha, Abigail, and Dolley often hosted and guided were not inconsequential: They allowed women to exercise some level of public power; they helped develop cultural unity and a distinctive American political style; and often the interactions and conversations held there became the "crucible in which the ideas of [male] politicians" were tested.[13] They viewed, as should we, their domestic realm with its myriad responsibilities as requiring skill and possessing dignity and worth as well as being critical to the well-being of not only their families but also their surrounding community and country. For many years it was not uncommon for earlier generations of writers to dismiss their work in the domestic sphere as being of only modest importance. However, historians have increasingly come to realize not only that there existed "a fully formed woman's domain in the public sphere" but also that it provided the opportunity for political and cultural influence.[14] It is through those avenues that the three First Ladies made significant public contributions.

Although all three, particularly Abigail and Dolley, knowledgeably considered, discussed, and wrote privately about political issues and the inner workings of the American government and held considerable influence, their deep immersion in broader political life was still unusual at the time as political power was viewed as essentially the realm of men. Yet the American Revolution had politicized many white elite females, including Martha Washington and Abigail Adams. When women like Martha and Abigail supported independence, they often took up their husbands' work at home, enabling men such as John Adams to serve in the Continental Congress or allowing others like George Washington to go to war. During the rebellion, many colonial women played an important role in the realm of political action through their opposition to British policies through the venues of boycotts and public protests via the economic domestic sphere, as well as by raising funds to benefit Patriot soldiers. They also served as military supporters and "exhorters of men to direct action."[15] In other words, women began to test their political influence.

In Philadelphia, for example, elite women had mounted a successful fundraising campaign, amassing significant donations on behalf of the Continental Army troops, which had effectively moved them and other females in New Jersey, Maryland, and Virginia "out of doors" into the public arena, enabling women to display considerable agency as they turned "civic consciousness to action." Indeed, Martha Washington, who was by then highly visible to colonial citizens as the wife of General Washington, was designated to receive the financial collections and help direct the funds to address the needs of the soldiers.[16]

Like many other female Patriots, both Martha and Abigail voiced their political opinions during the days of the Revolutionary War through strong support of their Patriot husbands and American soldiers, as well as more tangible and symbolic actions such as banning British tea from their tables and producing and wearing homespun. Women's efforts were appreciated and afforded them an opening in which to be viewed as "political beings."[17] Both future First Ladies would have undoubtedly agreed with their friend, the Boston writer Mercy Otis Warren, who maintained, "But as every domestic enjoyment depends on the decision of the mighty contest, who can be an unconcerned and silent spectator? not surely the fond mother, or the affectionate wife."[18] For Mercy as well as Martha and Abigail, family was their underlying source of political commitment.

The first three presidential wives were women whose lives reflected the realities of eighteenth- and early nineteenth-century life in the United States, and when studying them we need to retain the integrity of the past. In an era when women had no legislative voice, their primary connection to politics was through their husbands, all highly politically influential men, and for the most part Martha, Abigail, and Dolley approached political issues from the perspective of how they affected their spouses.[19] They were always quick to defend their husbands against any criticism by fellow politicians, journalists, or other members of the public, sometimes taking the heat themselves, and they also fiercely guarded the physical and emotional health of their spouses. In other words, they looked after *both* the personal and political welfare of their presidential husbands. For them, the private domestic and public spheres were not separate paths; one area influenced and interacted with the other in a reciprocal relationship.

Therefore their correspondence is often a melding of descriptions of momentous political events folded in with domestic themes, which included updates about household matters and the lives of family members and friends, with many references to health, illness, and child rearing. When Martha, Abigail, and Dolley ventured into public and even political life as the wives of America's first presidents, they likely viewed themselves first and foremost as carrying out their valued domestic responsibilities as good wives, who were also fulfilling their duty as patriotic Americans. Although republican ideology emphasized the domestic base of what would eventually be described as "republican motherhood" and "wifehood," at the same time it did not "entirely constrain women's work within the private household."[20]

Thus the three First Ladies were at times able to use those contemporary social and cultural ideals to their advantage. The founders of the United States had attempted to stabilize the new republic and build the framework for an emerging national government by maintaining, to a large measure, the traditional societal hierarchical relationships, and they believed in an appointed order of society. During this period, the question of human rights, which had so occupied the revolutionists, did not emerge as a main focus. But a new suggested path for women did gain traction. The new role for women as patriotic republican wives and mothers may have been intended to restrict women from full political participation, but there still remained room for women's agency. For many middle-class and elite American women, republican motherhood justified their interest and involvement in contemporary political and social issues. It also offered many an important and visible (although not overtly political) position for them as both the guardians of the next generation as well as the promoters of American moral and civic virtue as the nation developed a new culture of manners and societal guidelines that better aligned with the new type of republican government.[21]

Despite the plethora of studies about the founders, none has focused a lens specifically on America's first three presidents and their wives as a group during their presidential years, a period of time when their extraordinary, albeit far from equal, marital partnerships were most visible. Nor, for the most part, have the ways in which this *particular* trio of First Ladies navigated and at times expanded their public and private roles and how their experiences reflected changing cultural ideas about the proper role of women in American society received adequate attention.[22] The early American republic was an evolving experiment, and in that fluid environment, Martha Washington—the original First Lady—Abigail Adams, and Dolley Madison were often able to express considerable individual agency and influence that oftentimes extended to the world of politics before the parameters of women's sphere hardened in the coming decades, particularly during the Jacksonian era.

There has been a particular recent boom in books that have detailed the stories of the women who played such a central role in the lives of the male founders. A generation ago a number of historians and popular writers focused on several prominent founding mothers, most notably Abigail Adams, as examples of early pioneer feminists, at times anachronistically reading modern sensibilities into their lives. Even a few recent biographies have incorporated this theme of Adams as a "protofeminist."[23] Were these women poised to become nascent feminists, as some contended, or conventional eighteenth-century elite women, as others have affirmed? The reality probably falls somewhere in the middle, and certainly historians today acknowledge the complexity of the subject.

Nearly four decades after her essay first appeared, Linda Grant De Pauw's reevaluation of Abigail Adams and the question of her "feminist theory" still remains perhaps the most insightful analysis. As De Pauw points out, although Abigail was an uncommon woman of superior intelligence, with a sophisticated grasp of politics and liberal leanings, at heart, like her husband John, she was never an egalitarian. Both the Adamses hoped that, after the revolution, the new American government would allow for broader mass support. But at the same time, they believed in a hierarchical order that would not challenge the position of the elite. For the most part, American women of the eighteenth century, including Abigail, who exhibited concerns about the treatment of women, were focused narrowly on reform of the common law of coverture and legal equality, rather than on broad political equality.[24]

The political historian Rosemarie Zagarri has also suggested that, when post-Revolutionary American political theorists discussed human rights, they drew largely on Scottish philosophy, which stressed the strong connection between individual rights and duty to society. That resulted in the prevalent view that, although women certainly were entitled to "natural" human rights, they were "to be nonpolitical in nature, confined to the traditional feminine role of wife and mother." Yet Zagarri maintains that the early focus on natural rights had a positive effect because in reality it opened the door for discussion about the possibility of social and political equality for women in the future.[25]

The intellectual historian Lynn Hunt has broadened our understanding of that perspective and has shown how print, especially epistolary novels of the eighteenth century, encouraged empathy among even ordinary people, which led to an enlarged construct of the "self." That in turn influenced the development of the concept of the human rights of man, ultimately paving the way for the Declaration of Independence and the American Revolution, later followed by the French Declaration of the Rights of Man, and the "foundations for a new social and political order." Although those currents benefited many disenfranchised groups, women, who were not viewed as autonomous beings but as passive citizens, were not wholly included; they were broadly seen as entitled to fundamental *human rights* but not political ones. Still, like Zaggari, Hunt maintains that it paved a path for discussion about women's rights for the future as "the philosophy of natural rights had an implacable logic."[26]

During the era, women enjoyed few political rights, but that does not mean that women during the Revolution and in the early national period were wholly excluded from politics and had no voice. A number of elite women, like the three First Ladies, who possessed the education and leisure that enabled them to become involved in political life, occupied an often ambiguous position that blurred the demarcations between the private and public realms. If we view those spheres during their era as a continuum rather than as strongly bifurcated separate spheres, then their agency is brought into sharper focus. Moreover, it likely provides us with better insight into the manner in which contemporaries viewed them and how women of their class actually *saw themselves* during the late eighteenth and early nineteenth century. Although the three First Ladies lived in an era when women were not able to exhibit overt political voices and during a time when none of the three men they married—not George Washington, not John Adams, and not James Madison—would have endorsed granting the vote to women or allowing them to hold public office, they all regarded their wives as political partners and took their wives' political engagement and advice seriously.

Social gatherings were often effective vehicles for middle- and upper-class women to bridge the separate spheres and exert a degree of political influence in an era in which they could neither vote nor hold office themselves.[27] Later in Washington City, Dolley Madison would expand those occasions hosted by the two first presidential wives and other prominent women of their class to include ordinary citizens alongside the elite from both the Republican and Federalists factions. At the center of early political life in the United States, and having intimate access to a president's ear, the three First Ladies were better positioned than most women to make an impact, and all three corresponded regularly with other influential men and women who lived in various locations around the nation.

Abigail Adams even ventured into the wider emerging print culture in the United States. She kept a finger on the pulse of the leading newspapers of her day and provided "corrections" and comments when she felt editors had erred in their reporting or opinions.[28] If Martha Washington launched the first American political salon, Abigail transformed it into an intellectual hub, in which she participated fully and could hold her own in the most important political conversations of the day. Dolley was able to combine the talents of Martha as a skillful and highly congenial hostess with Abigail's keen understanding of politics, fusing both those threads to excel as a social and political force on behalf of her husband. Far more than many male politicians of her day, Dolley understood the central importance of compromise, accommodation, and the need to build consensus in a republican form of government.

The social events that they hosted and attended became an integral part of the political culture that developed around the new federal government. These very capable and sometimes path-breaking women helped shape not only their own roles as prominent Americans and First Ladies but that of the presidency and the development of American social culture and politics. Long before the development of mass media and the official White House press agent, Martha Washington, Abigail Adams, and Dolley Madison served as effective presidential public relations envoys and at times even campaign managers for their husbands, building political capital and a power base through the social realm. For, as a number of historians have pointed out, it was often behind the scenes at social events conducted in the drawing room—the acknowledged province of women at the time—in which the most effective politicking and lobbying occurred.[29] Thus social and political life was often permeable and clearly intertwined in the early republic, and traditionally defined separate spheres for men and women frequently intersected.

Lively conversationalists and astute judges of human character, Martha, Abigail, and Dolley moved easily in the unofficial social sphere, and they often called upon their extensive female networks for support. At the time, fine conversation was seen as a hallmark of gentility and class, and all three First Ladies excelled in the ability to interact with people from all walks of life. Their significance and influence, although often indirect, was far from inconsequential, and it is no exaggeration to assert that they served as the mainstays of support for their husbands' day-to-day existence on both a personal and public level. It is telling that Martha, Abigail, and Dolley were at times variously referred to as "The President's Lady," "Mrs. President," "Presidente," and "The Presidentess" as the political arena widened for these three women during and after the American Revolution and their husbands' presidential terms.

Although the early presidents and their wives may have displayed radically different personalities and temperaments, diverse political and social views, and varying outlooks about the ideal goals and structure of marriage, each of them shared the common desire to be supportive and caring partners to their spouses and nurturing and caring mothers to their children. Indeed, all three clearly viewed their domestic responsibilities as the most central and valued role in their lives. Examining their marital partnerships and their parenting styles lends them a corporeal presence that is often absent from many historical accounts and serves to humanize them. It reminds us that they were flesh-and-blood individuals who had to contend with personal, family, and public challenges in many ways similar to ours yet at the same time radically different from contemporary circumstances. And like most couples, their marriages endured ups and downs that included serious disagreements and disparate ideas about how best to navigate their complex lives. Yet it is telling that throughout their marriages, George Washington, John Adams, and James Madison all keenly respected the minds, work, and talents of their respective spouses.

Additionally, raising children in especially turbulent times often brought heightened burdens. Abigail Adams, for example, took the primary responsibility for caring for their children and capably overseeing the family farm and household during John's frequent absences as a member of the Continental Congress during a period when war and illness were constant backdrops. She also endured the heartbreaking loss of a stillborn daughter while John was in Philadelphia attending the Continental Congress, but her intense religious faith helped her overcome the grief, comforted as well by her husband's supportive letters. Martha and Dolley also often had to supervise their large and complicated households and deal with numerous personal or family illnesses without their husbands by their sides. But in the process, Martha and George Washington, Abigail and John Adams, and Dolley and James Madison forged enduring partnerships that encompassed not only the bonds of marriage and mutual affection and respect but also political, social, and even economic alliances as well. Nevertheless, it is important to note, as one historian has recently observed, that "even the best eighteenth-century unions viewed men and women as unequal."[30]

The noted early American historian Mary Beth Norton has carefully traced changing cultural perceptions of women's roles in America from the first early settlements in the seventeenth century through the American Revolution and the nascent republic of the late eighteenth century. She maintains that, before the late 1670s, "notions of rigid, gendered divisions between the terms public (male) and private (female) did not exist" and in reality public political roles much more closely reflected and were tied to social status rather than gender. However, by the mid-eighteenth century, the belief that women should be confined to what became termed the "private domestic sphere" "had become the assumptive norm," and by the advent of the Revolution, males dominated the public sphere, and even elite women had become marginalized politically.[31]

Yet the American Revolution disrupted those normal patterns of settled domestic life, blurring some of the lines that demarcated appropriate female and male behavior, at times breaking "the barrier which seemed to insulate women from the realm of politics."[32] Those new social constructs, brought into play by a war and crisis that affected women as well as men, changed the political landscape and launched Abigail's and Dolley's overt involvement. Even the self-proclaimed apolitical Martha Washington avidly followed newspapers reports about the war battles and later developments in the early republic, and George Washington is reputed to have discussed details of his military operations with her as she joined him every winter in camp during the eight years of the Revolutionary War. Her letters during that period certainly reflect a clear knowledge of ongoing political and military events.

Martha Washington, Abigail Adams, and Dolley Madison may have expanded their own female roles by conscious design or simply opportunity against the backdrop of new paths offered during the Revolution, but they did so within the framework of their acceptance and genuine appreciation of traditional societal norms.[33] For as Norton asserts, even for those women who had enlarged public experiences, "the developing notions of women's sphere carried weight."[34] Other historians, such as Karin Wulf, have also noted the new opportunities the Revolution created for women to expand their traditional roles to include political involvement, which continued on some level through the era of the Federalist administrations, but, as Wulf and other historians like Linda Kerber argue, those activities began to regress under Jefferson and then were submerged almost completely as time passed. Propelled by changing cultural ideas about women's roles, soon even women's indirect and supportive political roles were considered inappropriate, and their overall status did not change their opportunities.[35]

However, in a cogently argued thesis, Zagarri offers a fresh, convincing new perspective, in which she maintains that elite American women remained politicized in the new republic, certainly into the 1790s and even through the first decades of the nineteenth century before a "revolutionary backlash" became firmly entrenched by the 1830s. Female "politicians"—that is, women who understood and knowledgeably discussed contemporary political issues—took advantage of opportunities to engage in what we would today term "politicking," and moreover, this phenomenon was most apparent when women were part of a *political family*.[36] Of course, individual personality and taste played a role, but when applied to the first three First Ladies, Zagarri's thesis helps explain how and why, albeit to different degrees, Martha Washington, Abigail Adams, and Dolley Madison, all members of influential political families, became visible political actors. And, of course, all three were active *before* the height of the backlash to push women out of politics.

In the early United States, as the two-party system developed, both Federalist and Republican politicians found it in their best interest to win women as well as men over to their particular party ideology. Indeed, from the Revolutionary era though the War of 1812, women were crucial to the unfolding of party structure and the manner in which party conflict evolved. Loyal republican wives, Martha and Abigail became ardent Federalists in concert with and in support of their husbands. Dolley emerged as an enthusiastic Republican in alignment with her husband James and his mentor, Thomas Jefferson, the co-founders of their party. All three women counted themselves as staunch adherents of the policies and broad views of their respective parties and worked alongside their presidential husbands to fulfill their political vision. But because of her reputation for charm and her conciliatory manner, Dolley appeared, at least in the popular imagination, to be above partisanship. Ironically, it is only with the increasing vituperative divisions between the new political parties, which even at times resulted in violence, and the widening of male suffrage that women became totally excluded from politics (by the 1830s women were officially denied the right to vote in all states). They were increasingly relegated to the newly emerging domestic sphere through a backlash against active female political participation. To encourage civility in American society, especially in print, women were exhorted to remove themselves from sordid politics and the commercial world and instead reserve their feminine influence to being peacemakers and mitigating dangerous factional strife.[37]

Despite their unusual political involvement, all three women in this study were certainly influenced by the contemporary cultural norms referred to by Norton. Martha Washington and Abigail Adams especially were also informed by their strong religious beliefs, which included a highly cultivated sense of duty and long-held prescriptive views of marital roles, with the wife subservient to the husband in the vital family unit. Far from being merely theoretical, religious and cultural ideals were incorporated into their daily lives and world outlook. Although the religious and popular views of their era stressed that partners in a good marriage had "symmetrical" roles, that did not mean by any stretch of the imagination marriage was considered a fully egalitarian partnership.[38] As many historians have reminded us, each generation tends to reshape its images of the founders to adhere more closely to the prevailing outlooks of its own era, unfortunately sometimes in an anachronistic manner or from a present perspective. We need to look at the lives of these founders on their own terms and in the historical context of their times, not ours.

Clearly marriage was different in the eighteenth century. As the historian Edith B. Gelles reiterates, the socially prescribed form of marriage during the era was one in which the wife was automatically the subordinate partner in marriage.[39] Martha Washington, Abigail Adams, and Dolley Madison would have never even contemplated deviating from that norm. Marriage was also considered an unbreakable lifelong commitment, and although many early Americans undoubtedly married, in part, for love, frequently political, economic, and social considerations played a pivotal, if not primary role, in the decision to marry.

This outlook was evident at least on some level for America's early presidential couples, George and Martha Washington and James and Dolley Madison. Initially, they may very well have viewed their respective unions as marriages of convenience, which involved underlying practical financial and social considerations. Certainly marrying for money, security, and position was considered eminently sensible at the time, and social rank mattered. While he served as president, George Washington voiced this perspective very clearly in 1794 when he advised his step-granddaughter Elizabeth Parke Custis: "Do not then in your contemplation of the marriage state look for perfect felicity before you consent to wed. [Your prospective spouse] should possess good sense— good dispositions—and the means of supporting you in the way you have been brought up."[40] It was certainly a direction Washington had taken to heart when he courted Martha Custis over thirty years earlier.

Wealthy widows, who as unmarried *femes soles* could make contracts as well as own and devise property in colonial America, often exercised considerable economic and social power. However, they frequently re-married when faced with myriad estate and business challenges and the need to protect the interests of young children as well as the desire for companionship.[41] As a rich, lively young widow, Martha Custis attracted a number of suitors. From Martha's perspective, the impressive-looking, dignified, and responsible George Washington must have been an especially attractive marriage prospect. Similarly, once challenging legal issues following her first husband's death were settled, Dolley Payne Todd also found herself a comfortably off widow. However, marriage to fellow southerner and rising politician James Madison held the promise of increased social status for Dolley. It provided her with the opportunity to become part of an elite and wealthy planter family and a participant in national politics, as well as providing stability for her fatherless son.

The exception of the three couples was John and Abigail Adams, who were lifelong loving soul mates, but even their marriage has often been idealized. One wag has observed that the reason their marriage was so successful was probably because they were forced by political circumstances to spend so much time apart! All three couples represented to varying degrees an emerging companionate style of marriage. They were at times forerunners of an ideal in which the relationship of husband and wife was changing. The largely accepted view of the wife being totally dependent on her patriarchal spouse had been evolving to one that encompassed and emphasized mutual bonds of friendship, shared interests, and support—yet still remained within a hierarchal structure, with the husband as the unquestionable head of the household.

In other words, expectations for marriage, particularly among the upper classes, were beginning to change, transforming the institution from an often economic or social transaction motivated to a large degree by practical considerations to a union in which compatibility and love were becoming vital ingredients. Still, for many decades to come, husbands remained in full legal control. According to the rules of coverture, a married woman did not have the status of legal personhood, and her identity was subsumed under her spouse. To put it another way, she was "covered" by her husband, who had control of all her property and the children of the union, and she could not enter into binding legal contracts, even in the case of personal wills. Not until 1839 was the first American law passed to ensure women's property rights.

As Kerber and others point out, from a legal standpoint the American Revolution was fundamentally conservative. Even the more radical revolutionists had not envisioned or desired an underlying change in status for women (or for enslaved people or for working-class men, for that matter), although they were considered citizens. But women's active participation in the war had effected a subtle change on the perception of women's role. After the Revolution, new ideas emerged that popularized the concept of the idealized republican mother and republican wife as a way to reconcile the inherent contradictions between the formation of a new public role for women and the fact that they were excluded from formal political involvement.

Hearth, home, and the supervision and education of children were increasingly considered crucial to the development of the virtuous good citizens who were necessary to the success and continuation of the new republic. Therefore women, who as a group represented moral stability and virtue in the popular mind, were lauded as critical to American progress and afforded a quasi-political role, albeit from the vantage point of their prescribed domestic sphere.[42] In other words, their crucial moral role was validated. If we take into account the various perspectives offered by historians over the last decades, we can conclude that the Revolution closed some avenues for women and at the same time opened others.

In the final analysis, the American Revolution brought a "divided legacy to women," as they were increasingly relegated to the domestic sphere at the same time that their political, economic, and intellectual expectations were raised.[43] Something similar occurred in France. French revolutionary republicanism, too, had left conflicting legacies regarding both women's role within the household and in the larger state and political realm.[44] Looking back from the perspective of the twentieth century, Kerber later described the ideology of American republican motherhood as the belief that women had "an obligation, both to themselves and to the political society" in which they resided, "to educate themselves for economic competence and intellectual growth."[45] Perhaps Zagarri describes the situation best when she notes, "Republican motherhood preserved traditional gender roles at the same time it carved out a new political role for women."[46] Others, such as the historian Jan Lewis, see the "new and unprecedented" role of the republican wife to have been even more significant than that of republican mother. In Lewis's view, it was in that crucial position that American women could exert at least an indirect political influence.[47]

Martha Washington, Abigail Adams, and Dolley Madison clearly accepted and valued the roles of what Kerber characterizes as the republican wife and mother. Those categories are a construct introduced by Kerber to help make sense of the manner in which early elite women in the United States conducted themselves. She notes that women of the era often used those positions as a justification for their interest and involvement in political affairs. As Kerber puts it, "The Republican Mother integrated political values into her domestic life." Ironically, as men's political enfranchisement widened in the early nineteenth century, women's sphere of political involvement narrowed, for only males were allowed to vote. However, republican motherhood offered at least an indirect level of involvement in matters of state. Kerber further observes that "those who shared the vision of the Republican Mother usually insisted upon better education, clearer recognition of women's economic contributions, and a strong political identification with the Republic."[48]

Although they were certainly not consciously trying to adopt a persona that was first described centuries later, surely the ideals Kerber explicates are ones that resonated with Martha, Abigail, and Dolley. However, far from being "merely" helpmates in that appreciated critical domestic sphere, all three women in varying degrees were also not only essential to the comfort and happiness of their spouses and their concerns about education and economic stability for the women in their families but also to the development of their husband's political careers, their ascent to the highest office in the land, and in some cases even their sociopolitical outlooks. As the wives of men who served as the leaders of the emerging governing class, the First Ladies were better positioned than most elite women to participate in public affairs.

Martha Washington, in particular, surely appreciated the fact that, when she married in the 1750s, American women seriously discussing or writing about political events would have been "violating cultural norms,"[49] yet as First Lady she was widely appreciated as a skilled hostess who could converse comfortably on many subjects, including contemporary politics. Of the three women, she appears to have most conformed to a southern domestic feminine ideal of womanhood in which women remained (at least in the popular imagination) apart from the public or state realm. That outlook was clearly challenged for Martha and many women during the 1760s and 1770s in the days leading up to and during the American Revolution.

Although both John and Abigail Adams were deeply involved in American politics in those decades, even they were, according to Norton, also "influenced by the conventional wisdom that accepted a sharp division between the public realm of men and the familial province of women."[50] However, that division was probably more blurred than previously thought. It is noteworthy that the essentially socially conservative John exhibited a somewhat more progressive, although clearly ambivalent, outlook about women's political, social, and economic roles than most men of his time. No doubt his views were influenced by living with Abigail, whom he recognized as an exceptional woman, and he was visibly proud of her political abilities. One of her biographers declared that during her era she became "the nation's best informed woman on public affairs."[51] Even Thomas Jefferson, who generally viewed women as idealized domestic beings, found her a stimulating and well-informed conversationalist and "one of the most estimable characters on earth."[52]

Yet, even with the example of his unusually capable wife before him, John Adams envisioned only a very circumscribed political role for women in the newly formed United States, and he affirmed that he believed that they had a different relationship to the state than men. In this outlook, he was a disciple of conservative Scottish political theorists such as Lord Kames and David Hume. In the momentous year of 1776, John fretted disapprovingly to a fellow politician that if the franchise was widened and qualifications for voting extended beyond propertied males (a situation that John regarded as a very serious threat), the United States would be set on a slippery slope on which eventually even "Women will demand a Vote."[53]

Ironically and fortunately, history would prove Adams right, but women's suffrage was a long time coming. Early on, then, John was already foreshadowing his later Federalist vision, in which he and others in his party sought to maintain the hierarchical order of society. Later as president, John shared with youngest son Thomas his continued belief in the correctness of "true Family Authority. There can never be any regular Government of a Nation without a marked Subordination of Mothers and Children to Fathers." Yet, at the same time John acknowledged rather sheepishly that his opinion would not prove very popular with his wife Abigail. Apparently, unwilling to antagonize Abigail, John asked his son to keep his views "a Secret."[54]

John's hierarchical outlook reflected popular thought and extended not only to the place of women in the new nation but also to the question of enslaved people and of lower-class males. Although Patriot Revolutionary leaders had promised more opportunities for capable men based on a meritocracy, later many Federalists felt working-class men were to be encouraged to defer to the better-educated and politically sophisticated male elite. Too much emphasis on natural rights at the expense of duty and virtue, they warned, would lead to "social unrest, moral upheaval, and political chaos."[55]

However, the introduction of the theory of human rights proposed by Lord Kames and other Scottish philosophers had opened the Pandora's box that led to increased public discussion, often fostering paradoxical views. Even the opinionated and outspoken Abigail, who was an especially vocal proponent of robust education opportunities and legal rights for women and believed they were intellectually equal to men, felt that the two genders were designed for different but complimentary roles. Her famous "Remember the Ladies" letter to John during the revolution was primarily aimed at overturning the practice of coverture and safeguarding women from tyrannical or abusive husbands, but it was by no means a broad feminist appeal for women's rights and full political equality, as some past historians suggested.[56]

As late as 1814, when she was in her sixties, Abigail maintained that "I believe nature has assigned to each sex its particular duties and sphere of action, and to act well your part, there all the honor lies."[57] Although the American Revolution and her husband's tenure as vice president and then president had opened new avenues of political involvement for Abigail, clearly she still placed the highest level of value for herself and other women in the domestic realm. Still, humans are full of contradictions. For in addition to her domestic responsibilities, Abigail had also ventured successfully and capably into traditionally male dominated economic arenas by selling a variety of imported domestic goods to neighbors and, more daringly, investing in real estate and government securities during her husband John's many enforced absences from home on behalf of his country. During the periods she and John were separated, she clearly pined for him and often complained bitterly, but she also relished her position as the temporary "deputy husband," or interim head of the family household and farm, enlarging her family and community status and even economic power. Those roles also brought her immense satisfaction and confirmation of her self-worth as well as her own personal measure of independence.

In carefully composing her own will, which had no legal standing at the time (she could not own property or make contracts as she was considered a *feme covert* under the dominion of her husband), Abigail was demonstrating, if not an "act of rebellion," as the author Woody Holton termed it, then certainly a conscious desire to manage well the final actions of her life.[58] However, it is clear from the many vivid, revealing letters she penned to John, other relatives, and friends over the fifty-four years of the span of her marriage that she found her greatest satisfaction in traditional domestic roles and hoped to return to those endeavors as soon as circumstances allowed. Indeed, she may have seen the composing of her will as responsibly and capably carrying out her duties as a good wife, mother, grandmother, and aunt. What is perhaps more impressive than Abigail's composing her will is that John honored her wishes, even though he was not legally bound to do so. That's what enduring partnerships are all about, and it highlights their extraordinary relationship.

Shared life outlooks may also have been the reason that Abigail Adams and Martha Washington got along so well, held each other in such mutual high regard, and developed a lasting friendship that began when they served respectively as the wives of the first vice president and president of the United States. For, like Abigail, Martha also regarded felicitous domesticity as a most estimable and valued goal, as did the future First Lady Dolley Madison. With obvious admiration after meeting Martha, Abigail declared, "Mrs. Washington is one of those unassuming characters which create Love and Esteem" and averred she found Martha's simple dignity and elegant but unostentatious clothing more impressive than that of the British monarchs she had met while John Adams was stationed in England.[59]

It is interesting that the lives of the trio of First Ladies intertwined on numerous occasions during President Washington's tenure. They may have influenced one other's views, from visions for the future of the burgeoning nation and its nascent political structure to strong opinions about family life, child rearing, and matrimony. It was said that the Washingtons, especially Martha, even had a hand in encouraging Dolley's marriage to Congressman James Madison, whom both Washingtons admired at the time. Many elite women like Martha and others in her circle—such as Philadelphian Elizabeth Willing Powel and early New Jersey *salonnière* Annis Boudinot Stockton, an ally of the Washingtons who became an ardent Federalist—spent a good deal of time brokering matches between young emerging political figures and the daughters of prominent local gentry, and they played a role in the formation of the governing class in the new nation.[60]

In the memoir about Dolley Madison penned by her niece Mary Cutts, a perhaps apocryphal exchange between Martha and Dolley was reported and probably romanticized to fit Mary's vision of the proper feminine ideal of her own era. Cutts claimed that Mrs. Washington had declared, "He [Madison] will make you a good husband, all the better for being so much older, we [George and Martha] both advocate it."[61] Certainly, the Washingtons were well acquainted with Dolley, as her younger sister Lucy was married to George's nephew, George Steptoe Washington.

The lives of the three women also overlapped after the seat of the government moved to Philadelphia. Owing, in part, to Abigail's ill health, which forced her to return from the capital to Quincy, Massachusetts, for long periods, Dolley and Abigail never met in person, but they certainly knew one another by reputation. However, at various times each separately interacted with Martha at her famous Friday receptions, or "levees," where the fledgling American government's leaders and their wives mingled socially and built political alliances. All three First Ladies were clearly familiar with the constraints under which women in their social class had to function, but they devised ways to get around them, make their views known, and take advantage of opportunities for political influence as they arose. American women were considered citizens, but in the early United States, they did not possess all the rights of citizens. Yet the three presidential spouses demonstrate that they could still operate as insiders in the political culture, as they worked in partnership with their presidential spouses.

If George Washington was America's "indispensable" man, as one of Martha Washington's biographers so aptly put it, "Martha Washington was the indispensable woman to him."[62] Martha Dandridge Custis, America's first presidential wife, was a charming twenty-seven-year-old widow, perhaps the wealthiest widow in Virginia at the time, when she was first courted by George Washington in the late 1750s. When they married on January 6, 1759, Martha brought the ambitious Washington the social status and position he had long craved, as well as eighteen thousand acres of land, forty thousand pounds sterling in cash, and the two surviving children of the four she had borne to her first husband. Although the practical, down-to-earth, and personable Martha may not have been "intellectually sophisticated,"[63] she was certainly a capable manager and an avid reader who appreciated music and artistic culture and followed current events as well.

Shortly after her first husband's death, Martha dealt ably with his economic affairs and sought and retained the advice of sound, experienced business advisers. For at least a year, widowhood propelled her beyond the household into the largely masculine world of commerce. In one of her earliest extant letters, in 1757 Martha wrote confidently to the director of a prominent mercantile company in England to inform him of the untimely death of her first husband and the fact that "I have now the Administration of his Estate & management of his affairs of all sorts."[64] That is not to suggest that, by stepping into the business world, the conservative but resourceful Martha Custis was attempting to overtly expand her authority and autonomy beyond the domestic realm into the traditional male sphere. Like so many other colonial widows of means, she undoubtedly acted from necessity to help preserve the family fortune for her children, particularly that of her remaining son, and maintain her family's prominent position in the Virginia social order.[65] Although some married women at the time took part in economic ventures, the status of *femes soles* certainly provided expanded opportunities for widows like Martha.[66] It is noteworthy that Martha quite capably handled economic affairs and later during her second marriage often managed the extensive Mount Vernon household when Washington was away from home.

Much later in 1788, as the wife of the newly elected president, the self-effacing Martha maintained to a niece that she did not concern herself much about "politick" [*sic*].[67] But arguably Martha was more interested than she let on, for not only did she closely follow the newspapers of the day and was cognizant of the political challenges her husband faced, but she also zealously guarded her husband's public reputation and image as well as his health. And it is Martha Washington who is credited with introducing the country's first "political salon,"[68] an innovation followed by Abigail Adams and later brought to a new level by Dolley Madison, who excelled at converting social occasions into political capital.

Although they were modeled loosely on French salons, American salons were much more intentionally political in nature. According to the French historian Antoine Lilti, Parisian salons were never in reality platforms for deep intellectual, literary, or political discussion; rather, they operated predominantly as "social spaces of elite leisure." Moreover, Lilti maintains that the French women who hosted the salons were celebrated only for their social skills as hostesses and their ability to maintain "*politesse* and harmony," not for their intellectual or political contributions to the French Enlightenment or for their involvement in a "distinctively republican form of government," as the influential historian Dena Goodman had suggested earlier. According to recent scholars, it appears likely those salons may not have been quite the protofeminist salons or incubators for open political debate that a number of historians postulated between the 1970s and 1990s.[69] The drawing rooms and salons in the developing but still fluid United States, however, may indeed have allowed for more open types of conversation about potentially controversial topics that were forbidden under the Old Regime in France. In other words, despite the fact that they were not formal state actors, some elite women in the newly emerging democratic republic of the United States were allowed more public agency than their European counterparts in creating a viable political culture.[70]

Martha's disparaging remarks to her niece about politics may have reflected her belief that displaying overt political interest was unseemly and marred the image of feminine domesticity she wished to project. After all, Dolley Madison, one of the most intuitively political of women (and of men, for that matter), insisted in a letter to her husband James that "You know I am not much of a politician."[71] And many other early male American figures who aspired to the republican ideal of the repudiation of self-interest professed to be above politics, including George Washington and Thomas Jefferson, both highly skilled politicians.[72]

By temperament Martha may not have relished public life, but ultimately, she proved a great source of political support and encouragement to her increasingly influential and famous second husband. She also oversaw domestic details and social obligations with great efficiency and flair at Mount Vernon and in the temporary presidential homes in New York and Philadelphia that the Washingtons occupied during George's years in office. As the "President's Lady," or "Lady Washington," as she was respectfully and affectionately known, Martha became a popular symbolic political figure and pioneered the role of First Lady. Moreover, Martha helped Washington forge advantageous political alliances from the vantage point of the arena that has so felicitously been dubbed "parlor politics" by Allgor.[73]

For Martha, her husband's ambitions and comfort became paramount, and her primary goal in life was to become a "worthy partner" to Washington, as one newspaper obituary later described her.[74] Throughout their long marriage, first as the wife of a successful gentleman planter, then through his challenging days as commander of the Continental Army during the Revolutionary War, and finally as Washington became the first president of the new republic, Martha exhibited unwavering loving devotion, support, and concern. Washington, in turn, was known to have often extolled the married state on the basis of his own happy experience and demonstrated genuine concern for Martha's welfare and that of her remaining children and grandchildren.

During the war, Martha's active public service on behalf of and concern for the common soldiers earned her their sincere appreciation and respect, as well as having a political impact by raising George's popularity among his men. In essence, her experience as the wife of the leader of the Revolutionary Army served as a training ground in influencing public opinion that would serve her well in her later role as First Lady. The intellectually sophisticated and politically astute female Massachusetts Patriot and writer Mercy Otis Warren, who first met Martha in camp during the war, described her to Abigail Adams in the most complimentary, albeit romanticized, terms. Warren reported that Mrs. Washington exhibited "Benevolence of the Heart, and her affability, Candor and Gentleness Qualify her to soften the hours of private Life or to sweeten the Cares of the Hero [General Washington] and smooth the Rugged scenes of War."[75]

Although the term "First Lady" did first not come into common usage until decades later, Martha Washington was the originator and pioneer of the role. Ironically, Martha notoriously displayed great aversion for public life and claimed to have found her greatest source of pleasure and contentment surrounded by family members with George at her side at the Washington plantation at Mount Vernon. As she wrote to her niece, her fondest ambition after Washington retired as commander of the Continental Army was to be "left to grow old in solitude and tranquility together." Yet she was committed to supporting her husband's call to public duty as the nation's first president and observed that, despite her private wishes, "I am still determined to be cheerful and to be happy in whatever situation I may be, for I have also learnt from experience that the greater part of our happiness or misery depends upon our dispositions, and not upon our circumstances."[76]

In her position as the wife of the president, Martha Washington famously declared she often felt like a "State prisoner,"[77] locked into a highly visible public role that she neither desired nor enjoyed and that often prevented her from the informal lively social interactions she had previously and happily conducted. Yet she carried out her role as the president's spouse with great aplomb and grace and became popularly known as a dignified, accessible hostess who could converse with people from all walks of life and as Washington's helpmeet par excellence. She served as an engaging model for the position of "First Lady" for all her successors, lending her genial and diplomatic presence to all social affairs while her husband George served as president and softening his sometimes austere public demeanor. Perhaps more important, following accepted standards for eighteenth-century wives, she supported Washington through numerous serious illnesses and political stresses, enabling him to devote his full attention to presidential responsibilities. As Martha noted sadly to her husband's successor, John Adams, after Washington's death in 1799, following Washington's example, she had long accustomed herself "never to oppose my private wishes to the public will."[78]

More unusually for their era, the future second president of the United States, John Adams, and his wife, Abigail Smith, married for love. Their union was not the result of a quest for financial gain, security, or social position; rather, it was a deep emotional and intellectual partnership that characterized their over half-a-century-long marriage. As Joseph Ellis observes, the steady, practical, and intellectually gifted Abigail served as the ballast for the brilliant, brash, but far more mercurial John.[79] John Adams recognized from the beginning that his talented, strong-minded, and sometimes judgmental and stubborn wife Abigail was his intellectual equal and regarded her involvement as essential to all his endeavors, always turning to her first as a sounding board for his ideas and projects. They regularly discussed momentous political and social issues, and to his credit, John took Abigail's views seriously. She, in turn, was fiercely protective of his reputation. At times this proved to his detriment, especially when Abigail strongly (and unwisely) encouraged his signing of the notorious Alien and Sedition Acts, a key factor in his failure to gain reelection for a second term as president. But that incident does demonstrate that Abigail might have even exerted influence on political legislation, certainly something she was accused of by her detractors.

Abigail was always John's loyal critic and—as Gelles, the author of a fine dual biography on John and Abigail Adams, observes—John's "best support both as a theorist and as a politician."[80] As we have seen, the American Revolution had rocked some previously held views about appropriate roles for women, including within the realm of politics, an area that Abigail tested and found infinitely interesting and one that she often discussed with heated emotion and robust knowledge. While the

Adams family lived in England in 1785, when John served as the American ambassador, their daughter Nabby noted that during their frequent social calls Abigail was a lively conversationalist who visibly relished her "dish of politics."[81] Similarly, Mercy Warren noted that Abigail loved "a Little seasoning of that Nature [politics] in Every production [letter]" she received from her friend.[82] Abigail Adams became the epitome of what was then termed "a female politician."

Abigail was also John's emotional bulwark in times of distress. As John famously declared after his presidential inauguration to Abigail, who was still back in Quincy: "The times are critical and dangerous and I must have you here to assist me. . . . You must leave our farm to the mercy of the winds. . . . I can do nothing without you."[83] Although John sometimes had a tendency to be histrionic, he was indeed entering a most challenging period in American history, and once again he looked to Abigail for guidance, her stabilizing influence, and her political insight and skills. Theirs was a marriage grounded in deep mutual appreciation on many levels.

It was the infamous Philadelphia yellow fever epidemic of 1793 that first thrust Dolley Payne Todd Madison into her prominent role in American history.[84] Ultimately, it was that health crisis that led to her marriage to the rising politician James Madison. An attractive widow of twenty-six, Dolley would marry future president Madison, who at forty-three was seventeen years her senior, less than a year after the death of her first husband, the Quaker attorney John Todd, and their baby. It is clear that Madison was smitten with the charismatic Dolley, but financial stability and social status for herself and her remaining young son Payne were likely Dolley's initial overriding concerns. Since Dolley appears to have experienced a happy marriage with her first husband, it is understandable that it took her a bit more time to develop the deep and abiding affection and concern she came to feel for James. Eventually, he became the beloved centerpiece of her life.

Whether living in Philadelphia, in Washington, or in Virginia at Montpelier, the effervescent Dolley dazzled and sparkled. The gregarious and vivacious Mrs. Madison was much more than a mere decorative, supportive, and loving spouse during Madison's two terms as president. She carved out an especially visible role for herself as First Lady. Dolley was not only a consummately skilled hostess and diplomat, as so many of her contemporary observers and historians in our own time have noted, she was also a savvy and formidable political force in her own right, earning herself the nickname of "Mrs. Presidentess." As James Madison's political rival for the presidency Charles C. Pickney was said to have observed, "[I] was beaten by Mr. and Mrs. Madison. I might have faced a better chance if I had faced Mr. Madison alone."[85] She seemed to realize instinctively the political value of forming alliances through compromise and was able to successfully mold "a public arena" in which women were able to exert influence upon political men in her era.[86] Dolley became a celebrity even in her own day, widely viewed as a heroine for rescuing documents and Washington's portrait (what turned out in reality to be only a symbolically important copy) just before the British set fire to the White House.

Even after James died, Dolley Madison remained an impressive figure in Washington. Early American politician and statesman Daniel Webster was reputed to have dubbed Dolley "The only permanent power in Washington." He also was said to have claimed "all others were transient."[87] Although the quote is probably apocryphal, it illustrates the power of Dolley's reputation in the American imagination, even if we take the view that her political influence has been exaggerated. As her recent biographer Catherine Allgor has perceptively observed, Dolley grew especially skillful at building the necessary alliances that were essential for developing unity within the young nation. Although in many respects she was a conventional eighteenth-century woman, at the same time she was "an innovator as a politician."[88]

Martha Washington was born in 1731 in Virginia. Abigail Adams, over a decade Martha's junior, was born in the Massachusetts Colony in 1744. Dolley Madison, born in North Carolina in 1768, was the youngest of the three women and literally a generation below Martha and

Abigail. She grew up in Virginia, but her family moved to Philadelphia when she was fifteen, in the same year the peace treaty to end the Revolutionary War was signed between America and England. To what degree did their specific age differences, era, and region influence these First Ladies?

Was Martha perhaps the least "political" of the three women because of encroaching old age as well as common rigid views about public and private spheres for women in early eighteenth-century Virginia? Historians have traditionally viewed southern culture as a strict patriarchal society. Yet newer research has suggested that patriarchy had its limits in the region, and stereotypical visions of white southern privileged women who never ventured into the public area was a myth before sectional differences hardened by the 1830s.[89] Was Abigail the strongest and most outspoken political theorist of the three because in early New England the patriarchal model was more permeable and flexible than in other regions of the country? It appears that women in at least that region of the early American colonies were able to assert themselves to some degree in a variety of public and private roles within the larger social framework while still conforming to broader cultural norms.[90] Had Dolley, who grew up during the American Revolution, been the most influenced by the enlarged roles many women experienced during the war as well as by aspects of her early Quaker roots? Quaker women in early America often possessed significant authority in their churches and community.[91]

Despite these differences, all three women shared a common upbringing in which formal education for women was often rudimentary and primarily focused on training them to competently run households. However, the trio appears to have been educated in a manner superior to most American females of their era. Martha may have attended a local country school or received private instruction from a tutor hired by a group of plantation families. She was certainly literate and was said to have closely followed the newspapers of the day and personally purchased a number of books, including histories of the French Revolution, while she was First Lady.[92] And although her spelling was often idiosyncratic, her handwriting was neat, firm, and clear, and she was an engaging letter writer. Abigail Adams was educated by family members, what today would be termed "homeschooled," but she read widely and deeply. Her voracious literary appetite was fed by her parents, Mary and Pastor William Smith, her erudite brother-in-law Richard Cranch, and later by her husband, John Adams. The Quakers were known for providing a strong education for girls as well as boys, and it is possibly one of their early schools or simply her enthusiasm for learning and passion for reading that allowed Dolley to develop her strong writing and communication skills.

Another common thread that ties the three women together is the family tragedies they endured. Like most early Americans, they were frequently challenged by the ravages of epidemics and diseases. Before the advent of the hallmarks of modern medicine—antibiotics, antiseptics, and reliable anesthesia—life could be abruptly shattered by contagion and death. That stark reality was, of course, commonplace for early Americans, regardless of social status, but the founders in this study appear to have suffered disproportionately. The lives of the first presidential couples were especially filled with the loss of loved ones, perhaps ultimately strengthening their characters and making them more resilient in the face of adversity. Martha Washington lost her first husband and all four of her children to illness. John and Abigail Adams were predeceased by four of their six children, and Dolley Madison's first husband and their baby died during the notorious Philadelphia yellow fever epidemic of 1793, leaving her with just one young son, who would turn out to be her only child.[93]

While all three couples experienced strong marriages, they fared less well with their children. Martha's son, Jacky (John Parke Custis), and Dolley's son, John Payne Todd, were for the most part feckless men who proved a great disappointment to their parents on numerous occasions. Two of the sons of John and Abigail Adams, Charles and Thomas, were similarly challenged, and their only surviving daughter, Nabby Smith, endured a troubled marriage and sadly died when she was only in her forties of breast cancer. Although their eldest son, John Quincy Adams, achieved great political status, he was a dour, often embittered man, whose own marriage reflected more downs than ups.

Like all humans, America's early leaders were motivated by complex impulses. Of course, personal ambition and aspirations as well as individual temperament played a part in their rise to the pinnacle of political power and society, but in the eighteenth century the notions of duty and public service were ones that most Americans took very seriously. Indeed, members of the upper classes believed that public service was an obligation that was imposed upon them by their status. The Washingtons, the Adamses, and the Madisons were all influenced by a highly complex interweaving of religious, family, and Enlightenment-inspired shared values that formed the core of their desire to serve their country and fellow Americans in the early years of the new republic. Disciples of the Enlightenment, they all subscribed to the belief in the fundamental importance of working on behalf of the nation, and they all shared the conviction that public service, which emphasized unselfish devotion to the common good, was essential to the safeguarding and development of the republic. In other words, for the most part duty trumped their personal inclinations.

Over the span of their three administrations, America's early presidents and their First Ladies did indeed serve as "worthy partners" in relation to their spouses as well as the country. When the six were born, the American colonies were an integral part of the far-flung British Empire, and as the historian Alan Taylor has recently shown, by the mid-1700s, and even on the eve of the Revolution, Americans had become "more British than ever before."[94] They considered themselves English by birth, culture, and social orientation, and they were united by their allegiance to the British crown. In fact, the Washingtons and other members of the colonial elite prided themselves on their acquisition of imported English fine china, fabrics, and British tea, which would later become such a flash point of contention, as they viewed such accoutrements as tangible demonstrations of their British identity and links to the English gentry class. But the perceived violation of their rights as Englishmen and their fear that their western expansionist aspirations would be thwarted led to a traumatic war and revolution. By the time the Washingtons, the Adamses, and the Madisons served as presidential couples, the United States was an independent nation and a rising power. Each of them had witnessed the birth of the new republic, and each had an impact on the transformation of their country from an unwieldy fragile confederation of states to the early configuration of one united nation.

Dolley Todd Payne Madison was only a child in 1776. She might have understood that it was the beginning of a momentous new era, but she could not have imagined to what extent the revolution would change her world and the lives of future generations of men and women throughout the United States. All three witnessed cataclysmic changes during their lifetimes. While some of the founders' outlooks in this study about what constituted the appropriate bonds of marriage, wifely "duties," and women's roles may offend modern ears, we need to take a step back and examine their stories in the context of their times. Their experiences focus a lens on the development of the role of presidential First Lady, as it would become known over time, as well as evolving views of marriage and women's place in the early republic. This book aims to locate their stories as the initial First Ladies of the land into the larger personal and political context, for all three, especially Abigail Adams and Dolley Madison, forged deep marital *and* political partnerships with their presidential spouses.

During the presidential years, and indeed throughout their marriages, each of the presidential wives developed robust skills as a political spouse, as part of a *family unit*. Their involvement in the public sphere stemmed from their attachments as the wives of the most prominent political players in the United States, but that does not diminish the importance of their own contributions. Circumstances and inherent talent conspired to thrust Martha Washington, Abigail Adams, and Dolley Madison out of the domestic shadows and into the public realm, ultimately pivoting them onto the stage of American history. Indeed, Abigail Adams may be viewed as a bridge between America's first and third First Ladies and the growing development of the evolving formal and informal roles of the position of First Lady, from the more overtly social role that Martha primarily occupied, to Dolley, who was able to meld Abigail's political acumen with Martha's highly developed social skills. And without question, each of them played a critical role in shaping a new American identity at a critical juncture in the birth of the United States republic.

Their experiences demonstrate that the public world of men and the domestic world of women of their era were not as starkly separated as has been thought, and at least in the lives of these three admittedly elite women, those realms sometimes intersected and overlapped. They capably managed their complicated households and carried out the normal duties of women of their status, dealt with heartbreaking personal losses and life-threatening illnesses, and at the same time engaged in the political currents of the day. The trio helped develop the temperament and tone as well as public perceptions of their husbands' administrations. Whether always consciously or not, as First Ladies, Martha Washington, Abigail Adams, and Dolley Madison each constructed a public identity for themselves, and in the process, they played an influential role in nation building and helped shape the contours of the future of the new United States of America.

[ONE]

Martha Washington

THE ROAD TO THE FIRST LADYSHIP

I think our country affords every thing that can give
pleasure or satisfaction to a rational mind.

MARTHA WASHINGTON

to Janet Livingston Montgomery, January 29, 1791

When Martha Dandridge was born in Virginia in 1731, no one could have imagined that in little more than half a century, she would become known as Lady Washington, the wife of the first president of the United States and a central figure in the momentous events that occurred in Revolutionary America and the new republic. At the time of Martha's birth, Virginia was a loyal American colony in the far-flung British Empire. British monarchs of royal blood ascended to the throne through the long historical tradition of inherited Divine Right, and commoners, even wealthy ones, would no more have aspired to head countries than to have contemplated flying to the moon.

The government of the new United States was created on a virtually blank slate, and in many respects, its birth and development served as a grand experiment. As the fledgling nation's original First Lady, Martha Washington would have to craft the new role—albeit with strong direction (sometimes unwelcome) from the president and other members of his administration—and she certainly understood that her activities would serve as a precedent for her successors to follow. Martha may have undertaken her position reluctantly, but she proceeded thoughtfully and mindfully, carefully weighing her actions. Although her contemporaries recognized the critical role she played in her famous husband's success and she commanded great respect during her lifetime, today the stereotypical portrait of Martha often portrays her as a charming but reticent woman. In many accounts of their lives, Martha emerges primarily as a faithful wife who stood loyally but somewhat meekly by George Washington's side, attending to his personal needs and supervising mundane social events during the period he was viewed as the most famous and revered American of his era.

Yet on many levels Martha was central to Washington's military and political success. Born into a modestly prosperous planter family, Martha was raised from a young age to be an efficient and capable household manager, a responsible member of the larger community, a welcoming and congenial hostess who knew how to make guests feel comfortable, as well as a dutiful wife and mother. In other words, Martha's early training and life experience provided her with the skills to later succeed as America's initial First Lady. Moreover, on an even more practical level, the wealth she inherited through her first husband allowed George Washington to realize many of his ambitious economic, social, and even political goals.

Raised in an earlier generation and a southern cultural milieu characterized by more rigid gender spheres, Martha Washington's political vistas perhaps offered fewer avenues than those that opened up for her two successors, Abigail Adams and Dolley Madison. The dictates of eighteenth-century southern society held that a properly raised woman from the upper-class echelons should not exhibit a highly visible public role. And during her era, wifehood and motherhood were unquestionably considered the primary purpose of a woman's life. But in reality, as Martha's more recent biographers have suggested, she exercised more influence than has generally been acknowledged, ably helping to burnish George's public image and build support first among his army troops during the American Revolution and later with his political colleagues and the larger American community. It is highly improbable that Martha was demonstrating a conscious feminist sensibility, for that would be inaccurately reading the past into the present, but she likely would have considered her support reflective of being a good republican wife, one who was conscientiously carrying out her duty to her spouse and the nation as part of the Washington family unit.

In the early republic, the social and political realms intersected on a daily basis, and political capital was built on relationships that were cemented during dinners, balls, and receptions, such as the Washington's popular levees. Martha acquired new ceremonial duties, and in large gatherings held in the presidential mansion, she often entertained a mixed company of women as well as men, a tradition that would be continued by her successors. Martha may have privately disdained the public limelight, but that did not prevent her from presiding over, and helping to shape, the character of a variety of social events that en-hanced George's public reputation and brought other critical American political players into the new president's orbit. In other words, she was not a neutral bystander during a period when the position of chief ex-ecutive of the United States was still being tested and solidified, and by her demeanor and actions, she helped set the tone of Washington's administration.

Indeed, in reality it was Martha Washington who launched the first event for the Republican Court, as it came to be known—the popu-lar drawing room, which served a political as well as social purpose. It was supervised and guided by Martha and other elite women who lived alongside power and were drawn into the political sphere through their husbands, fathers, and brothers. For these early female members of America's governing elite, it was often a joint cooperative undertak-ing, an effort in which they participated actively as part of the family unit. That central social occasion, the drawing room, and the attendant levees and dinners played a critical role in defining a "style of manners" for the new federal government, which helped distinguish it from the Old World regimen that characterized royal courts in Europe. It often meant fostering an atmosphere that sought to highlight the desired characteristics of "republican equality," yet one that conveyed import and dignity at the same time.[1]

The concept of manners at the time extended far beyond mere social etiquette, for it placed special emphasis on upright personal character, virtue, and morality, seen as the bedrock of the infant republic.[2] For Enlightenment-inspired American leaders such as Washington and his new vice president, John Adams, those values ideally led to behavior directed toward the public good of the new nation. Both men realized that women like their wives could help shape and guide private behavior at social events that had broader public implications, including bring-ing politicians from diverse regions of the country into a closer national configuration. Although Washington could often be stiff and somewhat unapproachable, throughout her lifetime Martha was uniformly praised for her sociability, ready smile, and talent for skillfully and engagingly conversing with people from all walks of life, an approach to social interaction she had internalized from youth. Her mellowing presence brought a degree of much needed civility to administrative occasions, often populated by bickering male politicians who espoused different visions for the construction of the new nation.

Born on June 2, 1731, Martha, affectionately nicknamed Patsy, was the eldest of eight children born to John and Frances Dandridge. She received a typical upbringing and a somewhat superior education for women of her era and class. The modest-sized but successful five-hundred-acre Dandridge family tobacco plantation of Chestnut Grove was worked by a relatively small number of about twenty slaves and located in agricultural New Kent County, Virginia. Martha was taught (probably under the primary tutelage of her mother) dancing, horseback riding, sparkling conversation, and other social graces as well as the skills needed for running a competent eighteenth-century household that would have included cooking, baking, sewing, candle making, and growing vegetables and herbs that could be used as food or transformed into medicinal remedies. Certainly, from a young age, she learned to be a good domestic manager and socially adept gentlewoman, a skill set that stood her in good stead when she became the wife of the well-to-do plantation owner Daniel Custis and later, after her second marriage to George Washington, as mistress of their large Mount Vernon home.

In addition, Martha learned to read and acquired basic math and writing skills, which enabled her not only to enjoy novels, poetry, and history books but also to capably manage household accounts. The latter was particularly valuable after the death of her first husband and before her remarriage to Washington. Religion was central to the lives of most early Americans, and the Dandridges were known as regular churchgoers and faithful members of the Church of England. Martha, who was a lifelong devout Episcopalian, personally held deeply ingrained religious beliefs that sustained her during periods of grief and heightened her sense of duty to family and community.

Not only did literacy allow Martha to pray daily and read her Book of Common Prayer and Bible[3]—to which she was reputed to have devoted an hour daily after breakfast—but it also allowed her later, as the wife of Washington, one of America's most celebrated Revolutionary Patriots and noted military commanders and ultimately first president of the United States, to avidly follow newspaper descriptions of political events. After Washington retired from the presidency, Martha—and George—even subscribed to several books of essays published in 1798 by the American writer and women's rights supporter Judith Sargent Murray, in which Murray argued that women possessed robust intellectual capacities, and therefore, like men, they, too, benefited from a strong education. John Adams, then the president of the United States, also purchased these volumes, so Abigail Adams, Martha's successor as First Lady, was also exposed to Murray's progressive views on female education.[4]

When Martha married the wealthy Daniel Custis, she moved up in social and economic status and became part of the colonial landed gentry and chatelaine of the Custis's very comfortable and elegant home called White House, located on their Virginia estate in New Kent County. As a young woman, she enjoyed beautiful clothing and furnishings but tended to favor elegant simplicity over gaudy excess throughout her lifetime. Daniel, one of the wealthiest men in Virginia in his day, owned a number of tobacco planation farms in several counties as well as over two hundred slaves and a stately mansion in nearby Williamsburg, the capital and largest town in Virginia at the time. The local gentry enjoyed balls, plays, musical entertainments, and shopping in Williamsburg, and Daniel and Martha regularly visited the town, which was located about twenty-five miles from their main residence. In addition to running the busy household, supervising the work of the indoor enslaved men and women who acted as house servants, and bringing up their four children, Martha moved easily in Virginia social circles at parties and Sunday services and at other gatherings at St. Peter's Church, where her husband was a vestryman. Even as a young wife and mother, her cheerful, lively, and caring personality was evident.[5]

But wealth and power were not enough to protect Martha from the death of two of her young children and her husband from one of the many illnesses that ravaged Americans in the eighteenth century. Although the cause is uncertain, Daniel Custis appears to have died from complications from a severe throat infection, coincidentally similar to the illness that later led to George Washington's demise. Without the hallmarks of modern medicine, including antibiotics, reliable antiseptics, and anesthesia, a myriad of unidentified viruses and bacterial diseases claimed the lives of the rich as well as the poor with tragic regularity during their era.[6]

Daniel Custis died on July 8, 1757, at the age of forty-five intestate, that is, without having made a will. Fortunately for Martha, that meant in practice that she still received as a dower portion at least a third of his wealth (the rest being held in trust for her two surviving children), which included substantial property that totaled about 17,500 acres of land, but she was dependent on lawyers to execute the legal papers entitling her to take possession of the estate. Within days of her widowhood Martha, despite her grief and the needs of her young son, Jacky, and toddler, Patsy, was forced to turn to practical matters on the planation. In August, she was also already working on business related to Daniel's tobacco exporting business and other financial concerns. She ordered mourning clothes and an expensive tombstone for her late husband and began a brisk correspondence with his London agents.

Widowhood significantly enlarged Martha's economic power and personal independence as a *feme sole*. Soon Martha, with the initial assistance of her twenty-year-old brother Bartholomew (Bat), who was a lawyer, competently hired attorneys, business managers, and overseers to secure her legal rights and help carry out the work on the plantation farms and transactions related to selling their products. In a letter dated August 20, she firmly informed Custis's London factor, Robert Cary, that her late husband's "Affairs fall under my management . . . and I now have admon of his Estate. . . . I shall yearly ship a considerable part of the Tobacco I make to you which I shall take care to have made as good as possible and hope you will do your endeavor to get me a good Price."[7]

Given the social norm at the time that most elite southern women were expected to have little active interaction in the overtly public world of commerce, it is noteworthy that Martha almost immediately embarked on a surprisingly effective business campaign. She first acquired power of attorney for the estate, collected on outstanding debts, made personal loans, and penned her own letters to her creditors and bankers.[8] Many years later, presumably based on her own experience, she would advise a widowed niece to "exert yourself in the management of your estate. . . . A dependance is, I think, a wretched state and you have enough [funds] if you will manage it right."[9]

Before long, Martha turned to the question of remarriage. Colonel George Washington, who had made a name for himself during the French and Indian War, emerged among her suitors as a promising choice as a potential spouse. They shared many interests, with both George and Martha enjoying plays and music, and George especially was also a devoted and energetic dancer. At around six feet three inches tall, the imposing muscular military man towered over the petite, attractive Martha, who at only five feet tall was already inclined to plumpness. They may have met previously at a Virginia social function, but they appear to have been reintroduced at the home of a mutual friend in March 1758, and they were married the following year. Whether Martha "fell passionately in love with George almost immediately,"[10] as one of her biographers has claimed, is questionable, but she certainly developed a deeply heartfelt and abiding love and respect for him over the long years of their marriage, as he did for her. But in their day, marriage was often viewed as a strategic alliance. Men and women were expected to marry within their social set, and the Washington marriage brought advantages to both parties.

Although the two initially disagreed about which of their two plantation estate houses, White House or Mount Vernon, should become their home, Washington prevailed. George and Martha were married on January, 6, 1759. Within a few months, the newlywed couple, now a readymade family with the inclusion of Martha's two remaining children, moved into George's estate house, at that time a more modest edifice than the Custis family home. After their marriage, Martha re-acquired the designation of a *feme covert*, once again coming under the full dominion of a beloved and indulgent husband, but one who had full legal control over virtually all aspects over her life, including her land, slaves, finances, and even her children. Yet Martha appeared to be content with the arrangement, as did George, who informed a friend he was happily retired from the military world to Mount Vernon "with an agreeable consort for life."[11]

Mount Vernon was composed of five plantations, and with his new-found wealth, George purchased additional land and slaves to raise more tobacco. From the start of their marriage, the Washingtons set out to make their home one of the finest of its kind in Virginia, filling it with handsome furniture, beautiful paintings, ornate china and silver, and other exquisite household accoutrements. Many items were imported from England, as both the Washingtons considered themselves loyal British subjects. Many of the furnishings were chosen by George, who was determined to become a leading member of the local colonial aristocracy. At the same time, George gradually increased the size of the mansion, making it one of the largest residences in colonial America. As Martha moved from widowhood to a second marriage, she gave up the relative economic independence she had enjoyed and transferred all the former business dealings she had capably managed to George. He took over the supervision of all of the Custis plantations, which were spread over the New Kent, York, King William, Accomack, and Hanover Counties, as well as Martha's large retinue of slaves, the tobacco business, and a still unsettled lawsuit.[12]

Martha moved quickly back into the traditional female domestic roles, efficiently running the large household and gardens and overseeing the kitchen, smokehouse, dairy, and spinning work. Together with George, she selected what type of food supplies, furniture, and medicinal items to purchase. Both Washingtons admired fashionable clothing, and they often purchased fine imported dress items. In the early 1770s, for example, George ordered a white satin cloak and fine silk material for a gown for Martha from London, as well as several of the beautiful frilly lace caps she frequently wore.[13] However, for the most part, Martha dressed simply and neatly but always elegantly. As Abigail Adams was later moved to remark after her initial meeting with the First Lady, Mrs. Washington was "plain in her dress, but that plainness is the best of every article."[14] George devoted most of his efforts to running the planation farms. In addition to becoming a very competent agriculturalist, he also became a successful business merchant who oversaw the sale of salted fish and distilled whiskey from his plantation, and he also developed as an increasingly competent land speculator and investor.

Although it may not have begun as a love match (Washington was said to have carried a torch for another woman, Sally Fairfax, at the time of his engagement), by all accounts it was a marriage increasingly characterized by growing mutual admiration and fond compatibility. Washington proved to be a caring, affectionate husband and dutiful stepfather. In one of the few extant letters from George to Martha that survives, Washington informed Martha of his later appointment by Congress to lead the Revolutionary Army, unquestionably a momentous turning point in their marital life. He addressed Martha as "My Dearest" and then affirmed his reluctance to take on the military position, which he maintained [perhaps disingenuously] he only accepted out of a deep sense of responsibility and destiny. "I should enjoy more real happiness and felicity in one month with you, at home, than I have the most distant prospect of reaping abroad, if my stay were to be Seven times Seven years," George declared. Moreover, Washington stressed that Martha's happiness was his overriding concern and that his "earnest and ardent desire" was that in his absence she pursue a course that would bring her the most contentment and tranquility.[15]

Martha proved to be an affectionate and loving wife with a congenial personality. As one of her recent biographers has observed, she was a woman "who raised emotional support to an art form."[16] Unfortunately for posterity, Martha destroyed almost all of her correspondence with George, and she often tended to be matter of fact in her surviving correspondence, but in a fragment of a 1777 authenticated letter discovered in the 1990s (one of only two extant missives from Martha to George Washington that survives), Martha addressed her husband as "My love," reflecting their enduring and close relationship.[17] By the days leading up to the American Revolution, the Washingtons had forged an amiable marriage and a comfortable lifestyle. In 1774, Washington left Mount Vernon to serve as a Virginia delegate to the first Continental Congress in Philadelphia, probably unaware that this would mark the turning point in the couple's future in active public service. Both would become avid Patriots, even though in the beginning Martha had to defend herself against allegations that she harbored Tory sympathies as public attitudes opposing British policies hardened.

Content with their life at Mount Vernon, both Martha and George reluctantly acceded to the call of public duty at the beginning of the active conflict with England, though George was clearly more comfortable with the prospect of his going off to battle against the British in 1775 as the head of the Continental Army than his wife would be. Still, the thought of being separated from his spouse for long periods aroused palpable unease in George. In a letter written to his stepson Jacky Custis, Washington expressed his anxiety, revealing that "My great concern upon this occasion is the thought of leaving your Mother under the uneasiness" that would result and exhorted Jacky to use "every means in your power to keep up her Spirits."[18]

When Washington wrote to his "dear Patsy," as he affectionately referred to Martha, he had informed her that he was being dispatched to Boston and assured her of his reluctance to assume the role of commander. "I have used every endeavor in my power to avoid it," he maintained, "not only from my unwillingness to part with you and the Family, but from the consciousness of its being a trust too great for my Capacity." A few days later, as he left Philadelphia, he wrote Martha a short note and affirmed that he retained an "unalterable affection for you [Martha], which neither time or distance can change."[19] Later, after experiencing the bleak year of 1776 for the American forces, a worn down and often dispirited George was moved to declare to Martha from Morristown in early 1777 that "No one suffers more by my absence from home than myself." Clearly, Washington had developed a deep and abiding affection for his wife and appears to have been very dependent on her support.

Soon after George was appointed commander of the American army in June 1775, Martha's personal patriotic public spirit was tested in the social realm. During the perilous time of war, committees of safety throughout the colonies as well as the Continental Congress had strongly discouraged what they considered frivolous or expensive social events. That fall, Lady Washington, as she had been respectfully nicknamed, had been invited to such an event in Philadelphia, a ball scheduled in late November, but a group of four men from the committee met with her to persuade her not to attend. Martha clearly understood the political symbolism involved and that she had an opportunity to win public approval for herself and her husband. She graciously acquiesced to their request and, moreover, was reported to have informed the men "that their sentiments on this occasion, were perfectly agreeable unto her own."[20]

During the perilous eight and a half very long years of the war with the British, Martha was determined to join George at every winter camp, often leaving George's cousin Lund Washington in charge of the Mount Vernon plantation in her absence. Her experiences as the wife of the man who was probably the most well known figure in America served as a prelude to her later role as First Lady of the United States. In the face of hardships and real physical danger, she always managed to be by the side of her "Old Man," as she affectionately referred to her husband. Beginning in 1775, Martha left Mount Vernon annually for George's military winter quarters, although she was usually housed in superior, more comfortable locations at nearby farmhouses or homes. Under the most adverse conditions, she not only tended to Washington's needs but personally knitted and sewed for the troops and nursed the wounded, providing much needed moral support, comfort, and cheer to the officers and soldiers.[21]

Many American women provided encouragement for the Patriot war effort. It was no accident that when Philadelphia women, such as Benjamin Franklin's daughter Sarah Franklin Bache, collected funds to help the Continental Army soldiers, they designated Martha, as the wife of General Washington, to receive and help direct the use of those funds on behalf of the troops. In 1779, women who resided in a number of American states together raised the impressive sum of over $300,000, which at Washington's insistence was used primarily to provide shirts and other badly needed clothing items for the troops. Martha herself appears to have personally donated around $20,000 to the collection.[22] It is also interesting to note that earlier during the Revolutionary War the paths of Martha Washington, Thomas Jefferson's wife Martha Jefferson, and Ellen Conway Madison, the mother of James Madison and future mother-in-law of Dolley Madison, crossed. In the summer of 1780, in a letter to the senior Mrs. Madison, Mrs. Jefferson wrote to Ellen to inform her that Mrs. Washington had passed along news to her about the Philadelphia Ladies Association and its voluntary work on behalf of the Revolutionary cause. Mrs. Washington had suggested that a similar group be founded in Virginia.[23]

In fact, Martha's appreciation for the sacrifices that the American soldiers made propelled her to make one of her few overt political gestures when she later asked Congress to provide benefits for veterans after the war. Martha's efforts on behalf of American soldiers, both during and after the hostilities, were not mere window dressing, and they not only earned her personal popularity but boosted her husband's public reputation as well. Indeed, through her conduct during the Revolution, Martha became known as a model for virtue, sacrifice, and rectitude, which would help cement her position as First Lady.

While he was stationed in Philadelphia in 1775 as a delegate to the Continental Congress, John Adams wrote his friend Mercy Otis Warren back in Boston to praise both the Washingtons: "The General is amiable and accomplished and judicious and cool; you will soon know the Person and Character of His Lady [Martha]." He then offered a compliment to Mercy and his own wife Abigail by stating that he hoped Martha would have "as much ambition for her husband's glory" as the two women displayed, a goal Martha was destined to fulfill.[24] She became so esteemed by the general's troops that one of the regiments that fought at Valley Forge was named "Lady Washington's Dragoon" in her honor. When she served as First Lady, her personal generosity and advocacy for impoverished veterans helped set a precedent for the involvement of future presidential wives in a host of benevolent philanthropic causes, ones often related to children or poor families.

Moreover, the time that Martha spent at Washington's side during the war enlarged her world. She not only traveled far from home in a geographical sense, but she also encountered men and women from other regions of the country, who helped expand her social milieu. Although she and George may have not recognized it at the time, the war provided Martha with exposure to people with different backgrounds and world outlooks, which would gain her experience for her later role as First Lady. She not only interacted with the troops at camp headquarters, but also often entertained officers, members of the Continental Congress, and other visitors. As early as 1775, Martha traveled to Massachusetts, far from her comfort zone of Virginia, to join George in Cambridge as he commanded the American troops. She wrote rather proudly to her friend Elizabeth Ramsay back in Alexandria that, during a stop in Philadelphia, she had been treated very graciously. Martha reported that she had left the city "in as great pomp as if I had been a very great somebody." Although she found New England "a beautyfull country," she told her friend that she shuddered as she heard "cannon and shells from Boston and Bunkers Hill." And although the preparations for war were "very terrible indeed," she determinedly endeavored "to keep my fears to myself as well as I can,"[25] a stoic outlook she adopted not only during the war but during her stint as First Lady.

Throughout the Revolutionary War, Martha remained steadfast in her support of her husband and the troops as well as remaining a committed Patriot. When Boston's Mercy Warren invited Martha to be a guest in her home in light of the dangerous local circumstances, Martha politely thanked her and declined, but she extended her best wishes and that of General Washington's for the Warren family's "happiness" and her hope for "speedy, and honourable peace."[26] The Warrens and Washingtons remained on very friendly terms after the war had ended, but later after the Warrens became staunch Republicans, the two families parted ways.

Martha witnessed firsthand the daily hardships endured by the soldiers and the stresses her husband encountered, and they both politicized her and fueled her patriotic zeal. Writing to her sister in January 1776 from Cambridge during an especially precarious time for the military, Martha referred pointedly to "our cause." And later, from Valley Forge in 1778, she expressed her hope to Mercy Warren that "I hope, and trust, that all the states will make a vigorous push early this spring, if every thing can be prepared for it, and hereby putting a stop to British cruelties—and afford us that peace liberty and happyness which [we] have so long contended for."[27]

During the war, as her patriot zeal deepened, Martha had little empathy for British sympathizers. At the end of January, in a letter to her sister Nancy (Anna Maria Bassett) from Cambridge, Martha referred disdainfully to the number of Tories who resided in "that part of the world" of New York, who were unfriendly "to our cause," that of the Revolution and the army led by her husband General Washington. Later, after she relocated to Philadelphia, during August 1776 Martha wrote quite knowledgeably to her sister about the progress of military matters in New York, where General Washington actively continued to battle the formidable British forces.[28]

The 1781 Battle of Yorktown turned the tide for the American side, and it effectively served as the last engagement with the British before the execution of the 1783 Treaty of Paris, which formally ended the Revolutionary War. To celebrate the victory, George and Martha were feted in

Philadelphia, then the temporary seat of the government. But it was not until the closing days of 1783 that George Washington was able to finally bid his formal farewell to Congress after an emotional parting from his army officers the previous month at the Fraunces Tavern in New York City. When the final tally was in, Martha had spent nearly five years at her husband's side in the various winter army camps, periods of time that ranged from three to ten months. She had unquestionably sacrificed her personal comfort and time with her immediate family back in Virginia to serve her country through the essential support she provided for George.

At the conclusion of the war, in late 1783 the Washingtons were free at last to retire (at least temporarily) to Mount Vernon to tend their own "vine and fig"—a biblical reference often employed by the Washingtons, particularly George—and reunite with their family, which now included Martha's two adopted grandchildren, Eleanor Parke (Nelly) and George Washington (Wash) Custis. After the death of Martha's last child, her son Jack Custis, who tragically perished as a result of contracting typhus just as the war was ending, his widow Nelly remarried and allowed her two youngest children to remain permanently with the Washingtons.

Martha's young niece, Fanny Bassett, joined the household in 1784 and later married George Washington's nephew, George Augustine Washington. After her husband's return to Mount Vernon, Martha resolutely told a fellow female American Patriot that "The difficulties, and distresses we have been exposed during the war must now be forgotten. we must endevor to let our ways be the ways of pleasentness and all our paths Peace."[29] Martha was visibly back in her element at the family estate, surrounded by young people, and Mount Vernon, once again, became a successful enterprise under Washington's direct supervision. However, life was far from idyllic as Martha suffered a number of personal losses, which included the deaths of her mother and beloved younger brother, Bartholomew, who had been so supportive to her in her widowhood, leaving Martha with only one surviving sibling.

One of the many visitors to Mount Vernon after the Revolutionary War commented pointedly not only on the very apparent "solid happi-

FIGURE 1.1. *Washington and His Family.* George and Martha
Washington with grandchildren George Washington Parke
Custis and Nelly Custis. (Courtesy Library of Congress.)

ness" George Washington enjoyed in his retirement but the patriotism
Martha exhibited and the obvious pride she personally took in the ultimate success of the Continental Army. In 1785, John Hunter, an Englishman who was on a tour of Canada and the newly created American
republic, stopped to visit with the Washingtons for several days. He
recorded in his diary that it was "astonishing with what raptures Mrs
Washington spoke about the discipline of the army, the excellent order
they were in, superior to any troops she said upon the face of the earth
at the close of the war." Martha, who had initially viewed George's appointment to head the Continental Army with great apprehension and
reluctance, declared to Hunter that when she had viewed the troops in
full regalia before they disbanded, she found it a most "heavenly sight."
Moreover, she described military matters knowledgeably and noted with
evident satisfaction and pride how "melancholy" and tearful Washington's soldiers were at the prospect of parting from their beloved military
leader.[30]

But despite their obvious contentment, in 1787 the Washingtons were again thrust into public affairs. As the debates over the Constitution unfolded, a quartet of pivotal figures, composed of James Madison, Alexander Hamilton, John Jay, and George Washington, who presided over the Constitutional Convention, were key to guiding and influencing its ratification. Washington's national and international reputation virtually guaranteed he would be chosen as the individual to fulfill the inaugural executive position of the nation's first president within the new political framework created by the Constitution. Indeed, it was George's presence and involvement in the ratification process that was crucial to its successful adoption.[31] It was during that critical watershed period in American history that Martha rather disingenuously informed her niece Fanny that the only news she encountered focused on the debates and that "politicks" were of no concern to her.[32] That was patently untrue—she unquestionably understood that her future tranquility and happiness were at peril if her husband was persuaded to return to active public life, surely a "political" undertaking that was of immense personal concern to Martha.

Certainly, it was more of a severe disappointment than shock for Martha when the Washingtons were notified of George's election to the highest office in the land on April 14, 1789. Martha confided to her nephew she was saddened by her husband's election and maintained that, at age fifty-seven, "it was much too late for him to go into publick life again." By then, Martha was also showing the signs of age, and she was a plump, white-haired matronly woman who wore false teeth. However, to Martha's displeasure and dismay, once again, duty trumped their personal inclinations to remain at Mount Vernon in "solitude and tranquility." Yet despite her mixed feelings, Martha still worked to burnish the new president's public image and her own, later telling her friend Mercy Warren that, in accepting office, George had acted nobly "in obeying the voice of his country."[33] Just two days after George received official word of his election, he set out for New York City to be sworn in as the first president of the United States. Washington, who had been cheered and hailed throughout his journey from Virginia to New York, was treated to festive celebratory meals and even honored with a triumphal arch in Trenton, New Jersey, before he arrived in the new temporary capital on April 23 to set up the arrangements for the presidential household at 3 Cherry Street.[34]

Martha stayed behind, ostensibly to prepare the Virginia house for their prolonged absence. The Mount Vernon estate would be supervised in the interim by the Washingtons' nephew and niece George Augustine and Fanny Bassett Washington. However, through what appears to have been the passive-aggressive behavior of delaying her departure, in reality Martha may have simply been demonstrating her strong reluctance to return to public duty as well as her clear displeasure at the prospect of seeing her aging husband once more sacrificing their private happiness. Like the other presidential couples in this study, Abigail and John Adams and Dolley and James Madison, the Washingtons experienced an enduring partnership, but that does not mean they never disagreed or never held divergent opinions. After an emotional departure, Martha set out over a month later than her husband and began her journey from Mount Vernon accompanied by her two young grandchildren and clad in a modest brown homespun dress, clearly a symbolic patriotic gesture. Although Washington had apparently longed for her soothing presence beside him, Martha did not actually join her husband in New York until the following month in late May.

The new First Lady became a national public figure from almost the moment she left Mount Vernon, and like her successors, she soon realized she would be subject to constant scrutiny under the public eye. Yet it turned out to be an enjoyable trip for Martha in the company of her lively grandchildren. It was highlighted by a successful shopping excursion for luxury goods in the bustling port of Philadelphia, then the largest city in the United States. Lady Washington, as she was hailed, was greeted by admiring citizens in virtually every town she passed through on her journey. She stopped along the way in Baltimore, where she was celebrated with fireworks, and then in Philadelphia, where she was feted by city and state officials. Martha, in turn, rose to the occasion, and despite her personal misgivings, she responded with her typical warm sociability and ready smile, even offering a short rare public speech from her carriage to thank those who had welcomed her.

Conscious of their high-profile political status and Washington's desire to create dignity around the new executive office, George met Martha in Elizabethtown Point, New Jersey, on May 27, 1789. He then escorted her to New York on an impressively decorated presidential barge that had not long before ferried him to the new seat of the temporary federal government. It was an official and symbolic gesture that established the precedent that a presidential spouse occupied a "public role in the ritual and ceremonial aspects of the presidency."[35] The challenge for the presidential couple would be to project an image that reflected republican simplicity, political stability, and inspirational authority, all at the same time. After she was rowed to Manhattan Island by a crew of thirteen, Martha was "royally" welcomed in New York by the state's governor, George Clinton. Lady Washington was clearly flattered by the cheering crowds, an attendant parade, and the thirteen-gun salute in her honor, reminiscent to some degree of the extravagant rituals that had surrounded European kings and queens. Apparently being in the public eye was not quite as distasteful as Martha professed, as she proudly wrote her niece Fanny that "the paper will tell you how I was complimented on my landing."[36] It is quite obvious that the normally self-effacing Martha experienced some degree of exhilaration as she realized she had become a famous and perhaps even influential figure. Still, rather than receive the suggested honorary titles of Lady Washington or Marquise Washington, Martha preferred to be called simply "Mrs. Washington" and always referred to herself in that way.

From the first, Martha's life in New York was hectic. As she put it, "I have not had one half hour to myself since the day of my arrival,—my first care was to get the children [her grandchildren Nelly (Eleanor) and Wash (George Washington) Custis] to a good school."[37] Martha's first priority for education for her grandchildren clearly reflects her keenly

FIGURE 1.2. Portrait of Martha Washington from an original painting
by Gilbert Stuart. (Courtesy Library of Congress.)

felt responsibility as what we recognize today as a republican mother,
the need to ensure that the next generation would be provided with the
tools to become loyal and productive citizens. In addition, perhaps because of their own truncated access to schooling when they were young,
both Martha and George were staunch supporters of formal education for girls as well as boys as a broad goal for the new nation. Nelly,
with her energy and eager mind, thrived in the school environment, but
Wash, who preferred play to study, was assigned a private tutor to try to

encourage scholastic progress. By the fall, the previous arrangement for the lively little boy had been replaced with attendance at a small local school, and Nelly, who continued to take private music and art lessons, became a day student at the elite Mrs. Graham's local boarding school, where she studied French, grammar, spelling, and arithmetic, among other subjects.[38]

The handsomely furnished rented brick three-story house on Cherry Street that served as the presidential home featured a spacious drawing room and enough bedrooms to accommodate the immediate family as well as the seven enslaved servants the Washingtons brought with them from Mount Vernon. Also joining them were George's assistants, his personal secretary, Tobias Lear, who had originally served as the tutor to Martha's grandchildren, and aide-de-camp Colonel David Humphreys. Washington's nephew, Robert Lewis, appears to have served as a special assistant to Martha. He often accompanied her on excursions and helped out at the many events she hosted. Although the presidential mansion was large and dignified, it in no way resembled the massive lavish palaces that European monarchs occupied.

Reluctant or not, Martha Washington helped craft the first Republican Court, which developed the new protocol for "republican manners" that were carried out through a variety of social events. She was certainly aware that she now moved within a politically elite circle, and Martha soon found out that even the President's House, whether in New York or Philadelphia, was a political space. As the wife of the chief executive, her life, and that of her successors, would be both more public and political than other women's.[39] Although Martha was naturally gregarious, her initial displeasure with her role as First Lady likely stemmed from the prescribed narrow avenues that were suggested by Washington, John Adams, and members of Congress as they worked to construct appropriate parameters for the new government, including the official social style for the presidential couple. And as a very visible public figure, Martha also had to look her best at all times, so having her hair dressed daily and spending more time than usual donning formal clothes and receiving visitors became part of her regular routine. Of course, her role as First Lady was also constrained by contemporary gender parameters that considerably limited female political participation to the social realm of politicking.

An experienced hostess, Martha chafed under the new restrictions and rules placed upon her, for she had long been accustomed to moving freely in her native Virginia society. Washington and his advisers tried to adopt a social style that would be fitting for a modern republic. According to their decision, the president and his wife would not attend events such as private dinners or return most time-consuming social calls, as it might appear beneath the dignity of the head of government. These were practices that the sociable Martha, who had always interacted with many female relatives and friends, would undoubtedly have found both stifling and lonely. Fortunately, she retained close ties with some of her old friends, such as Lucy Knox, wife of Secretary of War Henry Knox, and Elizabeth Hamilton, the wife of Secretary of the Treasury Alexander Hamilton, who resided in New York with their politician husbands, and she soon developed an abiding friendship with Abigail Adams, the wife of the new vice president of the United States.

Some historians have dismissed Martha Washington as an intellectual lightweight, probably because of her strong focus on the southern ideal of female domesticity and her notoriously faulty grammar and spelling. That perception demeans the importance of women's domestic work in the colonial and early republic era, as well as her efforts on behalf of the new nation in the increasingly important social arena. Her letters often reveal a perceptive, thoughtful woman who understood political culture. In a 1789 letter written at the beginning of Washington's presidency to her friend Mercy Warren, Martha clearly explained her husband's primary motivation to promote the common good in accepting the presidency despite both their personal preferences for a return to tranquil private life. Although by this time some of Martha's semiofficial letters may have been edited or even drafted by her husband or his secretary, the Harvard-educated Tobias Lear,[40] they are consistent with Martha's views and sentiments exhibited in more informal letters to relatives and friends.

The December 1789 letter speaks volumes not only about George's motivations but also Martha's commitment to the republic: "I cannot blame him for having acted according to his ideas of duty in obeying the voice of the country," Martha averred, "of having attempted to do all the good in his power."[41] Among the founders, perhaps John Adams expressed this ideal about public obligation best when he earlier maintained that "Public Virtue is the only Foundation of Republics. . . . Every Man must seriously set himself to root out his Passions, Prejudices and Attachments, and to get the better of his private interest. The only reputable Principle and Doctrine must be that all Things must give way to the public."[42]

In any case, despite her initial discomfort, Martha recognized her "political" duty, which she carried out with her customary fortitude and became especially adept at hosting a number of events that came under the broad category of social receptions and, more specifically, drawing room salons. Those types of occasions were virtually all coordinated and hosted by women. Martha began her public role on the day after her arrival in New York as the hostess of the first of one of the many formal dinner parties in their spacious dining room, where primarily members of Congress were hosted on a rotating basis to ensure that men from all factions and states had an opportunity to interact with the president. It was a major undertaking, but Martha had a good deal of help in preparing for the official events, from enslaved servants who carried out much of the intensive physical labor, to New York tavern and innkeeper Samuel Fraunces, who was known for his culinary flair, and Polly Lear, the wife of Tobias Lear, who at times served as a quasi social secretary, assisting with invitations and other social arrangement details.

On Friday of her first week in New York, Martha presided over the first of her formal and popular receptions at the presidential mansion. These weekly drawing rooms became regularly well attended social occasions that also included members of Congress and their families, as well as visiting dignitaries and a wider group of both leading male and female members of the city's elite. Before guests were allowed to mingle around the room to converse with others, Washington's aides first greeted them. Next, they were presented formally to the First Lady, who was seated on a raised platform instead of a gilded throne like Queen Charlotte of England, and afterward they were officially introduced to the president. Although he often projected a stiff and regal demeanor, Washington could be affable, and once the protocol had been carried out, he often moved sociably among the crowd. For critics, these drawing rooms were too closely patterned on European court customs. Friday night events lasted from between seven and ten o'clock. However, as Martha became more confident in her role, she often encouraged the guests to leave closer to nine thirty to accommodate her husband's early bedtime.[43] Clearly Martha, as did most of her successors, viewed her position as First Lady as including seeing to her husband's welfare, and she was especially zealous about guarding his health and attempting when possible to reduce his workload, especially when he was ill or under undue strain.

At the official Thursday evening dinners hosted by President Washington, when only men were present, Martha generally sat at the head of the table, but when both males and females attended such event, Martha sat opposite George. After dinner, Martha usually retired upstairs with any female guests who were in attendance for coffee and more relaxed conversation, and they were later often joined by the president and the other men. Additionally, separate dinners and drawing rooms were hosted by Abigail Adams, and lesser functions were given by the wives of members of Congress or those who held other political posts. All served to develop an influential social and cultural network in which women could, if so inclined, speak freely about political and philosophical matters and foreign emissaries and other important visitors could be entertained.[44] As First Lady, Martha was looked upon as the reigning head of the group of female elite social leaders who fostered the behind-the-scenes interactions that helped define the character of the new style of federal government and that enhanced more effective communication, which was so crucial in those early days.

George Washington certainly understood that the role of the new executive president of the United States was a prime signifier of the unity and purpose of the country, and he consciously worked to bring the disparate states together into a seamless federal union. To accomplish this, he and several of the political advisers who surrounded him appropriated at least some of the old monarchical traditions to bolster Washington's authority as the nation's new leader while at the same time attempting to project the republican principles they had fought for during the American Revolution. Washington chose his cabinet members for their merits without realizing that some, like Thomas Jefferson and Alexander Hamilton, would soon become fierce political adversaries. During his first term, which was marked by peace and general prosperity, Washington experienced a successful honeymoon period as the head of the Federalist one-party government. However even during that period in the early 1790s, Jefferson and Madison introduced a second alternative political party, one that initially was known as the Democratic-Republicans and then later referred to as the Jeffersonian Republicans. Soon fault lines appeared in Washington's vision of an enlightened and harmonious republican government, and by 1793 radical divisions developed between the two nascent political parties, as each became aligned with their own partisan newspaper allies.[45]

Indeed, it is likely that, as the leader of the emergent Republican Party, Thomas Jefferson saw himself as a "republican patriarch" locked in a constant battle to "sustain the 'Spirit of '76" against "aristocratic" and "monocratic" Federalist leaders in the Washington and Adams administrations. Jefferson, once the personal friend and fellow comrade in arms of both Washington and Adams, increasingly viewed them as political leaders who schemed to fashion the new United States in the image of Great Britain and reverse the gains of the American Revolution.[46] By extension, Martha Washington and even his once-admired friend Abigail Adams, who also had hated the pomp of the French and

English courts while she resided in Europe, sometimes became targets of Jefferson's displeasure and anxiety.

In Jefferson's mind they and their husbands played a pivotal part in developing new quasi-monarchical rituals at their levees that mimicked the corrupt European courts. Jefferson's vision reflected his deeply in-grained belief that "true citizens governed themselves" and that politicians were merely servants of the people, not their masters.[47] Although Martha may have professed to eschew politics, she had to have been acutely aware of the criticism launched against her and her husband by Jefferson and other prominent Republicans. Certainly, years later she would disdainfully count Jefferson as an enemy of what became the Federalist Party, which coalesced around Washington. And while New York City served as the nation's capital, Martha was interested enough in politics to attend at least some congressional debates with other political wives such as Sarah Cornelia Clinton, the wife of New York's governor.

Aside from broader philosophical considerations about political style, on a practical level, it also soon became apparent that modifications were necessary to the unfolding social protocol of the United States government. In line with the ideals of the new republic, it was imperative that the president, in contrast to the royal monarchs of Europe, needed to be accessible to the public. But where was the appropriate line to be drawn that would enable the president to interact with American citizens but still allow him to carry out his myriad political responsibilities? Because the new president had initially been bombarded with visits from members of the general public, Washington began by restricting the days and hours that those callers without any official business to discuss could arrive unannounced, and he instituted a ceremonial schedule that included regular designated times for receptions, dinners, and levees.

At first, Tuesdays and Fridays from nine to three o'clock had been open to appropriately dressed male individuals without formal appointments. In addition, on Tuesdays from three to four o'clock in the afternoon, Washington "welcomed" even more ordinary men to drop in to a levee.

Overall, those events were not a success. Washington tended to be stiff in crowds, and the very formal atmosphere of his Tuesday levees alienated many and provoked criticism that the protocols that were followed there were not in keeping with the ideals of a republic. When Martha was present at social occasions, the ambiance was markedly improved. The First Lady was also said to be especially sensitive to the needs of former Revolutionary War soldiers, greeting them graciously if they came to visit, and although those gestures reflected Martha's private inclinations, they also served as effective and perhaps conscious public relations efforts that helped enhance George's reputation among veterans.

It is noteworthy that, in her role as First Lady, Martha presided over what was to become the first *political* salon in the United States. Enlightenment-inspired salons of the eighteenth century had been popular in Europe, especially in France, and a number of cultured elite French women who hosted those gatherings became prominent *sa-lonnières*. Those salons focused predominantly on social and intellectual interaction, but they sometimes included conversations with political themes. In recent years, historians have argued that the previously touted Parisian salons prior to the French Revolution were in reality much less egalitarian than previously thought, and political discussions, which were officially forbidden, were rare, if they existed at all. The French salons were primarily run and attended by members of the aristocracy, who were closely connected to the royal court, and according to recent scholarship, in practice the women who presided acted only as hostesses with little, if any, political agency other than being allowed to dispense limited patronage.[48]

But in the early American republic, the drawing rooms took on a somewhat different dimension, for they were *intentionally* political, albeit in perhaps a more practical way than their French counterparts. Although they were less formal affairs than the more official government administrative functions, the republican salons in New York— and later in Philadelphia and Washington—provided a forum for the national elite to meet for social interaction and lively conversation. At the same time, they were also places where political "alliances could be constructed or broken."[49] Moreover, those social gatherings provided a real public space for females, for the occasions primarily included political figures and their wives and other female family members and friends, and women took part in the conversation by sometimes vocally sharing their political opinions. In this relatively brief but fluid period when the United States government was in formation and political parties did not yet have a developed organizational apparatus, a great deal of politicking went on after hours when Congress was not formally in session.

Still it was clear that the ranks of national political leadership were consciously composed primarily of what they considered the "best classes." It was tacitly understood that elite women, who were part of the governing class and official society, took part in the conversation among friends and that they had a role in power brokering, sometimes working to expand or acquire influence for their own male family members. Moreover, elite marriages were also often initiated at social events, as alliances between powerful families were seen as playing an important part in the wider class formation.

Far from being simply a social entertainment, the regular occasions hosted by the Washingtons were consciously designed to merge "monarchial rituals with republican ideas" in order to connect the government more visibly with its citizens.[50] Although the new vice president's wife, Abigail Adams, was appalled at criticism aimed at Washington and the Federalist administration from the Republican Jeffersonian-backed press, newspapers like Philadelphia's *National Gazette* had a heyday firing barbs at what Abigail instead termed "Innocent action." Indeed, Abigail insisted in a letter to her sister that the president's Tuesday levees and Martha's Friday evening drawing rooms demonstrated "nothing which wears the least appearance of [royal occasions]."[51]

Yet Abigail tended to overlook some of the more obvious connections to European courtly customs, as well as her own appreciation for her own now-elevated social status. Earlier she had commented on the brilliant dress and jewelry of the women who had attended Martha's crowded New Year's celebration drawing room at the beginning of 1790, comparing them favorably to the level of high fashion exhibited by British women who attended social gatherings at St. James's Palace in London. Abigail also confided to her sister that, at some formal American government functions, female guests sometimes failed to remember that, as the wife of the vice president, Abigail was *always* entitled to be *properly* seated at the First Lady's right, but that they were soon gently corrected by the president. However, sensitive to the public mood of the time in regard to alleged royal-like behavior, in a sarcastic aside, Abigail then asked Mary Cranch to keep that bit of information confidential because "*all distinction* you know is unpopular."[52] Of course, major differences existed between the social formation and practices that had grown up around the French and English courts and that of the official society that was developing in the United States. But some elements of European style had been adapted to the American version as particular customs surrounding the governmental center of political power evolved under the Washingtons.

It was during that first summer of the new administration that Martha Washington and Abigail Adams first became formally acquainted. It was a relationship that blossomed into a strong friendship between the two women, who exhibited fundamentally different temperaments. Abigail had already met George Washington previously in his role as commander of the Continental Army in July 1775, when he was in Cambridge, Massachusetts, to assist the local militia in regaining control of Boston from the British. As the wife of John Adams, who was then a prominent Massachusetts delegate to the Continental Congress, Abigail had been one of the first Bostonians introduced to the general, who made a very positive impression on her.

Although she could often be critical, in this instance Abigail enthused to John that "You had prepared me to entertain a favorable opinion of him, but I thought the one half was not told to me. . . . Dignity with ease, and complacency, the Gentleman and the Soldier looked agreably blended in his face. Modesty marks every line and feture of his face. Those lines of Dryden instantly occurd to me: 'Mark his Majestick fabrick.'"[53] Abigail's remarks presage the adulation and cult of personality that would later develop around Washington when he served as president. During his administration, Republican opponents would frequently voice their outrage at the often hyperbolic praise directed at the nation's leader, declaring that in a republic no one man should be elevated to such a lofty king-like position.

From their first encounter, the wives of America's first president and first vice president expressed admiration for one another and exhibited a mutually supportive relationship. Both tended to be most comfortable among family and were somewhat reluctant participants in the necessary sociopolitical whirl of the early republic. Early on, Abigail described routine daily visits among the leading women of the New York area. Like the dinners and levees, these visits incorporated a political component. In addition to the female networks, sometime members of Congress and other prominent men also paid visits to elite women like Mrs. Washington and Mrs. Adams. Those occasions provided the opportunity for the females present to express their political sentiments to men who were in a position to act on them.[54] On Mondays, the Adams home at Richmond Hill, located on the then outskirts of New York City (what is now Greenwich Village), was open to ladies and gentlemen who partook of coffee and tea and chatted for half an hour so before returning to "Town," located around a mile and a half away. During her time in New York, Abigail usually attended Martha Washington's Friday evening social events "once a fortnight," and the two often sat side by side to greet guests at official functions.[55]

Abigail was drawn toward Martha's natural dignity and elegant simplicity, as well as her warm, cheerful, and nurturing personality. Abigail's prolific correspondence provides us with a firsthand description of her first meeting with Martha in June 1789 in the nation's temporary capital of New York City. From Richmond Hill she reported to her sister Mary, "I took the earliest opportunity (the morning after my arrival) to go & pay my respects to Mrs. Washington. . . . She received me with great ease and politeness. She is plain in her dress, but that plainness is the best of every article. She is in mourning. Her Hair is white, her Teeth beautiful, her person rather shorter than otherways . . . Her manners are modest and unassuming, dignified and feminine, not the Tincture of ha'ture about her."[56]

Abigail had made an astute observation: Martha may have worn elegantly simple gowns, but like her husband George, Lady Washington had long appreciated fine, high-quality accoutrements, which they viewed as a mark of gentility. The presidential couple understood that dress reflected position and that the elaborate costumes worn by European royalty had signaled both political and social power. Indeed, aspiring American statesmen like Washington believed that urbanity, civility, and polish, long associated with European courtly behavior, demonstrated their ability to lead. Despite its association with aristocratic values, even after the American Revolution, courtly refinement remained a valued trait in the new republic because gentlemanly manners appeared to help inspire trust.[57] Clearly, political power and social reputation were interconnected.

When Abigail had interacted with the English royal couple when John was stationed in London, she had observed firsthand that, donned in their finery, the royal family appeared enveloped in privilege. In the new republic of the United States, the challenge would be to convey the dignity and strength of leadership and at the same time reflect the egalitarian ethos that informed popular opinion. After all, in France, Marie Antoinette had lost her crown and her life, in part, over issues revolving around dress. While exuding authority and the fine taste that befitted a leading member of the political elite, George Washington attempted to transform the excesses of European luxury into republican virtue.[58] Martha's more restrained dress and conspicuously proper demeanor was something Abigail not only admired but tried to emulate when she later assumed the role of First Lady.

Although Abigail was unable to meet that day with the president, who was ill, she was clearly taken with his wife's deportment, sense of fashion, and friendly reception. As Abigail's remarks reveal, Martha may have exuded republican simplicity, but she loved beautiful clothing as well as superior decorative objects, such as fine china and silver. Abigail herself tended to be conservative in dress and often deplored the excesses of French and even British royal fashion, but, she, too, had an aesthetic appreciation for attractive gowns and jewelry. Yet, compared to the future First Lady, Dolley Madison, Martha and Abigail appear as plain sparrows alongside a peacock.

Martha's first forays into public entertainment were temporarily sidelined within a short time after she arrived in New York when George was temporarily felled by what was described as a painful inflamed tumor, or "malignant carbuncle," a malady that today would probably be diagnosed as a staph infection that developed into a fast-growing infected abscess. Although it was successfully excised, it confined him to bed for six weeks, and Martha and his physicians had feared for his life.[59] Martha even stepped in for the president when he was ill at a memorial service to honor the life of deceased Revolutionary War hero General Nathanael Green. According to Abigail, who paid a sick call in July 1789, President Washington was forced to lie on a cot set up in his carriage when he ventured out. He was often accompanied by Martha, whom Abigail again praised for her elegant, neat, but simple style of fashion and for her always pleasant "countenance & unaffected deportment which renders her the object of veneration and respect."[60] This time Abigail was invited upstairs to meet George. The president was still forced to recline on a sofa because of his malady, but his dignified and welcoming manner made a very positive impression upon her.

It is also Abigail Adams who provided future historians with one of the most detailed descriptions of Martha's "fryday 8 o clock" drawing room receptions, at which Martha hosted a tea for men and women, which at times even included ordinary citizens. Guests were announced by the Washingtons' servants and met at the door by Humphreys and Lear, who then "handed" them to the seated Martha Washington, to whom they curtseyed before being seated. As the wife of the vice president, Abigail was seated on Martha's right. After the initial standard ritual was performed, President Washington then greeted individual ladies and left the company to enjoy an intentionally simple "republican" array of refreshments that omitted spirits but included coffee, tea, and "homely . . . Ice Creems and Lemonade," as Abigail put it.[61]

In the early republic, the president and his wife often had to walk a fine line between what were perceived as detested Old World monarchial practices and those that appeared to reflect more republican virtues. Newspapers that supported the Jeffersonian Republican faction quickly denounced George's levees as "court-like" and Martha's formal events as "queenly drawing rooms," comparing them to European royal courts.[62] Martha typically sat on a raised seat to greet guests, and critics such as Jefferson viewed the practice as a signal of creeping monarchy, akin to kings and queens who were seated on thrones. That Martha sometimes wore simple white muslin gowns at the events she hosted may have reflected her desire to deflect criticism by attempting to appear more republican than regal. By 1793, the Republican political faction loudly decried what they considered "courtly rituals" and overtly criticized the president and his wife through print campaigns as increasingly distancing themselves from the common people. They maintained that the alleged anti-republican nature of the events that the presidential couple hosted, which they perceived as compromising the principles of the American Revolution, was moving the country away from the desired level of simplicity that should have characterized the new republic.[63]

Abigail Adams was reputed to have been the first who dubbed the social side of the early presidential administration the "Republican Court" but, in her case, to distinguish it *favorably* in her opinion from its European counterparts.[64] She apparently continued to describe events hosted by the Washingtons over the coming years in a similar manner, for later from Philadelphia in February 1791, she wrote her daughter Nabby to inform her that she had "dined with the President, in company with the ministers and ladies of the court. . . . He [Washington] was more than usually social."[65]

Increasing criticism about the Washingtons' court style clearly stung Martha. It might have been another ingredient that influenced her negative comments to her niece Fanny, in which she famously maintained that she often felt like "a state prisoner" in her role as First Lady. Yet even presidents felt constrained by the dictates of the highest public office, and over a century and a half later, President Harry Truman only half in jest referred to the White House as "the great White jail."[66] As we learned previously, at first, under the direction of Washington and his closest advisers at the time, Martha's duties were often rigidly prescribed, and her schedule much more constricted, than the more amiable social lifestyle she had enjoyed at Mount Vernon. This was likely why she informed her niece that her life was circumscribed and "very dull" in New York, as she felt obligated to keep within the strict parameters set for at the same time by both her detractors as well as several Federalist leaders. Martha claimed to Fanny that "as I cannot do as I like I am obstinate and stay at home a great deal," for the most part only venturing out for visits with close friends.[67]

Yet in letters to Mary Cranch, Abigail Adams mentioned many enjoyable visits and outings with the Washingtons, so Martha's social interactions were likely not as limited as she suggested, and she was perhaps only venting her frustrations over what she perceived as unfair public opinion about the presidential couple's lifestyle and the strict guidelines for entertaining with which she had been presented. George enjoyed plays, and the Washingtons often attended the theater in New York with friends including Abigail and members of his cabinet such as Alexander Hamilton and Henry Knox and their wives. Moreover, by the end of 1789, Martha assured her friend Mercy Otis Warren of Massachusetts that she had grown accustomed to her role as First Lady and that she was pleased that her husband had received the "respect and affection" he deserved during his northern tour in New England. In addition, she was gratified that "The difficulties which presented themselves to view upon his first entering upon the Presidency, seem thus to be in some measure surmounted: It is owing to this kindness of our numerous friends in all quarters that my new and unwished for situation is not indeed a burden to me."[68]

Martha also confided to Mercy that, although she personally would have much rather been allowed to remain home at Mount Vernon than to "occupy a place [as First Lady], with which a great many younger and gayer women would be prodigiously pleased," she was not, "God forbid," as she put it, expressing dissatisfaction with her "present station." Too many considerate people around her had extended their best efforts to "make [her] as contented as possible" for her to complain. Yet she managed to still reveal her natural preference for a more tranquil private life out of the limelight: "I have too much of the vanity of human affairs to expect felicity from the splendid scenes of public life."[69] Still, as always, duty and her partnership in a family unit were the overarching guiding principles for the resilient Martha, and she was determined to carry out her role resolutely and with as much grace as possible. Six months later, Martha reiterated her outlook in another letter to Mercy. Martha informed her friend that she was as content in New York as it was possible for her to be outside of Mount Vernon and that she would have been very ungrateful if she did not acknowledge "that everything has been done which politeness, hospitality or friendship could suggest, to make my situation as satisfactory and agreeable as possible."[70]

By the fall of 1789, the relationship between the Washingtons and the Adamses had even developed to the degree that, before the president left for his New England tour, the two families joined for a break from the demanding pace of work for a relaxing day excursion by boat to Long Island to visit the "Princes Gardens." The friendship between Martha and Abigail helped create a reasonably good working partnership between the president and vice president, whose personalities and political styles were often at odds. As it turned out, Martha found a trip by water somewhat anxiety provoking, so it was decided that the men would set out early on October 10 for the gardens by boat and Abigail and Martha would leave later in the morning and travel instead by "Mrs. Washingtons coach and six" to meet the gentlemen's party at a halfway destination. The two ladies were accompanied by Abigail's pregnant daughter, Nabby Smith, and Martha's granddaughter, Patsy Custis, and the quartet rode together to an inn known as Mariner's Tavern, located in upper Manhattan overlooking the Harlem River. The outing proved very agreeable to all, and Abigail reported with obvious satisfaction, "We live upon terms of much Friendship & visit each other often." She also, once again, praised Martha's gracious manner: "Mrs. Washington is a most friendly, good Lady, always pleasant and easy, dotingly fond of her Grandchildren, to whom she is quite the Grandmama."[71] Coming from Abigail, who had a tendency to be critical, this was a high compliment indeed.

The relationship between Martha and Abigail remained steadfast, and when President Washington set out in the fall of 1789 on his tour of the northern states to take the pulse of popular sentiment toward the new government, the two women met often to dispel their loneliness. As Abigail observed, "While the gentlemen are absent we propose seeing each one another on terms of much sociability."[72] While President Washington was away from New York on the month-long tour of New England, Abigail clearly made a great effort to keep the First Lady company. In mid-October, for example, when Martha invited the Adams family to dinner, she also noted that she planned to accompany Abigail to a concert that evening. In fact, before John Adams left town, he and Abigail joined Martha for a musical concert, and they also dined again at the Cherry Street presidential mansion in George's absence. Similarly, in early November, Martha told Abigail that she was disappointed that bad weather kept Abigail from a planned visit but that she was looking forward to dining at the Adams home at Richmond Hill the following Saturday, along with a group of friends that included Washington's secretary of war General Henry Knox as well as a number of female guests.[73] After John departed New York for Braintree soon after Washington left, Abigail and Martha continued to socialize. Abigail later wrote her sister that, not only did she hope that Mary would have the opportunity soon to meet with "our worthy President," whom Abigail described as "a favorite of mine," but she also asked her to inform John that Martha had a small gift for him, which she promised to bestow when he returned to New York.[74]

During 1790, social events under the administration continued unabated. When New Year's fell on the day of Martha's regular "publick day," she hosted her usual event but with heightened celebration. As Abigail noted, she continued to take her regular place beside Martha as "My station is always at the right hand of Mrs Washington." When female guests sometimes mistakenly sat in Abigail's customary spot, President Washington tactfully reminded them of the proper Republican Court etiquette, and they soon learned to rise whenever she approached. Abigail, who admired George Washington, was also a shrewd observer of human nature. She noted that, while in the final analysis the president's opinions nearly always prevailed, he accomplished this in such an affable manner that people did not realize the steely strength of his will. As Abigail astutely observed, "if he was not really one of the best intentioned men in the world he might be a very dangerous one."[75]

The Washingtons and Adams also continued to meet at occasions that held symbolic political importance. After Benjamin Franklin's death in April 1790, the presidential couple as well as the vice president and his wife joined members of Congress and a number of foreign ministers for a well-attended memorial service in New York for the late statesman and Revolutionary Patriot leader. Franklin was still venerated as a hero, and at Franklin's funeral in Philadelphia, an astounding number of over twenty thousand people had gathered to pay their respects.

The friendship between Martha and Abigail deepened further during 1790 while both still resided in New York, and Martha sometimes dropped in for afternoon tea at the Richmond Hill home with other women whose husbands were involved in the thick of political life, such as Mary Alsop King, the wife of the senator from New York, Rufus King.[76] By late February, the Washingtons had moved into a new, elegant, and spacious leased presidential mansion on Broadway, where they resided until their move to the temporary capital in Philadelphia. By the spring, George had became dangerously ill but recovered. In one of the modest number of letters that Martha Washington penned that survive, she wrote Abigail to inquire "how the Vice-President and Mrs. Adams are to day—Mrs. Washington is happy to inform that the President [who had contracted influenza and then a dangerous case of pneumonia] is a little better to day than he was yesterday."[77]

A year after Abigail first shared her observations about the Washingtons' social functions, she elaborated about the continuing receptions they hosted weekly. She emphasized that they were quite modest events without a hint of the frivolity or the "dissipation" that characterized European nobility, as some of the Boston papers had critically suggested. Abigail, who had experienced the practices of royalty firsthand in France and England, was more qualified than most Americans to assess diverging customs in the Old World and the United States. She tartly observed to her sister that "faction and Antifederalism may turn every Innocent action to evil." Jumping to the defense of the Washingtons, according to Abigail, "the Presidents Levee of a Tuesday and Mrs Washingtons drawing of a fryday" lasted only two hours for the former and about three hours for the latter, in contrast to the far lengthier events at the European courts. In summer, Martha offered "Tea, coffe, Cake, Lemonade & Ice Creems" to her guests, and to Abigail, these innocent amusements were far superior to alternative entertainments in taverns or at extravagant supper parties, where expensive fine wines flowed freely.[78]

Brought into close proximity in their complimentary roles as the wives of the nation's two highest-level leaders, the friendship between Martha Washington and Abigail Adams flourished. They often enjoyed one another's company, even apart from formal official government-related events. In early June 1790, for example, Martha and Abigail took a trip by coach together to New Jersey, an excursion that Abigail reported with obvious pleasure to her sister: "I last week accompanied

Mrs. Washington to the Jersies to visit the [water] falls of Pasaick [Passaic]. We were absent three days and had a very agreeable Tour."[79]

That autumn, a large party of American political leaders and their wives—which included John and Abigail Adams; their son, the young lawyer and future president, John Quincy Adams; Thomas Jefferson; Henry and Lucy Knox; Alexander and Elizabeth Hamilton; and the Washingtons—traveled by coach to visit the site of one the battles of the Revolutionary War. At the time, during the honeymoon period of the first Washington administration before political party fractures became full blown, all of the participants were still on cordial terms. Washington noted in his diary that the group assembled at Fort Washington at the upper end of Manhattan Island and then joined together for supper at a home that had once served as Washington's headquarters. The house had originally belonged to the prominent Tory Roger Morris, who had moved to England at the beginning of the war.[80]

The friendship between Martha and Abigail had progressed to the point that, when Martha left for Mount Vernon at the end of August in 1790, Abigail noted that she hoped her separation from Martha would be short and that she would part with the First Lady with "much regret. . . . No Lady can be more deservedly beloved & esteemed than she is, and we have lived in habits of intimacy and Friendship."[81] The relationship extended even to the two women's grandchildren, for later Martha issued an invitation to Abigail's granddaughter, the child of Nabby and William Smith, to join Martha's grandchildren Nelly and Wash for their regular lessons with their European dancing master, James Robardet.[82]

The Washingtons left New York in the late summer of 1790 for a three-month respite at Mount Vernon, but not before they were cheered by large crowds and afforded a thirteen-gun salute as they boarded the presidential barge. The site of the nation's next temporary capital moved to Philadelphia for an agreed-upon ten-year period, and the presidential couple arrived there in late November. Martha carried out her duties and continued to host numerous social gatherings at the rented President's House, the vacated Morris family mansion on Market Street, beginning with her first official reception in early 1791. As she wrote a friend at the end of January, "since my arrival in this place the business of settling in a new habitation receiving and returning visits have left me no time for myself."[83] However, Martha also found in Philadelphia a more comfortable social milieu than she had experienced in New York. In Philadelphia, not only was Martha able to reunite with old friends, such as the leading Bingham, Morris, Penn, and Powel families, but some of the more rigid social rules that the Republican Court had operated under in New York had been relaxed, and the presidential couple was able to return visits to acquaintances. Martha also appears to have had the opportunity to spend more time in the kitchen on tasks she enjoyed, such as brewing her own morning coffee and tea for the family.

Still, the Philadelphia events were perhaps somewhat more elegant and more cosmopolitan than those Martha had overseen in New York, and Martha, in turn, was sometimes criticized for the lavishly decorated and British manufactured gilded coach she sported as she rode about town. Martha's Friday night drawing rooms in the new seat of government frequently included elite female members of Philadelphia society, who often appeared in French-inspired beautifully fashioned ensembles, and Martha herself indulged in acquiring an attractively stylish black velvet gown. Perhaps Martha felt the dress was a match for George's favored black velvet suits. Henrietta Liston, the wife of the British minister Robert Liston, also took part in these social events and noted that "publick tea parties seem to be an amusement of which the Ladies of this Country are particularly fond, and mine will have the advantage of *Cards* over Mrs. Washington," who, in line with her more austere personal style, did not approve of card playing.[84]

Moreover, as the new temporary capital, Philadelphia provided increasing opportunities for educated upper-class American women to participate in the evolving political culture, albeit in an informal manner. In addition to Martha Washington, a number of other prominent

Philadelphia women also hosted their own salons, including, most visibly, the accomplished and well-read Anne Willing Bingham, the wife of Federalist senator William Bingham. Mrs. Bingham, who was a strong proponent of female education, had spent time in France during the same period Thomas Jefferson resided there. She had participated enthusiastically in Parisian salons and admired what she perceived as the robust involvement of French women in lively intellectual discussion on a wide variety of topics.

Jefferson, however, who idealized the domestic role of women, held ambivalent views about politically minded women like those he had encountered in France. Jefferson particularly detested the intrigue and corruption he viewed surrounding European court culture and believed there was far too much unacceptable meddling by aristocratic women who had been accorded too much power. Although he acknowledged that cultured women could participate intelligently and valuably in "public spaces," he drew the line at formal politics because he felt such involvement was fundamentally in conflict with women's natural and lofty domestic role. For Jefferson, the political world was the exclusive purview of men, and women needed to be kept at a distance from the messy practice of politics.[85]

In a famous letter to Jefferson, however, Mrs. Bingham forthrightly lauded those intellectual women she had met in France for asserting "our [Female] Privileges" and likely looked to the French salons as a model for her own highly popular and influential events. Later, Jefferson lectured Anne Bingham by maintaining that she and other women should be "too wise to wrinkle their foreheads with politics" but should rather confine themselves to "soothe and calm the minds of their husbands returning ruffled from political debates."[86] In reality, however perhaps both Jefferson and Bingham were exaggerating the political power of Parisian *salonnières*, who have increasingly been viewed by scholars as accomplished social hostesses who exerted very little real political or intellectual impact.[87] However, in Bingham's mind French women were inspirational, and back in Philadelphia, she undoubtedly prided herself on both the high level of discourse and the civility between her guests, even those who held radically different political opinions. The attendees at Bingham's occasions, which occupied a space between the overtly public and the private sphere, included friends who were some of the most prominent political players among the governing class at the time, including the Washingtons, the Adamses, the Madisons, and Thomas Jefferson.[88]

By now more accustomed to their roles, both Martha and Abigail Adams moved more freely in Philadelphia society and attended a number of Bingham's salons, as well as hosting many of their own entertainments, most of which had at the least an indirect but significant political influence. For instance, "The men and women who frequented the social gatherings . . . were consciously aware that these occasions functioned to smooth over the variety of political and personal differences among guests" so the government could function.[89] In other words, a fortuitous conjunction of social, cultural, and political forces combined in Philadelphia during the early republic to actively thrust elite women into the center of politics, and they took advantage of the opportunity to take part in the national conversation, including to what extent aristocratic traditions should play in the new American sociopolitical culture. During that period of time, both Federalists and Republicans attempted to win over their female connections as allies in support of their own particular national goals. Thus the Republican Court presided over by Martha, and later by Abigail, as well as the satellite salons hosted by other elite women such as Eliza Willing Powel and her niece Anne Willing Bingham, were far from mere private domestic entertainments, as were common in France, and the American version served as a conduit to knit disparate elements in the new republic together and foster wider support, performing a vital function in the process of nation building. The salons were, in essence, a broadly defined public site where "gender, politics, and society intersected."[90] That is not to say that women played a formal, official role in governance. But along with Anne Bingham, Martha Washington, Abigail Adams, and later Dolley Madison surely understood that the events they hosted were helping to shape the emerging national political and social culture and that what occurred in the capital would radiate out through all regions of the country.

By late spring, Abigail Adams had already returned to what she considered the more "salubrious" climate of Massachusetts to help repair her often fragile health as well as the family finances, but Martha kept tabs on her friend from Philadelphia, where residents were already beginning to feel the effects of oppressive heat and humidity. She also insisted that her promise to keep in touch with Abigail was one that she intended to keep. In May 1791, Martha wrote that she hoped Abigail's health would be reestablished in Braintree and that regrettably she could not provide Abigail with much information about the local "fashionable world hear [*sic*]—you know I am not much in it at any time," particularly as many residents had already fled the heat to move to summer homes in the country. Martha herself was unable to leave for Mount Vernon until late July as her grandchildren were still in school, but in the meantime she presented her "complements to the Vice President" and her "Best wishes for the health and happy ness of yourself and family."[91]

By mid-June, Abigail was sufficiently recovered to reply with a lengthy letter to the First Lady. She acknowledged her appreciation of Martha's interest in her health and related that she had been "so weakened and debilitated as to be unable to walk alone." She continued by expressing her happiness that President Washington had returned safely to Philadelphia in good health from his "Ardous Southern Tour" and related that, when she herself had traveled home to Massachusetts, people along the way had expressed their satisfaction with the "administration of their Government." This reflected the fact that during his tenure, Washington had undertaken a tour of all thirteen states to assess the health of the nation and encourage support for the new federal government. Abigail concluded with the hope that she would hear again from her "dear mrs Washington," whose Health and happiness" remained the sincere concern of her "affectionate friend and Humble servant."[92]

Anxiety over the health of her own family members sometimes distracted Martha and even prevented her from socializing with friends in Philadelphia. Having lost her own four children to disease, Martha was understandably extremely sensitive to the effects of any illnesses contracted by her grandchildren. In the fall of 1791, she penned a letter to Abigail apologizing for not answering a letter she received in late June as her grandson Wash "Was confined to his bed with a cruel fevor for three weeks in the Months of July and August. . . . The fatague and anxiety, which I underwent, were almost too much for me." With her grandson on the mend, Martha returned to her obligations and wrote of her relief that Abigail had overcome her bout with "ague." She also informed Abigail that she planned to soon travel with President Washington to Mount Vernon in the hope that the "change of air" would benefit their grandchildren. Reiterating that she hoped to see a fully recovered Abigail back in Philadelphia in October, Martha signed the letter as "your affectionate friend."[93]

It should come as no surprise that Martha was unhappy but resigned over George's decision to serve a second term as president. Still, she dutifully attended his rather modest inauguration on March 4, 1793, and remained cordial to all the attendees. As political divisions deepened, the animosity between Jeffersonian Republicans and the Hamiltonian Federalists, led by Secretary of the Treasury Alexander Hamilton, became more open, and the Washington Republican Court came under increasing attack for its alleged "aristocratic" leanings. By Washington's second term, most newspapers served as blatant partisan organs for one or the other of the two political parties. Philip Freneau, editor of the *National Gazette*, and Benjamin Franklin's grandson, Benjamin Franklin Bache, editor of the *Aurora*, were especially strident critics of Washington, who had enjoyed relative immunity from public criticism at the start of his presidency. As the schism between Washington and Jefferson widened, Martha and the Adamses drew closer together. Abigail Adams noted the more frequent virulent attacks against the presidential couple in a letter to John written at the beginning of 1795, when she wrote: "Present me most dutifully to the President and Mrs. Washington. They are both too good to be persecuted."[94]

Republicans were especially incensed by the unpopular excise tax on whiskey that resulted in the infamous Whiskey Rebellion by western farmers. Martha was obviously well aware of the insurrection and unsurprisingly supported the Federalist position. In late September 1794, she informed her niece that "the insurgents in the back country has carried matters so high that the President has been obligied to send a larg body of men to settle the matter—and is to go himself tomorrow to Carlyle to meet the troops."[95] The support of the 1795 Jay Treaty between the United States and Great Britain carried forward by Washington and other Federalists also invoked Republican ire. Although it played an important part in improving Anglo-American relations, some like Jefferson viewed the Jay Treaty as further proof of the administration's monarchist tendencies exhibited by economic support of England and the betrayal of France, the country that had served as such a staunch ally during the American Revolution.[96] Washington's former friend and supporter, Mercy Warren, who had originally idolized George, became highly critical of him as president and denounced him for his "coldness to the cause of France, his love of adulation, his favouriteism."[97] The Federalists, in contrast, feared that Republicans encouraged too much French influence in the United States. In fact, the Jay Treaty would come back to haunt John Adams during his presidency as the French reacted to it vehemently by illegally seizing American ships, nearly precipitating an outright open war between the United States and France.

Both George and Martha felt the keen pressure of the factional fractures, but, ironically, although she longed to return to Mount Vernon at the end of George's second term, Martha seemed to have had a more pleasant experience as First Lady during that period. Although she still bristled at any criticism of her husband, she was able to charm at least some of Washington's detractors. She also appears to have found her role more satisfactory in Philadelphia, where she enjoyed more social interaction, especially hosting teas for small groups of her close female friends.[98] It was during Washington's second term that Martha and Dolley Madison, the new wife of the prominent congressman James

Madison, crossed paths more frequently. According to Dolley's niece, the Washingtons were said to have had a hand in encouraging Dolley's 1794 marriage to James Madison. Mary Cutts, who painted a rather rosy and unobjective picture of Dolley's life in her memoir, also claimed that, when the Madisons returned to Philadelphia in the fall of 1794, it became Dolley's "duty, as well as a very great source of pleasure to grace with her beauty the Republican Court of Lady Washington!"[99] Dolley's sister was married to George's nephew, and as friendly newfound "relatives," Dolley and Martha were reputed to have exchanged recipes, and Martha was said to have gifted Dolley with a valuable and delicately decorated porcelain milk pitcher.[100]

Of course, it was Martha Washington who largely superintended and helped set the tone at the court salons and other similar events in both New York *and* Philadelphia. Although Martha mounted a defense of the president in her personal correspondence and conversations with guests who attended her hosted events, she never ventured to offer her opinion in print in the increasingly influential media outlets of the day. Perhaps she felt her writing skills were too limited or that it was beneath the dignity of the First Lady to become involved in such a publicly visible role. Yet a well-known female ally of the Washingtons, the prominent American writer and poet Annis Boudinot Stockton, did attempt to influence public opinion by publishing poetic work that praised the Washington administration in one of the new nation's leading newspapers, the pro-Federalist *Gazette of the United States*.[101]

As time passed, although they were geographically separated, Abigail and Martha continued to keep in touch. In the spring of 1794, Abigail took the opportunity to send a letter to Martha via her son John Quincy, who had recently been appointed by President Washington as ambassador to the Netherlands as a reward for his support. A proud Abigail was unable to resist pointing out the part she had played in her son's political training, noting that "at a very early period of Life I devoted him to the Publick." Despite the possible danger during the Revolutionary era, Abigail asserted that she had allowed her son to accompany her husband to Europe so that he could be exposed to his father's patriotic influence and political wisdom. Abigail concluded the letter with a reference to her own loyalty to the American republic, noting that "I derive a satisfaction from the hope of his becoming eminently useful to his Country."[102] Her remarks provide us with rare insight into the manner in which leading political families of the time schooled their offspring to participate and excel in public life. Certainly, both Abigail and John had guided and groomed their eldest son for political greatness.

And in a letter written at the end of 1795 to Abigail from her husband John, he made a special point to let her know that "The President and Presidentess" [George and Martha] always send their Regards to you. Madam [Martha] invites you to come next Summer to Mount Vernon and visit the Federal City [what would become the nation's capital of Washington, DC]." It is interesting to note that John referred to Martha as "Presidentess," so that sobriquet was not used first to refer to either Abigail or Dolley Madison when they each assumed the position of First Lady. Moreover, John told Abigail that he had informed "La Presidante [Martha]" that in 1800, when the capital of the United States was scheduled to be permanently located in Washington, with Congress "set" there as well, it was entirely possible that Abigail would pay a visit to Mount Vernon to see her old friend.[103]

With the election of John Adams as president in 1797, the Washingtons were at last free to return to their beloved Virginia home, much to the relief of Martha. As early as January, she wrote with great anticipation that "A few weeks now, will place me in the shades of mount Vernon under our own vines and fig tree."[104] Henrietta Liston observed the presidential couple's pleasure at the prospect firsthand: "Washington is preparing for retirement with a very cheerful Countenance—Mrs. Washingtons heart seems a little melted, as she never expects to see Philadelphia again." Mrs. Liston also noted that, only the week before, a day of celebrations culminating with an elaborate evening ball that had been given to mark Washington's last birthday as president was mounted "with all the splendor the Country could afford."[105] Over a thousand people, including the future First Lady, Dolley Madison, attended the gala, which again provoked Republican criticism over Federalist courtly flourishes. Still, even though Martha was pleased at the visible public appreciation for her husband, she longed to return home. Just the day before she and George left Philadelphia, Martha wrote her old friend Catherine Miller, widow of Revolutionary War General Nathanael Greene, about her hope that "the curtain will fall on our public life, and place us on a more tranquil theater."[106]

George Washington's retirement reflected an enduring hallmark of American democracy, the peaceful transfer of power to a new leader and administration. The Washingtons began their journey back to Mount Vernon shortly after attending John Adams's inauguration. That Abigail continued to hold Martha Washington in high esteem is vividly reflected in a letter Abigail wrote in early 1797 as she prepared to assume the role of First Lady after John's election as the second president of the United States. Abigail insisted she would have far preferred that Martha had remained in the position and that the former First Lady's conduct had reflected "so exemplary a Character as irreproachable whilst it cannot fail to excite an Emulation in the Bosom of your Successor [Abigail]." She then implored Martha to give her advice and "communicate to Me those Rules which you prescribed & practiced upon as is respected receiving and returning visits, both to strangers and citizens as it respected invitations of a publick or private nature." Obviously, Abigail was concerned about following proper social and political protocol, an area in which she felt Martha had excelled and even blazed a trail. She maintained that "Your experience and knowledge must render your advise particularly acceptable to me . . . from a desire to do right, and to give occasion to no one."[107] Abigail certainly understood the importance of her new position as First Lady for bolstering support for her husband John and the critical role social interactions played in the developing political culture of the new republic. She clearly realized that the president's wife held the unofficial power to help build or sabotage vital political alliances and public support for the president.

Abigail's admiration for Martha's personality continued unabated over the years. In one brief message to the First Lady, Abigail reaffirmed the "high esteem and regard" she entertained for Martha.[108] When Abigail later resided in Philadelphia as First Lady herself in 1798, she continued to entertain guests, including Elizabeth Parke Custis Law, Martha Washington's eldest granddaughter. Abigail noted with approval that Mrs. Law "seems to inherit all the benevolence of her Grandmother," and unlike many of the other "formal Ladies of this city," she exhibited an easy, unaffected manner.[109] And Abigail was clearly pleased when George and Martha Washington invited her and John to visit them at Mount Vernon after Congress recessed in the summer of 1798.

That the first presidential couple had very much looked forward to their return to Mount Vernon was expressed graphically in a letter written by Martha to her friend Lucy Knox after George left public office. Martha told Lucy that "I cannot tell you, My dear friend, how much I enjoy home after having been deprived of one so long, for our dwelling in New York and Philadelphia was not home, only a sojourning. The General and I felt like children just released from school or from a hard taskmaster."[110] Still, frequent visitors to Mount Vernon brought political news, and Martha noted the progress of the "Federal City"—the new capital—when members of a commission informed the Washingtons "that the Public buildings were going on with great activity."[111] Sadly, George Washington was only able to spend two years on his plantation before he succumbed to a virulent throat infection, which was treated with repeated bleeding that led to shock and his demise.[112]

The death of George Washington in December 1799, just as the eighteenth century was drawing to a close, plunged the citizens of the United States into grief. Henrietta Liston, the wife of the British ambassador, astutely observed, "It is difficult to say what may be the consequence of his Death to the Country, He stood the barrier betwixt the Northernmost States and Southernmost States . . . and such was the majic of his name that his opinion was a sanction equal to law."[113] And Abigail Adams had surely understood the challenges Washing-

FIGURE 1.3. Print of President George Washington holding the proposed plan for the new capital city of Washington. (Courtesy Library of Congress.)

ton's stellar reputation had placed upon her husband John as the first president's successor, made even more visible by the former president's rather sudden death.

Yet despite the fragility of political life, Abigail articulately captured the mood of the young nation and her own admiration for Washington in a letter to her sister Mary: "This Event so important to our Country at this period, will be universally deplored. No Man ever lived, more deservedly beloved and Respected. The praise and may I say adulation which followed his administration for several years, never made him forget that he was a Man, subject to the weakness and frailty attached to human Nature. Possest of power, possest of an extensive influence, he never used it but for the benifit of his country." Although her focus was on Washington, Abigail could not resist a bit of praise and a plug for her own esteemed husband: "Our Mourning is sincere, in the midst of which, we ought not to lose sight of the Blessings we have enjoy'd and still partake of, that he was spaired to us, until he saw a successor [President Adams] filling his place, persueing the same system which he had adopted."[114]

Abigail wrote a similar letter to her younger sister Elizabeth, noting that "There is not any part of the united States, where the knowledge of the death of Washington has been heard but with Sorrow lamentation and mourning." That she admired Washington was clear, but she also tried to put his life in more realistic perspective by attempting to counteract the cult of personality that had grown around Washington. Abigail emphasized the former president's humanity: "The Virtues which embalm his memory, add Dignity to the Character of the Hero and Statesman, and the gratitude of his Country, has been upon this occasion commensurate with his past Services—In some instances, the Orator and Eulogists have forgotten that he was a Man and therefore subject to err, that it is only now when Mortality has put on immortality, that he is incapable of human frailty—Washingtons fame stood not in need of any such exageration."[115]

Following George Washington's death and burial in Virginia, a major public memorial ceremony was held for the late president in Philadelphia, and Federalists utilized the event to bolster their political position. Abigail reported that at her regular Friday drawing room reception, the "father of the country" was highly celebrated, and it "was the most crowded of any I ever had. Upwards over a hundred Ladies, and near as many Gentlemen attended, all in mourning."[116] She also recorded that her nephew William Smith Shaw had been dispatched to Mount Vernon as an envoy to offer official condolences to Martha Washington on behalf of President Adams and Congress. Overcome by grief, Martha could not bring herself to attend her husband's funeral, nor did she feel up to later entertaining Shaw in person, but Abigail noted that Martha wrote her a letter that expressed appreciation of Abigail's sympathy as well as the depth of Martha's "anguish of mind." According to Abigail, Washington's secretary Tobias Lear had informed Shaw that Martha "had not been able to shed a tear since the Genlls. Death, until she received the Presidents and my Letters."[117] Abigail undoubtedly viewed that as a tribute to her close friendship with the former First Lady and the depth of their mutual appreciation.

It is likely that Tobias Lear helped Martha answer the many letters of condolence she had received, but the sentiments expressed by Martha were genuine. In one missive that has survived, Martha revealed, once again, how much her religious faith had always sustained her in times of sadness. She told the Washingtons' old friend Jonathan Trumbull that "For myself I have only to bow with humble submission to the will of that God who giveth and who taketh away looking forward with faith and hope to the moment when I shall be again united with the Partner of my life."[118]

Although under pressure and always highly cognizant of her public duty, the grief-stricken Martha reluctantly agreed to President Adams's request to have George's remains be reburied in Washington. Fortunately, Congress dithered about the proposed memorial vault, and both the President and later his First Lady were interred at their beloved home of Mount Vernon. In March of the year following George's death, Congress honored Martha by conferring franking on all her mail, thereby making its postage free and sparing her a considerable expense. It is interesting to note, however, that President Adams closed his letter to Martha Washington with a declaration of "the profound respect which I personally entertain for your Person and character."[119] Adams, who at times sometimes disagreed with President Washington, had no similar qualms about the First Lady. He had observed Martha at close hand for well over a decade and appreciated the manner in which she had carried out not only her official duties but her resilience in the face of personal challenges and her devotion to both her husband and the nation.

Far from being apolitical in her last years, Martha remained a staunch Federalist. She received the many visitors who came to Mount Vernon to pay homage to the late president with her usual grace and good manners. But as was the case with her successor as First Lady, Abigail Adams, Martha was acutely sensitive to what she perceived as disloyalty or slights to her late husband. As the leader of the Republicans, Thomas Jefferson had earned the ire of Martha as well as Abigail, both of whom had earlier counted Jefferson as a friend. And like many female Federalist party supporters, Martha was known to bemoan Jefferson's victory as the newly elected president in February 1801 over the Federalist candidate John Adams. The friendship between Martha Washington and Abigail Adams, however, was an enduring one. When Abigail left Washington, DC, in 1801 at the end of John's presidential term, she made it a point to stop at Mount Vernon on her journey home to Massachusetts to visit Martha. In 1800, during the first summer of her widowhood, Martha had also entertained a future president and First Lady, James and Dolley Madison, along with Dolley's sister Lucy, who was related to Martha by marriage to George's nephew.

After Washington's death, Martha also appears to have sometimes discarded her former reticence and commented very overtly and candidly on public political affairs. According to the Reverend Manasseh Cutler, who visited Martha at Mount Vernon the following year in 1802, the former First Lady averred that she was very pleased that Cutler and his entourage "were all Federalists," but she referred sarcastically and disparagingly of "the new order of things and the present [Jefferson] administration." Cutler, who was trained as a clergyman and physician, had been a supporter of the American Revolution and served in Congress from 1801 to 1805. He went on to record in his journal that Mrs. Washington frankly "spoke of the election of Mr. Jefferson, whom she considered one of the most detestable of mankind, as the greatest misfortune our country has ever experienced." Cutler also noted that it was apparent that Mrs. Washington missed her husband's presence at all times and that her feelings "were naturally to be expected, from the abuse [Jefferson] had offered to General Washington while living, and to his memory since his decease."[120] Martha Washington only outlived her husband by less than three years, and died at the age of seventy in 1802.

Looking back over her life in her last days, surely Martha Washington took significant pride in the roles she and her husband had played in the founding and growth of the United States. Despite her initial reluctance to assume the role of what would become known as First Lady, she must have appreciated Abigail Adams's remarks about how admirably she had carried out her duties. For Martha admired and respected her successor, and Abigail's opinion likely served as a balm for Martha's many misgivings about public life. That the second First Lady sought her advice indicated that Abigail viewed Martha as a successful role model. Abigail and many of her contemporaries as well as future Americans commentators have acknowledged that not only had Martha Washington created the role of First Lady without any established precedents to follow but she also was a woman who had successfully, in the most challenging of times, navigated a difficult position that would inspire future presidential spouses. In essence, she had been the author in style and substance of a uniquely American role.

[TWO]

Abigail and John Adams

THE LONG APPRENTICESHIP
TO THE WHITE HOUSE

The happiness of our family seems to have been so interwoven with the Politics of our country as to be in a
great degree dependent upon them.

NABBY (ABIGAIL) ADAMS SMITH
to John Quincy Adams, September 28, 1788

Was not every Fireside, indeed a Theatre of Politicks?

JOHN ADAMS *to Mercy Otis Warren, July 27, 1807*

Like her predecessor, Martha Washington, Abigail Adams was an unlikely candidate to have played such an important role among America's founders during the Revolutionary and early national periods and to have been destined to become one of the most well known First Ladies in the history of the United States. Although her father was a prominent liberal Congregational minister and her mother stemmed from a well-known Massachusetts political merchant family, Abigail's future husband, John Adams, although highly intelligent, well read, and educated, was descended from a long line of modestly successful, respectable, middle-class yeoman farmers.[1]

Moreover, all the members of both the Smith and Adams families were loyal English subjects in the mid-eighteenth century, and the Massachusetts colony was a proud outpost of the British Empire. At the age of twenty-two, King George had ascended to the British throne in 1760, when Abigail was only a teenager herself. Still, Abigail had long been exposed to a legacy of public service, both through her politically active maternal grandfather and her parents, who steadfastly tended to the needs of the residents of their local community. Even more critically, her loyal marital partnership with John, who became a pivotal American political figure; the turbulent and momentous era in which she lived; and her own personal predilection for political theory all combined to ultimately thrust her onto the national stage. Because Abigail was involved in public life from almost the beginning of her marriage to John Adams, who became one of the new nation's most visible citizens, her "apprenticeship" for the later role of First Lady unfolded over three decades. Thus her life during the American Revolution, her time in Europe, and her position as the wife of the first vice president of the United States merit close examination.

Abigail Smith Adams was born on November 11, 1744, in Weymouth, Massachusetts. Recurrent childhood illnesses kept her from attending school in her hometown. Weymouth was then a small hamlet with a population of about twelve hundred, located about fourteen miles from Boston. Abigail's mother, Elizabeth Quincy Smith, appears to have been especially overprotective of the sometimes frail Abigail and probably wanted to keep her isolated from the general population by schooling her at home.[2] Her parents' concerns were not unfounded. In 1751, for example, when Abigail was only six, a serious diphtheria epidemic broke out in Weymouth, killing one in eight people, and it took a particularly high toll among children. Abigail's father, Pastor William Smith, kept a diary during the time that recorded the loss in only three months of thirty residents, including twenty-one children.[3]

Abigail's mother made sure her three daughters were raised to be capable wives and mothers,[4] and it is clear that fear of contracting one of the many virulent diseases that circulated during the era was not the only factor in homeschooling them. As was common at the time, her parents did not subscribe to the notion of advanced formal education for women, and both Mary and Elizabeth, the other two Smith daughters, also learned to read and write at the parsonage. However, all three, particularly Abigail, became highly articulate, literate women. Abigail was descended from respected prominent Puritan stock, raised in a highly devout family, and lived in a world dominated by faith. Although the young Abigail did not attend school, her well-to-do and well-educated minister father and her locally respected mother also made sure that her voracious appetite for reading and knowledge was well fed in both religious and secular subjects.

As she matured, Abigail developed a deep and abiding faith in the liberal religious tenets espoused by her father, and without exception, she saw the hand of Providence in all aspects of life, the sorrows as well as the joys. She also became especially familiar with classic literature, Shakespeare, and works on politics and philosophy. Abigail also avidly followed local newspapers, and much of what she read later influenced her own writing style and life outlook, making her a valuable and skilled commentator on early American politics in her private correspondence, which still resonates with us today.[5] Her later facility managing the

Adams family household finances suggests she was also taught some mathematical skills. Thus Abigail and her sisters were educated at home and probably in a manner superior to most New England females of the era. Moreover, as a pastor's wife, Elizabeth Smith served as a role model for all three of her daughters as a female community leader. She kept her finger on the pulse of congregation members, visited the sick and elderly regularly, offered emotional and physical support in times of crisis, and was considered an exemplary figure in the neighborhood.[6]

After a two-year engagement, on October 25, 1764, Abigail Smith married John Adams, future Revolutionary leader and American president. Despite being delicate, she was a very determined young woman. Abigail's feelings for John were so strong that she married him despite the apparent disapproval of her parents and especially her mother's belief that the fiercely intelligent but brash young lawyer was beneath their daughter's social station and that his career prospects were limited. Even as a teenager, Abigail was able to appreciate John's sensitivity, dry humor, and fierce sense of loyalty under the sometimes tough exterior. When she wed, the slim, petite Abigail was nineteen years old. John was nine years her senior and, at around five feet six inches tall, he was half a foot taller than Abigail and already on the road to stoutness. Adams was born in Braintree, Massachusetts, on October 30, 1735. From the beginning of their marriage, Abigail kept the brilliant and principled but sometimes vain, prickly, and erratic John grounded, and her natural serenity and optimism were a strong influence on taming his often mercurial temperament. As the historian Joseph Ellis put it, Abigail provided John's "ballast."[7]

By all accounts their long marriage of almost sixty years was a loving and enduring partnership, attested to by well over a thousand affectionate letters. And from the beginning, it appears that John recognized and appreciated Abigail's keen intelligence, strong character, resilience, and generally cheerful disposition. Even in the face of frequent separations, their marriage endured because of shared values, deep mutual affection, and respect, as well as their being closely matched in intellect. In an

FIGURE 2.1. *Portrait of Abigail Smith Adams as a Young Woman,*
by Benjamin Blyth. (Courtesy Library of Congress.)

oft-quoted letter, Abigail presciently described the bond that would
hold them together for over half a century as "a tye more binding than
Humanity, and stronger than Friendship, which makes us anxious for
the happiness and welfare of those to whom it binds us. It makes their
Misfortunes, Sorrows, and afflictions, our own."[8]

At the same time both Abigail and John believed in and accepted
the underlying contemporary eighteenth-century notion of a divinely
inspired hierarchical society and family structure, with the husband's
position as the undisputed head of the household, women subordinate

to men, and all members of the unit enjoined to perform their particular duty. But in New England that patriarchal model had always been relatively fluid, allowing for a valued prominent female role. As John Demos put it in his classic study of early Plymouth family life, *A Little Commonwealth*, despite the husband clearly being regarded as the master of the household, "Yet the wife had her own sphere of competence and a corresponding measure of authority."⁹

Moreover, all members of the family unit were duty bound in a reciprocal relationship, which rather seamlessly led to the ideal of prescribed duty being tied to broader public service, an outlook that played a central role in the way both Abigail and John navigated their lives. Certainly, it was a worldview that Abigail had internalized from girlhood and that was graphically reflected in a letter she wrote to her cousin Isaac Smith, Jr., in 1771: "Women you know sir are considered as Domestic Beings."¹⁰ As an eighteenth-century woman, Abigail clearly regarded her primary role as a partner and helpmeet to her husband John and as a mother who should care for, and provide appropriate guidance to, the couple's four surviving children: Abigail junior (Nabby), born in 1765; John Quincy, who followed in 1767; Charles, who came next in 1770; and their youngest son Thomas, who arrived in 1772. She also viewed the running of a smooth and productive household (assisted by the family servants) as her paramount concern. In other words, she viewed her domestic duties as real work, which was both respectable and respected. At the same time, her independent spirit and intellectual curiosity sometimes chafed at the constraints that restricted her full participation in the public world, constraints that were placed on women of her era, a subject that commanded her attention throughout her adult life.

During the first year of their marriage, the notorious British Stamp Act set John as well as Abigail on their first steps toward ultimate separation from England. Under that tax, all legal documents required a stamp, and as a lawyer it especially affected John adversely. The Adams family moved to the much larger town of Boston for several years beginning in 1768 (they returned to Braintree in 1771 largely because of John's ill health) so they could see more of one another, be closer to John's growing law practice, and take a more active role in the political affairs that led to the American Revolution and the War for Independence. That first year in Boston, Abigail gave birth to a second daughter they named Susannah, after John's mother, but sadly, like so many children in an age of high-infant mortality, she died not long after her first birthday. By then, John had become a fairly successful middle-class professional. According to Massachusetts governor Thomas Hutchinson, at the time, John's busy law practice and health precluded him from participating in the early and extensive involvement in public affairs displayed by his cousin Samuel Adams.[11]

However, John and Abigail were still keenly interested in unfolding events, and in Boston, with its population of around sixteen thousand, they had easy access to the growing press. Each read several newspapers daily to keep abreast of developments. Both were equally incensed with Britain's encroachment on liberty in the colonies and increasingly felt that separation from the Mother Country was both desirable and inevitable. From the beginning of John's political involvement, Abigail served as an able adviser and sounding board, and she became increasingly politicized. And like so many colonial women, she used her domestic role to make a political statement by officially renouncing British tea. Two weeks before the 1773 Boston Tea Party, Abigail Adams had already expressed her outspoken opinion on the contested beverage. In a 1773 letter to her friend, the noted Massachusetts author Mercy Otis Warren, Abigail revealed her strong Revolutionary political sentiments: "The Tea that bainfull weed is arrived. Great and I hope Effectual opposition has been made to the landing of it. To the publick papers I must refer you for perticuliars. You will there find that the proceedings of our Citizens have been United, Spirited and firm. The flame is kindled and like Lightning it catches from Soul to Soul. Great will be the devastation if not timely quenched or allayed by some more Lenient Measures."[12] American women like Martha Washington and Abigail Adams were able to become political actors during the American

Revolution and participate in Patriot networks as dutiful "daughters of liberty" through their traditional household responsibilities, including favoring homespun clothing over British imports and renouncing tea.[13] Indeed, women's support and sacrifice were both courted and appreciated by Revolutionary era men, from leaders to common soldiers.

During the early 1770s, John Adams took the controversial step of defending the British soldiers charged in the Boston Massacre, witnessed the heartbreaking death of his young daughter Susannah, and also played a key role as a member of the Massachusetts Assembly just as increasingly unpopular British measures fueled colonial protest. In February 1771, Adams appears to have suffered a "collapse," characterized by weakness, anxiety, and "Pain in my Breast and complaint in my Lungs." Whatever the real cause of his sickness, which, according to John, "seriously threatened my Life," it kept him away from pressing work for months, and on the advice of his physician, he even traveled to Connecticut to visit the mineral springs to improve his health.[14] The return to Braintree in 1771 may indeed have been prompted, in part, by health concerns and the feeling that a hiatus from politic strife and controversy would restore his former health. As John wrote to a relative, "I must avoid Politicks . . . or I should soon have shaken off this mortal body."[15]

According to the historian Edith B. Gelles, who has written extensively about various aspects of Abigail's life, the family's relocation back to Braintree and John's temporary retreat from politics also coincided with "a new consciousness, a budding awareness of unfair gender disparity" for Abigail. Gelles cites the letter noted above from Abigail to her childhood friend and cousin Isaac Smith, Jr., to demonstrate that, not only had Abigail made the point that women were "considered as Domestick Beings," she had also noted that, despite their high intelligence, social constraints prevented women from having the access to wide travel that was accorded to men during the era.[16] By the fall of 1772, a return to better health and practical issues related to growing John's law practice sent him back to Boston, where he bought a house on Queen Street. Abigail and the rest of the family followed him there in November after Abigail gave birth to their youngest son, Thomas, in September. Over the next two years, John, with Abigail's strong support, became increasingly involved in the growing discontent and resistance to Great Britain's policies, which they viewed as aimed at unreasonably curtailing the liberties of colonial Americans. It appeared fitting to both Abigail and John that he should participate actively in the political discussion about potential separation from the Mother Country.

In August 1774, John left Boston to begin his first stint in the Continental Congress, which assembled in Philadelphia. Abigail and the children returned for a time to Braintree to distance themselves from the growing volatile political situation in Boston. As the breach between Great Britain and the North American colonies widened, from afar Abigail assured her husband of her unfailing support. But she realized from the start that if "the Sword be drawn" and John remained in the center of the conflict, she would be bidding "adieu to all domestick felicity."[17] By the time he returned to Massachusetts in October, Adams regarded eventual war with the Mother Country as inevitable. Indeed, Massachusetts was often the most vocally radical of the colonies. As the political crisis intensified and John emerged as an increasingly committed leader of the growing revolutionary spirit, in June 1775 Abigail declared she was willing to sacrifice her personal happiness for the good of the colonies as she became more convinced of egregious behavior by the British government and King George. Despite her heightened worries and the challenges surrounding her husband's absence, she was visibly proud of John's role. According to Abigail, "the fate of Empires depend upon your wisdom. . . . I must intreat you to be careful as you can consistant with the Duty you owe our Country. That consideration alone prevaild with me to consent to your departure, in a time so perilous and hazardous to your family—and with a body [John's] so infirm as to require the tenderest care and Nursing."[18]

During John's absence in Philadelphia, the war played out almost literally on the Adams family doorstep as Massachusetts became the site of intense conflict between the British and American forces. Abigail and her eldest son, John Quincy, witnessed the memorable and terrifying Battle of Bunker Hill on their own from a position near their home in Braintree. As always, her strong faith and religious views served as a bulwark against the ravages of war, family illnesses, and personal losses, but she was greatly relieved to have John back home for a brief respite from Congress during the heat of the summer of 1775. As soon as her husband returned to Philadelphia, Abigail was assailed by yet another critical health crisis, an unusually virulent dysentery epidemic that sickened Abigail and some of her children and left her maidservant and her beloved mother dead. By this time, it was clear that John's political allegiance had been firmly affixed to his vision for the country and a life committed to the "public Cause of America."[19] Yet, despite personal costs, Abigail appeared to have been content with her supportive role, and in the month before the Declaration of Independence was signed, she affirmed to John that "I can serve my partner, my family and myself, and injoy the Satisfaction of your serving your country."[20]

Abigail was left on her own for the foreseeable future as the "deputy" head of the household and all their personal affairs. Although John often offered advice from afar, it was Abigail who took over the day-to-day supervision of the children's education, which in normal times had been the traditional purview of the father. She sorely missed her husband's presence, especially during periods of illness in the family, and at times she internally railed at John's absence in her heart and mind. But their enduring partnership meant that Abigail had also committed herself to unwavering support of her husband's public role, which she regarded as essential to the success of the new nation, and she resolutely willed herself to carry on as their worlds separated. Their letters became the lifeline that held Abigail and John Adams tethered together during their increasingly frequent, lengthy separations. As the war ground on, she remarked to her cousin John Thaxter, who served as a tutor to the Adams children and, later, as John Adams's secretary, that "I resign my own personal felicity and look for my satisfaction in the Consciousness of having discharged my duty to the public."[21]

Although John Adams was at best ambivalent about what place, if any, women should have in formal politics, he clearly appreciated Abigail's political acumen and the role she played in shaping the nation. A number of the American revolutionaries, including Adams, were strongly influenced by Scottish Enlightenment philosophers who emphasized an underlying principle of human rights, but from a basically conservative perspective. They argued that women, as well as men, were entitled to fundamental human rights but that those benefits also carried the responsibilities of duty. However, human rights did not automatically confer political rights; in the case of women, who were not considered autonomous beings, their obligations of duty were viewed as being tied primarily to the domestic arena.[22] This was a view John had certainly incorporated into his world outlook, but he was also cognizant of its inherent contradictions. His mixed feelings on the subject were revealed in several letters that he wrote to Abigail and also to his longtime friend James Warren as the colonies marched down the road toward independence. Although, owing to political differences, John and Abigail later parted ways for many years with James and Mercy Otis Warren, the four had been close comrades in arms during the war.

Abigail first met the erudite Mercy, who was sixteen years her senior, in 1773, and for many years she looked up to her as a role model. A shared interest in literature and politics, as well as support of the American Revolution and their concern over the well-being of their respective families, bound them together in a nurturing friendship during the war years. In the summer of 1774, John wrote to Mercy's husband James concerning his hopes for the "enterprise to Philadelphia . . . a Nursery of American Statesman," where John would become a leading member in the Continental Congress. John maintained that "Politicks are an ordeal path" one must follow from duty. At the same time John declared that, due to their overwhelming schedules and frequent absences from home, "We must recommend it to Mrs. Warren [Mercy] and her Friend Mrs Adams [Abigail] to teach our Sons the divine Science of Politicks: And to be frank I suspect they understand it better than we do."[23]

Yet in 1775 John praised the wife of a fellow politician for avoiding the discussion of politics in mixed company in public and for being "totally silent [on the subject] as a Lady ought to be."[24] Abigail herself had ambiguous and sometimes contradictory views about the role of women in the public sphere. In 1776, Abigail, who consciously or not also adhered to a version of Scottish theory about human rights in regard to males and females, would assert to John, "To be adept in the art of government is a prerogative to which your Sex lay an almost exclusive claim."[25] Whether that remark was meant as tacit agreement or criticism is not quite clear.

In a 1775 letter written from Philadelphia, John informed James he had received a letter from Mercy, and it had compelled him to try to clear up an unfortunate "misunderstanding." John asserted that far from believing that "either Politicks or War, or any other Art or Science was beyond the Line of her Sex; on the contrary I have ever been convinced that Politics and War, have in every age, been influenced, and in many, guided by her Sex." Although John felt that he would prefer that women should be "excused from the arduous Cares of War and State; I should certainly think that Marcia [Mercy Warren's pen name] and Portia [the pen name adopted by Abigail Adams], ought to be Exceptions, because I have ever ascribed to those Ladies, a Share and no small one neither, in the Conduct of our American Affairs."[26]

Certainly John Adams understood that he was married to an unusually astute and capable woman, and he held Mercy Warren in high regard as well. But in his letter to James Warren, he was most likely referring to the sacrifice their wives had made for their country rather than advocating for full political rights for even "exceptional" females like the two women. Many years later in 1805, Mercy published a popular three-volume history of the American Revolution. The Adamses both vehemently believed that Mercy's work had presented an unflattering and undervalued portrait of John's critical role in the Revolution; as John querulously commented, it reflected "a disposition to lessen me."[27] The long friendship was fractured, but Mercy and Abigail, at least, later reconciled in 1812.

In any case, while John was away from home on behalf of the American government, Abigail's own political consciousness grew. As the wife of an emerging congressional leader, she was sometimes invited to dine with visiting military commanders, and, of course, she frequently saw close family members, who lived nearby. However, Abigail was often on her own during the long, lonely evenings without her husband's presence, and she regularly scoured John's extensive library for works about history, philosophy, and government. She also avidly followed her husband's letters containing details about the workings of the Continental Congress. Increasing literacy and the burgeoning of a robust commercial print culture played an important part in bringing women like Abigail into the public world.[28]

Abigail became engaged in the world of political ideas early on, and she began to develop her own opinions about the struggle for independence from England, which she came to support with a fervor equal to, if not more intense than, John's. Unable to take the same political path as her male contemporaries owing to societal constraints, Abigail turned to correspondence for a semblance of political influence. She wrote to both men and women, including Catherine Macaulay, a female British historian whom both she and John respected and admired, often sharing frank outrage against English policies and astute observations about political and military developments. She wrote even more frequently and frankly about political issues to her sisters, other relatives, and Mercy Warren. Letter writing afforded Abigail a path into the male-dominated political arena and an opportunity to at least indirectly exert an influence in the public sphere.[29]

While John circulated his important essay, "Thoughts on Government," in which he outlined and supported his ideal form of government, a three-branched republic, Abigail felt confident enough to offer her own personal advice for governance (directed to the Congress via John) about taxes and monetary policies. Perhaps, most important, she ventured into the controversial subject of slavery, an institution she felt fundamentally contradicted the underpinning of the American struggle for liberty as well as religious precepts and moral principles. John realized that from a practical standpoint a strong stand on slavery would place an irreparable wedge between the northern and southern colonies as they battled the British. Although Abigail held ambiguous, complicated, and sometimes racist views about individual African Americans, she decried the *institution* of slavery. And she fearlessly spoke her mind (at least to her husband): "I have sometimes been ready to think that the passion for Liberty cannot be Eaquelly Strong in the Breasts of those who have been accustomed to deprive their fellow Creatures of theirs."[30] John and Abigail's eldest son, John Quincy, was undoubtedly influenced by his parents' views about slavery and came to strongly believe that slavery was incompatible with the ideals of the Declaration of Independence. After he completed his one term as president in the 1820s, he later became a public voice in support of the abolitionist cause.[31]

Even more unusual, perhaps, was her introduction of the subject of women's rights, which she moved to soon after fervently announcing, "I long to hear that you have declared an independency." Although Abigail's famous call for John to "Remember the Ladies" when he helped compose the "new Code of Laws" was far more limited than many writers in past generations have claimed, it still represented an incursion into previously uncharted territory. As many historians today have pointed out, Abigail was predominantly making a plea for legal and educational rights for women and protection from abusive husbands, not for full political equality and the right to vote. While some of her language was, indeed, bold, including admonitions not to "put unlimited power into the hands of Husbands" and the threat that "if perticuliar care and attention is not paid to the Ladies we are determined to foment a Rebelion," Abigail ended her missive with a conventional outlook about the traditional hierarchical roles governing men and women.[32] She concluded, "Regard us then as Beings placed by providence under your protection and in imitation of the Supreem Being make use of that power only for our happiness."[33]

Still, Abigail's musings were a forward-thinking and progressive view of women's rights for an eighteenth-century female to have offered. Abigail had enough confidence in John's sensitivity to the ideal of human rights and his affection for her to make what might have been seen as an inappropriate demand, even if it was perhaps couched in the vocabulary of what constituted the accepted women's sphere of the era. It is noteworthy that Abigail arguably came closer to an equal partnership in her marriage than was the norm for the era in which she lived. The views of Scottish philosophers concerning human rights, and the concomitant obligations and responsibilities they imposed, influenced post–Revolutionary era American political thought and at least wedged open the door for further contemplation. Vocal elite women, like Abigail Adams, were willing to discuss questions related to the exclusion of women from formal political power and the parameters of their roles as citizens of the newly formed United States, but for the most part it was done *privately*. Few, including Abigail, "made their ideas known publicly or expressed their concerns in print."[34] But her lifelong engagement with political ideas demonstrates that it was a subject in which Abigail was deeply invested.

Once John was elected to national office, however, Abigail was not reticent about trying to influence newspaper editors and influential politicians behind the scenes. Abigail's first and modest foray into actual print was a short introduction to an essay by Mercy Warren. Mercy's article was written in response to the Earl of Chesterfield, a prominent British writer who had criticized women's capabilities in a popular work. Mercy's piece, along with Abigail's comments, was published in a local newspaper in 1780, but in accordance with the accepted norms of propriety at the time, both female authors remained anonymous.[35]

The intent of John's tongue-in-cheek joking response to Abigail's famous "Remember the Ladies" letter has been debated by scholars for decades. He referred to American women as yet "another Tribe more numerous and powerful than all the rest were grown discontented" and concluded with the assertion that in practice male supremacy existed only in theory "as in Practice you know We [men] are the subjects."[36] It is most likely that his turn to humor to deflect the seriousness of the subject reflected his own ambivalence about the role of women in the wider world, yet in the end, he still rebuffed her overtures. Despite his radical commitment concerning separation from England and his relatively progressive views about republican forms of government, at heart Adams was basically conservative in his ideology and believed that the United States should be led by members of the "natural aristocracy." In other words, John's fundamental goal was to shore up his status and that of other elite white males in the new emerging order. Thus John had been an unlikely candidate to have advocated for the overturning of the accepted separate social and cultural spheres for men and women or to fully integrate females into the proposed political system.

During the Revolution, John Adams used his typical dry wit to deflect a serious discussion about the relationship of women to the state that he did not want to embark upon. In a 1776 letter to Boston author Mercy Warren, he praised ladies as "the greatest Politicians I have the Honour to be acquainted with" because he claimed they approached the subject with more honesty and less hot-headed impulsive zeal than men caught up in active public life.[37] Abigail later took this view one step further when she declared that, indeed, since women could not vote or hold office, their patriotism and political involvement was on a more lofty plane then men's, as it was "The most disinterested of all virtues."[38]

Yet in Abigail John had had beside him a living example of a woman of exceptional talent and incisive and forthright intelligence. Throughout their long marriage, John accorded her the personal respect and appreciation of her formidable competency and political acumen that she had requested for all American women in her dramatic plea. John's implicit intention in his reply was likely to table the discussion of women's rights so he could turn to what he considered the more pressing demands of the unfolding of the American Revolution. He also likely believed that women would lose their moral authority if they became involved in messy partisan politics. But Adams surely also realized that the upheavals of the era made women as well as men avid followers of political events and that they, too, had a stake in the future direction of the country. Soon he sent Abigail a copy of the Declaration of Independence for her personal edification as well as for safekeeping.

Although Abigail tried to bring Mercy Warren into the conversation about the grievances she had submitted to John in her letter, Mercy did not reply. However, Abigail's underlying commitment to the subject of women's human rights did not let her allow the matter to rest. In a final parting shot to John, Abigail brought up the inherent contradictions she observed in the fight for independence, often incorporating some of his own past arguments to refute the authority of the British monarchy. Adopting revolutionary rhetoric, she bluntly proclaimed, "I can not say that I think you very generous to the Ladies for whilst you are proclaiming peace and good will to Men, Emancipating all Nations, you insist upon retaining an absolute power over Wives. But you must remember that Arbitrary power is like most other things which are very hard, very liable to be broken—and notwithstanding all your wise Laws and Maxims we have it in our power not only to free ourselves but to subdue our Masters, and without voilence throw both your natural and legal authority at our feet."[39]

Although most of Abigail's political interactions were not in the public sector but in what we consider the private sphere, where she preferred to work behind the scenes, at times she stepped into a wider role, particularly after John's election to national office. But as early as April 1778, Abigail also experienced a modest but nevertheless active "political" public role when the Massachusetts Colony General Court in Cambridge appointed her to a committee to question local women who were alleged Loyalists. It was common at the time for the Patriots to identify and isolate ideological enemies. Abigail wrote John that a "Number of Gentlemen . . . thought it highly proper that a Committee of Ladies should be chose to examine the Torys Ladies, and proceeded to the choise of 3 Mrs. [Hannah] Winthrope, Mrs. Warren and your Humble Servant."[40]

That Abigail was named to the committee, along with the governor's wife and the well-known Mercy Warren, was a testament to Abigail's growing prominence and the public respect she was accorded for her unwavering revolutionary commitment. Moreover, it provided her with at least a modest political voice. The next month, John noted her new assignment and half-jokingly informed her, "As you are a Politician, and now elected into an important Office, that of judges of the Tory Ladies," she would now have influence with other women, and he exhorted her to use the position to encourage them to influence their "Gentlemen." This was a theme that would reappear frequently in the ideology of the new republic. Women, who were popularly acknowledged as holding superior moral authority, would often be asked to use that power to influence male family members to support one political party or the other or to stand behind a particular political position. At the conclusion of the letter, on a more serious note, John plaintively shared his personal reaction over his increasingly stressful role in Philadelphia with Abigail and sought her reassurance and approval: "What shall I do with my Office—I want to resign it for a Thousand Reasons. Would you advise me?"[41]

After the American Revolution, Abigail appeared to have given more serious, if fleeting, thought to the subject of women's voting rights. Aware by the late 1790s that New Jersey had granted unmarried women who possessed the sum of fifty pounds limited and short-lived suffrage (it was overturned with little fanfare in 1807), she told her sister Mary that "if our State [Massachusetts] constitution had been equally liberal with that of New Jersey and had admitted females to vote, I should have certainly have exercised it."[42] Yet her outlook on the political role of women at the time reflected her still contradictory feelings on the subject. At the beginning of the decade, in 1790 she had asserted that "Tho' as females we have no voice in Legislation, yet is our happiness blended and interwoven with those who have, that we have every reason to rejoice in the improvement of science and advancement of civilization which has proved so favorable to our sex, and has lead mankind to consider us in a much more respectable light than we deserve."[43]

Despite her keen interest, practical family responsibilities often took Abigail away from thoughts about such philosophical matters. In the summer of 1776, with John still in Philadelphia and preoccupied with developing political events and the drafting and details surrounding the adoption of the Declaration of Independence, Abigail was left to cope with health battles on the home front back in Braintree and Boston. From 1775 to 1782, smallpox was endemic in North America, and New England was especially hard hit. In June 1776, a virulent smallpox epidemic struck Boston, infecting thousands, and numerous local residents and visitors rushed to be inoculated at a group of homes that became temporary smallpox clinics.

John Adams was keenly aware of the public health situation in Boston as well as the potential of the disease to devastate the Continental Army. In June he wrote his wife from Philadelphia with concern, "The small Pox! The small Pox! What shall we do with it?" and concluded it was "Ten times more terrible than Britons, Canadians, and Indians together."[44] In early July, while the Continental Congress was in frenzied session as it edged toward independence, the Boston ban against small-pox inoculation was lifted for nearly two weeks. The ban had been instituted because some physicians still considered the procedure harmful. Although inoculation was meant to produce only a mild case of small-pox and confer lifelong immunity, at times fatalities occurred. Abigail had long desired that she and her family be inoculated against the dread disease. However, until then she had abided by her mother's insistence that they not be subjected to the potential danger of immunization. In July 1776, just a week after the Declaration of Independence had been adopted, Abigail left Braintree for Boston and the hospitality of her Uncle Isaac Smith's mansion so her four children—and another thirteen family members and servants—could be inoculated. Under Abigail's talented pen the seriousness of the disease and the fear it aroused in the public, as well as what it was like to be inoculated, were graphically portrayed: "I yesterday arrived and was with all 4 of our Little ones inoculated for the small pox," she wrote to John. "Our little ones stood the operation Manfully. . . . Such a spirit of inoculation never before took place; the Town and every House in it, is are as full as they can hold. God Grant that we may all go comfortably thro the Distemper. The Phisick [medical regimen] part is bad enough I know."[45]

By the next day Abigail reported to John that "The Little folks are very sick and puke every morning but after that they are comfortable." At the end of the letter Abigail managed to sneak in a "medicinal" request for the then politically controversial tea, noting "A Little India herb would have been mighty agreeable now."[46] Meanwhile, John alternated between worry over the fate of his family and the increasing reality of widespread debilitating and virulent smallpox within the Continental Army poised for battle. "The Small Pox," John reported to Abigail anxiously, "has done Us more harm than British armies, Canadians, Indians, Negroes, Hannoverians, Hessians, and all the rest," and he placed the blame for the American retreat from Quebec on the disease.[47]

Because of the tense political situation, inoculation for Abigail and her children had been a more harrowing ordeal than John Adams had experienced during the procedure shortly before his marriage. However, on July 18, while the children were in various stages or recovery, Abigail was able to personally witness the momentous public reading of the Declaration of Independence at the Massachusetts Statehouse, gratified that she and especially her husband had had a central role in launching the colonies on the road to liberty.

For Abigail, once again, political affairs and domestic responsibilities vied for her attention. However, the health of her children remained paramount in Abigail's mind, and she wrote John in Philadelphia, "Nabby has been very ill, but the Eruptions begin to make its appearance upon her, and upon Johnny. Tommy is so well that the Dr inoculated him again to day fearing it had not taken. Charly has no complaints yet, tho his arm has been very soar."[48] From afar John worried about the possible side effects of the inoculation for his family and admonished them to get plenty of fresh air. He also sent Abigail's doctor instructions compiled by Dr. Benjamin Rush, a fellow Revolutionary and Philadelphia's leading physician at the time, about administering the procedure. In Boston the physicians recommended the use of calomel, a form of mercury, to aid its success. During the eighteenth century the poisonous qualities of mercury were unknown, but in hindsight its deleterious effects appear to have left Abigail extremely weak and fatigued.[49]

The first inoculation successfully produced the desired pustules that confirmed the patient had been successfully infected with smallpox, both in Abigail and her son John Quincy, but Nabby, Charles, and Thomas had to be reinoculated, as did many of those who had undergone the procedure in Boston that summer. Abigail and John were relieved when Thomas and Nabby finally displayed the lesions, even though Nabby's case produced a spectacular mass of the pustules and fear that scars might mar her appearance. As Abigail put it in her letter to John, "Nabby has enough of the small Pox for all the family beside." John's advice to his daughter Nabby, his "Speckled Beauty," as he termed her, would be to keep out of the sun to avoid permanently damaging her face. Abigail also strongly expressed her ever-present fervent wish of seeing her husband soon. Always concerned about possible overwork on John's part, she urged him to return to Braintree from Philadelphia as "Your Health I think requires your immediate return."[50]

Six-year-old Charles Adams would prove especially resistant to inoculation and in the end contracted the disease the "natural way," through physical contagion from another smallpox victim. Frail by nature, Charles became violently ill, and Abigail nursed him anxiously for many days, extending her stay in Boston to nearly two months. Learning of his son's symptoms, John would share Abigail's fear and distress, but by the first week in September their young son was weak but, according to Abigail, recovering with the aid of "the Bark"—the common name for the medication quinine, which was formulated from cinchona tree bark—and she was expressing regret that she had needlessly worried her husband. With evident relief Abigail ended her letter reporting that in the Boston area "Tis Here a very General time of Health."[51]

In John's absence, Abigail, like many colonial women, honed her economic competency and served as the primary support for the family during the Revolutionary War and later while John was deployed to Europe on behalf of the United States. Despite the challenges of finding reliable labor and rising inflation, Abigail not only ably managed the Adams farm for a number of years before renting it out to tenants, but she also eventually started a small but thriving business selling imported French luxury notions, trims, and household items. She also successfully acquired property for the family and even speculated in government securities and currency. As time went on, she became increasingly confident about her economic prowess and sometimes disagreed openly with John about the manner in which to best increase their family holdings and keep their finances on a firm footing. Commercial growth in the colonies and strong ties with sources for goods had provided increasing opportunities for a number of elite and middle-class women to successfully engage in the market culture during the Revolutionary period, and Abigail became an adept and even proud economic participant.[52] Moreover, she would come to exhibit a rather radical notion at the time—that some of the money she had earned belonged to her exclusively. She once referred to it as "money which I call mine," an insistence that flew in the face of the accepted laws of coverture.[53]

Many years later, in 1788, when Thomas Jefferson served as minister to France, he acknowledged Abigail's financial acumen in a letter to James Madison. Commenting on Abigail's direction of the Adams "pecuniary affairs" while John was stationed in Europe on behalf of the American government, Jefferson approvingly noted that Abigail was the one of the "most attentive and honourable economists."[54] Although Jefferson often espoused an idealized view of domesticity and a narrow public role for women, he certainly appreciated the significant and indispensable contribution American women made to their households.[55] Before Abigail assumed a more visible political persona when John later served as the first vice president and then as the second president of the United States, during the period they both resided in France, she likely embodied Jefferson's vision of the ideal American woman. To Jefferson, Abigail appeared highly intelligent, well read, and cultured, but she made the needs of her husband and children her primary concern. Above all, she always operated as part of a family unit, what Jefferson regarded as the fundamental aspect of American strength and exceptionalism and the cornerstone of the national order. Unquestionably, the concepts of what came to be termed "republican wife" and "republican mother" resonated favorably with Jefferson.

As the wife of a prominent member of the Continental Congress during the Revolution, Abigail also became acquainted with many American patriots, including George Washington and, initially at least by reputation, with his wife, Martha. From their first encounter, Abigail had formed an extremely favorable impression of the future president. Writing to John from Braintree in the summer of 1775 after she met the general, she observed, "I was struck with General Washington. You had prepared me to entertain a favorable opinion of him, but I thought the half was not told me. Dignity with ease and complacency, the gentleman and soldier, look agreeable blended in him."[56] Mercy Warren's very enthusiastic assessment of Martha Washington the next year certainly predisposed Abigail to form her own positive estimation of the general's wife, even before Abigail met her personally years later in her role as the wife of the first vice president. Yet, by all accounts, even without Mercy's endorsement, it appears that virtually everyone who met Martha Washington appreciated her easy charm, amiability, and ability to converse and empathize with people from all walks of life.

In April 1776, Mercy had the opportunity to meet Mrs. Washington, her son John Parke Custis, and his wife Eleanor in Cambridge, Massachusetts, when Washington commanded the military there at the time. Abigail, who avidly followed all the news concerning the war, begged Mercy to share her impressions of the general's family: "How do you like Mrs. Washington?" she queried.[57] Mercy reported that Martha had greeted her "with the Ease and Cordiality of Friendship of a much Earlier date. . . . I think the Complacency of her Manners speaks at once to the Benevolence of her Heart." Mercy likewise found Martha's son and daughter-in-law very "agreeable."[58] John Adams had formed a similarly elevated assessment off Washington's capabilities. Indeed, he was the delegate who had first recommended Washington's appointment as the head of the Revolutionary Army. Adams had been clearly pleased to learn that his advice had been heeded after he returned to Philadelphia as a Massachusetts delegate to the Second Continental Congress in the spring of 1775.

Abigail's views on women's rights over the years were a complicated, complex, and sometime contradictory blend of her firm, unwavering commitment to the correctness of the prevailing notion of the proper female domestic sphere and what might be considered more radical views at the time concerning women's educational and legal rights, which she hoped could be won by constitutional means. As Gelles has astutely observed, "As an eighteenth-century woman, Abigail did not question male authority, but in the spirit of the revolutionary era, she was concerned about justice . . . an unusual gender awareness for her time."[59] That dichotomy and tension is born out eloquently in a letter Abigail wrote to her younger sister Elizabeth many years later in 1799: "I will never consent to our Sex considered in an inferior point of light. Let each planet shine in their own orbit, God and nature designed it so. If man is Lord, woman is Lordess—that is what I contend for, and if a woman does not hold the Reigns of Government, I see no reason for her not judging how they are conducted."[60]

Another subject related to the role of women that Abigail frequently focused upon was education, an element she likely believed was essential in developing the skills to examine issues with sound judgement. Both John and Abigail were passionate about the value of education for Americans but differed in degree as to what was appropriate for women specifically. John, for example, did not support Abigail's plan to allow their daughter Nabby to learn Greek and Latin, subjects he felt were only suited for male scholars. Abigail, however, firmly viewed female education as central to the development of a strong and enduring republic. This reflected the ideal of the republican wife and mother, who, in her opinion, required the educational tools to raise virtuous male American citizens. Not long after the Declaration of Independence was issued, Abigail made her case in a letter to John when she expressed her hope that "our new constitution be distinguished for Learning and Virtue. If we mean to have Heroes, Statesmen, and Philosophers, we should have learned women."[61] Although at the time, her ideas were considered controversial, John expressed his at least tacit (and tactful) support: "Your sentiments on the Importance of Education in Women, are exactly agreeable to my own," he affirmed.[62]

Perhaps influenced by the British historian Catherine Macaulay and a contemporary book titled *On the Management and Education of Children*, which conservatively advised offering women a basic knowledge of literature and history,[63] at the height of the American Revolution Abigail's own strong thirst for knowledge expanded even further, and she became an even more zealous advocate for the education of women.[64] Although educated privately at home, Abigail and her sisters had received a superior education compared to most girls of their era. Still, even as an adult she felt that it was unfair that her feckless only brother William was exposed to far more formal educational advantages. "Why should children of the same family be thus distinguished?" she pointedly asked her cousin, John Thaxter.[65]

In June 1778, when John was stationed in Paris as an ambassador on behalf of the American government, Abigail wrote to express her relief at finally receiving a letter from him that assured her of his safety. John often spiced his letters with political tidbits from the international scene, and she wrote with updates on family affairs as well as larger philosophical issues. In one of her earliest letters to John while he was abroad, Abigail took the opportunity to lament the general state of education of American women, but at the same time she subtly complimented John on what she considered his more progressive views on the subject than were common among his contemporaries. In response to the praise (often unwelcome) she heard from John about the "brilliant accomplishments" of French women, Abigail maintained that she regretted "the trifling, narrow, contracted education of the females in my own country . . . in this country, you need not be told how much female education is neglected, nor how fashionable it has been to ridicule female learning; though I acknowledge it my happiness to be connected with a person [her husband John] of a more generous mind and liberal sentiments."[66]

To Abigail's relief, John finally returned to Massachusetts from Europe in the summer of 1779, and he soon turned to local politics as he authored the state's new constitution. It was a document that reflected his underlying conservative views about human nature and the need for enforced limits of power, a political guideline that endures in Massachusetts to this day. But the long-awaited hiatus back in America was again short-lived, for in October, Congress assigned Adams a new diplomatic task in France. And far from it being the first time, Abigail's patriotic mettle and self-reliance were tested as she remained behind in Braintree to manage the family finances against the backdrop of continuing war. But convinced that John's direct participation was pivotal to a successful outcome for the American cause and bolstered by her religious faith and commitment to duty, she became increasingly confident of her ability to manage her expanded role. For example, Abigail ably solved her labor shortage problem during the time by renting the farmland to tenants, and she made a number of shrewd investments to help pay taxes and build a nest egg for the family. John, in turn, seems to have had great confidence in his wife's economic acumen, and for the most part, he was happy to allow her to take charge of their finances.

In November 1779—and this time accompanied by sons John Quincy and Charles—John returned to France as an American minister to negotiate peace and commercial relations with England. This turned out to be somewhat premature, as the war did not go well for the Americans in 1780. It would not be until after the Battle of Yorktown in late 1781 that Great Britain would view further hostilities as futile, and Adams did little to endear himself to either Franklin or French diplomats while he marked time there during yet another period of stress and anxiety. Congress ended up removing John as minister plenipotentiary in France, and instead, he became a member of a five-man delegation to negotiate a peace settlement with the British and to also further America's interests in Europe.

It was Adams himself who decided that his interim mission while he was in limbo would be to garner financial and moral support for American independence in the Netherlands. In late 1780, John relocated to a house overlooking a canal in Amsterdam, and over the next several years he served there as minister plenipotentiary and eventually achieved great success in his economic diplomacy. In Amsterdam, the normally hardy Adams became seriously ill with what he termed a "nervous fever of a dangerous kind," which was likely acute malaria. He apparently lapsed in and out of consciousness for several days and even lay near death: "For five or six days I was lost, and so insensible to the Operations of the Physicians and surgeons, as to have lost my memory of them."[67] Without Abigail at his side John always seemed more susceptible to illness, and he was probably made vulnerable to disease by exhaustion and depressed spirits after learning he had lost his initial diplomatic commission. John remained weak after his health crisis, and his recovery was prolonged. He did not return to his normally highly active schedule for some months.

In the meantime, back in Braintree, in addition to supervising the family household, Abigail conducted her own modest active foray into public politics when she served as a vote counter in the Massachusetts election and also tried to influence male voters by her powers of persuasion. She provided John with her opinion about the capabilities of the politicians running for office and her belief that the more capable candidate, whom she campaigned for and supported, would lose to his more popular, charismatic opponent, the well-known John Hancock. Abigail detested Hancock, whom she viewed as a charlatan and lacking in integrity, but she correctly predicted he would be voted in by what she described as the misguided "Lovers of the tinkeling cymbal." Yet she rather proudly alluded to her interest in, and talents for, political analysis and her modestly visible role in an era when women could not vote by trying to influence male voters through political discussions and her correspondence. She wrote John, "What a politician you have made me? If I cannot be a voter upon this occasion, I will be a writer of votes. I can do some thing in that way but fear I shall have the mortification of a defeat."[68]

As the war wound down, Abigail would take the opportunity to reflect on the status of women in the new republic and particularly the role she had played behind the scenes to support not only her husband's work but also the wider nation. She forthrightly accorded "praise to myself" because she had "sacrificed so large a portion of my peace and happiness to promote the welfare of my country." In addition, Abigail very clearly spelled out the political limitations she and other females still faced, despite the fact that they displayed heroic American patriotism prompted by what she termed the "most disinterested virtue." Even though they were "excluded from honours and from offices [and] we cannot attach ourselves to the State or Government from having held a place of Eminence," as well as "deprived of a voice in Legislation, obliged to submit to those Laws which are imposed upon us," females continued to exhibit the most admirable unselfish commitment to the public welfare. Abigail used her letter to openly, passionately, but still rather tactfully remind John that she and other women could neither vote nor hold public office and that their property still remained under the control of their husbands, even in "the freeest countrys."[69] Whether Abigail intended this as a "feminist statement," as the historian Woody Holton has suggested, is debatable, but surely it indicated that the political status of women was a subject to which she gave serious thought. Still, she ended her philosophical musings with a practical list of a number of textiles she requested that John send her from Holland to use as merchandise to sell in her increasingly successful business.

Following his success in the Netherlands, where Adams signed an advantageous economic agreement in 1782, John was later redispatched to France to help negotiate the long-awaited treaty with England. After a series of tension-producing complications, the Treaty of Paris was finally consummated and ready for his final signature in the fall of 1783. Although John had repeatedly entreated Abigail to join him, she still dithered over traveling to Europe, but while he was in Europe with their sons, John Quincy and Charles, Abigail certainly worried from afar.

Despite John's encouragement, fear of the long, potentially dangerous sea voyage and concern for her other children and her elderly father William Smith, who still lived in Braintree, had long made Abigail reluctant to join her husband in Europe. But finally Abigail concluded that their current separation, which had stretched over four years, was untenable. In April, she wrote to John to tell him that she had decided to banish the "Idle Specters" of her fears and declared, as she had so many times in the past and would continue to do in the future, that "the desires and request of my Friend are a Law to me. I will sacrifice my present feelings and hope for a blessing in pursuit of my duty."[70] Although she was terrified by the thought of crossing the ocean, Abigail gathered her courage and even hoped that she would be "benefitted by my voyage as my Health has been very infirm and I have just recoverd from a slow fever."[71] Abigail and her daughter Nabby sailed from Boston on June 20, 1784, accompanied by two servants, and once on board, they all became wretchedly ill. To her sister Mary Cranch, Abigail described her sea-sickness as the "most disheartening . . . malady," and reported that "we crawled on deck when able." The party finally landed on July 20. "Heaven be praised, I have landed safely upon the British coast," Abigail proclaimed in relief.[72]

John Quincy was dispatched by his father from The Hague to meet his mother and sister in London on July 30, and John Adams joined the family a week later in August. Once land was firmly beneath her feet, and she had recovered from the rigors of the voyage, Abigail traveled with John to France along with their son, daughter, and servants. They settled into a luxurious, spacious home in the Paris suburbs, in Auteuil on the banks of the Seine. Even after so many separations, it appears that Abigail and John were able to continue their marriage with the same enduring partnership of shared interests, trust, and mutual affection that had marked the union from the start. In Europe, the respite from her myriad family and economic responsibilities during the war and from the related anxiety over the fate of the nation and the safety of her husband and sons allowed Abigail more free time to read, think, and socialize. Her letters to her sisters clearly reveal a period of relative domestic serenity that characterized Abigail's more leisurely life in France. Yet, like her husband, Abigail disapproved of much she found in the pleasure-loving French society, especially the excesses of the royal court, and she witnessed the fact that those closest to the king and queen in the complex levels of aristocratic rank held the most power and privilege. In addition, evidence of what she viewed as Parisian immorality assaulted her at every turn. Although she professed to enjoy French plays, she complained they often left her with a headache.[73]

Over time Abigail began to appreciate aspects of French culture and developed several close friendships while she resided in the country, including one with Thomas Jefferson, whom she viewed at the time as a highly cultured, intelligent man and delightful conversationalist. Jefferson, then stationed in the country as one of the American ministers, similar to his friend Abigail, held ambivalent and often negative views about French society. But Jefferson became at least a partial Francophile. Although, like Abigail, he deplored the corruption and dissipation of the French court, at the same time he deeply admired French art, music, literature, and the high level of intellectual discourse and sociability that permeated the French salons he attended. Jefferson also admired Abigail for her devotion to her husband and children and the highly competent manner with which she fulfilled her domestic role within the Adams family. For a central tenet of Jefferson's republican vision for the future of the United States was an idealized domestic harmony that began in the home and flowed outward from the family unit into the larger American society and the nation's governance.[74] In other words, he longed for a successful republican nation that was built on tens of thousands of tranquil homes headed by benevolent patriarchs, supported by nurturing, accomplished, and competent women.

As the historian Brian Steele has suggested, Jefferson viewed the proper structure for family life in America as being governed by a patriarchal model, which would serve as the cornerstone of the nation's future success. For Jefferson, America provided the perfect environment in which the Enlightenment-inspired goals of happiness and progress could best flourish.[75] Moreover, Jefferson generally espoused only very circumscribed political roles for women, an attitude that became only more ingrained over time. By 1788, in a letter to George Washington, Jefferson maintained that women's happiness was best served by their focusing on traditional domestic roles and that females should, therefore, be excluded from the public duties and rights conferred by citizenship in the new republic as it would distract them from their more essential, but valuable, responsibilities.[76]

Perhaps Abigail and Thomas viewed themselves as such kindred spirits while they resided in France at the same time because they both critically viewed French society as dissipated, and both repeatedly extolled the virtues of their native country. When the Adamses later left France for England, Abigail told Mary that "I shall really regret to leave Mr. Jefferson; he is one of the choice ones of the earth."[77] While in Europe, Abigail wrote frequently to her uncle Dr. Cotton Tufts, who had graciously agreed to supervise the Adams economic interests back in Braintree in her absence. Like Jefferson and her husband John, Abigail clearly believed that the new American nation was superior to the Old World. In an early 1785 letter written from Auteil to Tufts, Abigail reaffirmed her underlying appreciation for American life: "I know not whether I shall be able to content myself to tarry out my two years. My Heart and Soul is more American than ever. We are a *family by ourselves*."[78] It is interesting to note that the metaphor of family was frequently employed by both Jefferson and Mrs. Adams.

In her correspondence from Europe, Abigail often folded in astute observations about "politicks," as she termed it, with financial matters, and she also revealed a great deal about her role in the Adams marriage. As was the case with many American women during the Revolutionary War, Abigail had taken on many formerly male duties in her husband's absence, and those realities sometimes caused a subtle shift in the balance of the family relationship. John granted Abigail more autonomy and authority in her household than many of her female contemporaries experienced. She once told Tufts that as a longtime and committed American statesman, John had little interest in the particulars of their day-to-day domestic and economic affairs, generally leaving it to Abigail to "write and think about them and give directions." Yet her views about their supportive, affectionate, but often unequal marital partnership, which she likened to monarchical structure, were clear: "Tho I am very willing to relieve him from every care in my power, yet I think it has too much the appearance of wielding instead of the sharing of the Scepter."[79]

From the earliest days of her marriage, Abigail had always taken a keen interest in public affairs that remained with her for her entire life, and she took an active role in American political life as she stood alongside avenues of power through her husband's prominence and position, including the time they resided in Europe together. Increasingly, Abigail became John's ally, sounding board, and intellectual and emotional confidante. Abigail kept abreast of contemporary politics, not only to satisfy her own formidable intellectual curiosity but also to arm herself to be able to defend John's—and later her son John Quincy's—political position. As much as she and her predecessor as First Lady Martha Washington would have preferred a more tranquil domestic life at home alongside their families, they both realized that the successes of their marriages were tied to their husband's ambitions. In other words, Abigail may have been reluctant to see herself and her husband thrust onto the political stage, but she felt the necessity of accommodating John's goals.[80] Abigail and John's prolific correspondence is filled with political discussion and musings, and she also ventured well beyond the family circle when she later discussed political topics knowledgeably with

American leaders such as Jefferson and the well-known Philadelphia physician and signer of the Declaration of Independence, Dr. Benjamin Rush, among others.

After John was appointed the American ambassador to the English Court of St. James in 1785 in an effort to promote better relations between the two countries, John Quincy returned to America for college, and John, Abigail, and Nabby relocated to a fine home on Grosvenor Square in an elegant neighborhood in London. There, Abigail continued her active correspondence with many relatives back in America, including Dr. Tufts. In one letter, she pointedly asked her uncle to "Excuse my being so busy in them [politics] but I am so connected with them that I cannot avoid being much interested.[81] Indeed, from almost the earliest days of her marriage, Abigail was part of a political household. But Abigail's biographer Edith B. Gelles makes the important point that the highly intelligent, extremely well informed, and often independent Abigail still always approached political issues from the perspective of how they affected her family members, especially her husband John, concluding rightly that "she was a woman before she was republican."[82] In other words, for Abigail, connections to family and loyalty to her spouse overrode abstract principles and personal inclinations.

Abigail had spent only eight months in France, but she would reside in England for about three years. When she was younger, Abigail had complained about the virtually nonexistent opportunities for women to travel unfettered, as many men had done. In Europe, Abigail's world literally expanded, and she was exposed to other cultures and political models. In both Paris and London, she encountered very powerful royal courts and moved in aristocratic circles. Abigail had the opportunity to view the monarchical form of government firsthand and compare it to the nascent American republic, and she found the European model decidedly lacking. To her sister Elizabeth, she carefully described her view of the key elements in American society that she felt made it politically and socially superior to what she encountered in both France and England: "When I reflect upon the advantages which the people possess in

America," she observed, "the ease with which property is obtained, the plenty which is so equally distributed, the personal liberty and security of life and property I feel grateful to heaven who marked out my Lot in that Happy Land."[83] And while she was in Europe, contemporary political subjects clearly remained on her mind. As her daughter Nabby reported, during their frequent social calls while the family resided in London, Abigail proved a lively and popular conversationalist who visibly relished her "dish of politics."[84]

For Abigail and John, life in London became a whirl of both political and social obligations and cultural opportunities. The city was also a hub of commerce at the time and a shopper's paradise, offering goods that rivaled Paris shops. Abigail and John, as well as Nabby, were officially presented to the British king George III and his queen Charlotte not long after their arrival, and for the occasion Abigail dutifully appeared in an elegant dress and fashionable jewelry and observed the social niceties. Abigail and John, as well as their compatriot Thomas Jefferson, well understood that in the European courts manner of dress took on great significance as a reflection of rank and importance.[85] Accordingly, all three made a studied effort to conform to acceptable standards of Continental fashion, and as Abigail noted to her sister Mary from Paris, "Fashion is the Deity everyone worships in this country and from the highest to the lowest you must submit."[86]

She grumbled about the cost of her unaccustomed finery but appeared to take secret pleasure in her fine appearance as well as the opportunity to glimpse life at the royal court. After standing in line for hours, she was greeted in a polite, admittedly even gracious, but rather perfunctory, manner by the royal couple, whom for the most part she found rather dull, and Abigail wrote her sister Mary that she was relieved when her ordeal was over.[87] Abigail crossed paths with the royal couple on a number of occasions, including a visit to St. James's Palace in the winter of 1786 to mark the queen's birthday celebration. She clearly understood the social hierarchy of the English royal court and the highly complex and inflexible rules and the calibrations of rank that were exhibited there.

More than a decade later, after she became First Lady, Abigail would studiously conduct herself in a manner different from the heads of state she had encountered in Paris and London, but the British experience paved the way for her official behavior on the national level.

Understandably, the English did not always enthusiastically welcome the couple who had played such a pivotal role in the American Revolution, and Abigail often felt that she and John were snubbed and made unwelcome by much of the British aristocracy. At the same time, John was often criticized in the English press. Abigail felt that English women were decidedly inferior as a group to their American sisters, and she viewed her rather cool reception as an opportunity to reflect upon the political and social differences between the two countries, which convinced her even more emphatically of the superiority of the new American republic. To her sister she maintained, "I know I am looked down upon with a sovereign pride, and a smile of royalty is bestowed as a mighty boon. As such, however, I cannot receive it. I know it is due to my country and I consider myself complimenting the power before which I appear as much as I am complimented by being noticed by it."[88]

Moreover, she was highly critical of a political system that in her opinion oppressed the lower classes: "When I reflect upon . . . the millions who are loaded with taxes to support this pomp and show, I look to my happier country with an enthusiastic warmth."[89] Still, the Court of St. James was more to Abigail's liking than the French Court of Louis XVI had been, and she was relieved to be able to converse in English as her command of French had been rudimentary at best. In addition, in England Nabby Adams would meet and marry William Smith in 1786, and at the time both her parents were pleased with the match to the promising young man, then secretary to the American legion. In 1787, the young couple became the parents of John and Abigail's first grandchild, and Abigail was delighted with her new role as "Grandmamma," as she reported to a niece.[90]

While in England, in addition to his diplomatic duties, John turned to a task close to his heart: a discourse on political philosophy that he hoped would move the American government in the right direction of a balanced government, one in which three separate but equally robust branches would work against dominance by any one faction. In the late summer of 1786, Abigail and John had visited Holland, and both were likely impressed, at least at first, by its new infant republican government, which may have influenced his political views. Balance and equal access to opportunity were fundamental to his vision for an ideal American republic. But John also believed in what he termed a "natural aristocracy," as well as a strong executive leader with decided authority. For some American politicians like James Madison, Adams's plan initially conjured up repugnant images of a monarch who was simply given another name. As always, Abigail, who served as John's valuable sounding board and as a capable political theorist in her own right, was generally defensive about any outside criticism of her husband. To her son, John Quincy, she proudly described the volume, titled *A Defense of the Constitutions of Government of the United States of America,* as "an investigation into the different Forms of Government, both ancient and modern, Monarchical Aristocratic Democratical and Republican." Furthermore, in Abigail's opinion John had very correctly demonstrated the links between a country's "happiness or misery in proportion of their different balances."[91]

In Abigail's eyes, John's recommendation for good government had achieved the perfect balance, something she would later see as critically lacking in the outcome of the French Revolution, which for both the Adamses had reflected the horrendous pitfalls of the unchecked excesses of democracy. His European experiences had made John more fearful than ever of the threat of aristocratic encroachment on the American republic; only virtuous dedication to the public good could counter the quest for personal gain among the powerful. And only a powerful executive could deflect powerful members of Congress. But even Abigail understood that his emphasis on the role of the executive would lead to the perception that John was advocating for the "sitting up a King."[92] Always sensitive to criticism, John was stung by the reaction of some of his detractors, and as he did so frequently, he looked to his intellectually gifted and loyal wife for validation. As Gelles aptly put it, "His best support, both as a theorist and as a politician, was Abigail."[93]

While in Europe, Abigail continued to expand her mind and educational vistas by attending not only the theater but also a series of scientific lectures, including talks about experiments dealing with electricity and magnetism, both innovative and much-discussed topics at the time. The lectures also provided her with the opportunity to, once again, pointedly criticize the lack of robust female education in the United States. She commented to her niece Lucy Cranch that the exposure to scientific subjects was "like going into a Beautifull Country, which I never saw before, a Country which our American Females are not permitted to visit or inspect."[94]

In that letter written in the spring of 1787, Abigail continued to share her views with Lucy about the importance of female education, but what is really eye-opening are the sentiments she first put to pen in the *draft*. In that version, Abigail was very frank about what she clearly understood as the inherent contradictions between progressive ideals and the role of women in the new United States republic. Although she clearly subscribed to the popular notion of republican wife and mother, believing an educated woman could be "a pleasing companion to the man of Science & of Sensibility" and "form the minds of her children to virtue & to knowledge," as well as continue to steward the "domestic economy of her family," at the same time she advocated for enlarged opportunities for women. Although Abigail toned down her rhetoric in the final letter she sent to her niece, perhaps feeling her initial thought might be considered too radical, originally she wrote passionately that it was her hope that soon women could wander beyond "the limits of the dressing room & the kitchen, to which even some men of sense have been illiberal enough to wish us confined." She felt progress for women was possible "as mankind appear in the present age to acquire more freedom of thought & action in politics," and she was somewhat optimistic that those new currents would extend to the improvement of the female mind. Yet even in the revised version of her letter, she may have felt she had ventured too far because she ended the letter to Lucy with a self-admonishment that she had wandered off tangent and that she resolved to end her missive by returning to "the Female sphere" and "talk . . . of fashions."⁹⁵

While in Europe, Abigail also kept abreast of American political developments at home. When news arrived about Shay's Rebellion, a popular anti-tax uprising in Massachusetts in 1786, she expressed her outspoken and harsh view of the incident freely to her then still admired friend, Thomas Jefferson. In contrast to John, who at first took a milder, more measured view, Abigail branded the rebellion leaders "Ignorant . . . desperadoes, without conscience or principals."⁹⁶ Jefferson famously replied that "I like a little rebellion every now and then. It is like a storm in the atmosphere."⁹⁷ As the situation worsened, even John became concerned about the new nation's ability to function, which had influenced his decision to undertake his composition of the *Defense*. Although John officially resigned as the United States minister to England at the beginning of 1787, he did so with the understanding that he would remain in the position another year, until a replacement could be chosen. But in the interim, Abigail and John set their sights happily on a much anticipated return home to America.

In March 1788, Abigail was in Bath, England, for her health, but even on vacation, her appetite for American politics continued unabated. She wrote to John, who had remained behind in London, to excitedly inform him that a letter had arrived for her son-in-law, William Smith. The missive had conveyed the welcome information that "Seven States [including their own state of Massachusetts] had accepted the Constitution," which had been under debate. She then proceeded to offer detailed information about the voting and told John that William had been informed that "he may consider the constitution as accepted, and beginning to operate at the commencement of another year." With obvious optimism for the future of the United States, Abigail informed John that "I think we shall return to our country at a very important period . . . May Wisdom govern her [America's] counsels and justice direct her operations."[98]

Within a month, Abigail and John set sail back to the United States as they looked forward to a peaceful resumption of their domestic life. They were not yet aware how soon they would be called upon to play a continued prominent role in the young nation's development. However, John undoubtedly hoped to reactivate his political career, and in many ways Abigail's European experiences had prepared her for her own future endeavors on behalf of her beloved country. When she left England in 1788, Abigail was a mature woman of forty-three. Her youngest child, Thomas, was already a young man of sixteen, and she was also a grandmother.

Although Abigail still regarded her roles as wife, mother, and now grandmother as primary, during her time in Paris and London, she had stood face to face with the heads of Europe, observed European society firsthand, and had the opportunity and leisure to attend educational lectures and converse about political and broader philosophical topics with some of the best minds of the era. All that she encountered in the Old World polished her political and cultural sensibilities but also left her more convinced than ever of the superiority of the American nation. She would later incorporate what she had learned and absorbed into her future positions, first as the wife of the country's first vice president, and then as the second First Lady of the United States.

When they returned from London in June 1788, the Adamses were grateful to be home in Boston after enduring a lengthy seven-week voyage. Soon Abigail was busy setting up their new household in a two-story house undergoing renovation in Braintree, which they had purchased sight unseen while still in England. Compared to the luxurious quarters they had occupied in Paris and London, the new residence was very modest, but they grew to appreciate their homestead, which they named Stonyfield, or Peacefield, as it was more often fondly known. As Mount Vernon became for Martha and George Washington, Peacefield served as a welcome refuge and touchstone for Abigail and John and became the site for numerous Adams family gatherings.

Although political divisions in the new nation were already beginning to develop, George Washington had emerged from the protracted Revolutionary War as arguably the most popular man in America, and he even became an international hero, so it was not surprising that he was unanimously elected to the nation's highest office. However reluctant Washington may have been to exchange private life for public service, once again, he felt compelled to accept the call to duty and was inaugurated as America's first president on April 30, 1789. In contrast, Adams, already plagued by the emerging political factions and the rise of political parties, was elected to the vice presidency by just the slimmest margin. Although he had not campaigned for the position, as it would have been considered decidedly lacking in accepted proper political protocol at the time, John certainly hoped to be centrally involved in the historic new government administration.

The political differences between the Federalists and anti-Federalists—or the Republicans, as they would become known—soon widened. Washington's own cabinet members were often at odds, and some of Adams detractors accused him of favoring a new version of a monarchy when he suggested that new heads of government receive impressive new titles. John's critics derided his suggestion to address Washington as "His Excellency" and viewed it as further proof of his anti-republican outlook. Although John had mellowed with age, his tendency to speak his mind bluntly and blunder in sensitive social and political situations was exacerbated without Abigail at his side. Still, both John and Abigail looked forward with great hope for the future for the new nation and their own family.

During the years John held national office, Abigail traveled back and forth from their home in Braintree (later renamed Quincy in honor of Abigail's grandfather John Quincy). But even before the couple learned formally of John's election as vice president, she avidly followed her husband's political progress. In mid-November of 1788, Abigail was on her way to New York for a visit to join her daughter Nabby, who was soon to give birth. But that did not mean Abigail had eschewed her own

FIGURE 2.2. Engraving of John Adams from an original painting by Gilbert Stuart. (Courtesy Library of Congress.)

interest in the unfolding political scene. From a stop in Connecticut, Abigail wrote John that she hoped he would share any news he heard about the elections and told him, "I shall want to know a little of politics."[99] The two may have pretended to be indifferent to the election outcome, but that obviously was far from the truth.

Abigail was back in Massachusetts when John was officially sworn in as the nation's first vice president on April 21, 1789. But she still managed to critique his formal speeches from afar, and she later joined him in June in New York City, then the seat of the federal government and the new nation's temporary capital. With a population of over thirty thousand, it was the largest city in the country at the time. John and Abigail were both undoubtedly relieved when she arrived safely in New York, having set out on the journey in mid-June via a gale-tossed ship voyage from Newport, Rhode Island.

We are indeed fortunate that Abigail Adams was not only a prolific correspondent but also on unusually articulate and gifted writer. Many of her letters were written to her sisters, especially to the eldest Smith daughter, Mary Cranch. Their correspondence not only casts an intimate lens on family issues but also reveals a broader story about the political development of the new United States, especially when Abigail joined John during the periods he served as the nation's vice president (two terms under Washington) and his single term as its president. She wrote from all three of America's capitals, first New York, then Philadelphia, and finally Washington, and she provided posterity with a firsthand, if partisan, account of the growing regional divisions, political factions, and challenges in the new nation. She also documented the initial rocky relationship between the United States and France after the French Revolution, as well as contemporary life in the late eighteenth century.

Abigail could be sharp-tongued and critical and was unfailingly and sometime almost blindly loyal to her husband John and his political outlook, but at the same time, she generally exhibited an optimistic and generous nature and was a keen, highly intelligent observer who rarely minced words, at least not with her close family members. She was rarely shy about providing political advice to first her husband and later her son John Quincy. Although, like Martha Washington, Abigail would prove herself a capable hostess, manager, and helpmeet, she involved herself more closely in the political debates of the day than her predecessor or probably any other First Lady of the nineteenth century, with the exception of her successor, Dolley Madison. And although Dolley excelled in what the historian Catherine Allgor has dubbed practical "parlor politics,"[100] she did not exhibit the same grasp of political philosophy that became second nature to Abigail.

Although leaving her beloved home in Braintree behind in June 1790 was wrenching, Abigail was entranced with the family's newly rented New York house at Richmond Hill, which was surprisingly affordable on John's comparatively modest $5,000 a year salary. In contrast, President Washington received $25,000 yearly, which John probably took as additional evidence that his position was indeed one of the most "insignificant" ever created. John had written Abigail in late May to let her know that he had secured "a large and handsome house, in a beautiful Situation." As it was two miles "out of the City," the rent was more modest than they would have paid for a less impressive house in the center of town. John urged Abigail to join him as soon as possible and advised her to make arrangements to send some of their own furniture and household items, as well as some his most essential books about political philosophy. He also informed Abigail that the wife of the new president "Mrs. Washington will be here before you, without doubt," as she was "expected daily."[101]

After settling in, Abigail waxed poetic as she praised the Richmond Hill site overlooking the Hudson River to her sister Mary as a "Situation where the hand of nature has so lavishly displayed her beautifies, that she has scarcely anything for her handmaid, art, to perform."[102] One of the factors that made the New York location especially attractive to Abigail was that her beloved only surviving daughter Nabby Smith and her grandchildren would also reside at Richmond Hill. An added bonus was that her son Charles also joined them there, while Thomas, who was at Harvard, and John Quincy, who was preparing to pass the Massachusetts bar, continued their studies in the Boston area. Still, politics were never far from Abigail's thoughts, and she also took the opportunity to proudly inform her younger sister Elizabeth that John, whose responsibilities included many long hours seated in his chair presiding over the Senate, "has never been absent from his daily duty in Senate a single hour from their first meeting." Additionally, she expressed her satisfaction with Jefferson's nomination for secretary of state and John Jay's as chief justice, among a number of other American men appointed to the new government who exhibited "the greatest talents and abilities . . . Thus have we the fairest prospect of sitting down under our own vine in peace."[103] Abigail clearly viewed the era as one of great promise for her country, and at that point in time still held Jefferson in high esteem.

Although Abigail claimed she heard less about "politicks" in New York than she had in Massachusetts, she then proceeded to comment in detail about deliberations in the House and Senate and criticized the now anti-Federalist congressman Elbridge Gerry for his lack of understanding about "the Great National System which must Render us respectable abroad & energetic at Home."[104] During her time in New York, she also became fond of John Jay's wife, Sarah, and beginning in February 1790, Abigail indulged her taste for politics by joining Mrs. Jay and other political wives to listen to debates in the House of Representatives. Those occasions allowed Abigail access to witness discussions of national import beginning with Hamilton's proposal for funding the United States debt. Attending congressional debates also provided her with an introduction to many rising politicians, including Virginia's James Madison.

As the vice presidential couple settled in at Richmond Hill, they were thrust into a whirlwind of social engagements. Soon after she arrived, Abigail took her quasi-official place in society as the wife of the nation's first vice president, and she wrote her sister Mary that "Our House has been a mere Levee ever since I arrived morning & evening." The first morning after she breakfasted, she and Nabby went to "pay my respects to Mrs. Washington," who immediately made an extremely favorable impression on Abigail for her "modest, dignified and feminine" ways.[105] In Abigail's estimation, Martha Washington personified female republican virtues and served as a stark contrast to the haughty royalty she had encountered in Europe. At the same time, Abigail appeared to enjoy her newly elevated station as her "Ladyship" and regarded with pleasure the relationship she and John had developed with the Washingtons. In

July, she noted that, during his recovery from an infected abscess on his leg, President Washington had even stopped at Richmond Hill to rest one day when he had undertaken a coach excursion, and she later proclaimed that "We live upon terms of much Friendship [with the Washingtons] & visit each other often."[106]

As time passed, the initial cordial relationship between the president and vice president remained; however, since the two men exhibited such different personalities, they never developed as close a friendship as their wives had. Washington tended to rely on his cabinet members for guidance and advice rather than on Adams, but he was always courteous and respectful, and at times even genial and quite friendly toward his vice president. Martha and Abigail, on the other hand, seemed to genuinely enjoy one another's company. An obviously pleased Abigail reported to John in the fall of 1789 that not only had Mrs. Washington visited Richmond Hill and joined Abigail for tea on one fall afternoon in 1789, but a few days later she also invited Abigail and the rest of the Adams family in New York to join her for dinner and the last local concert of the season after supper.[107] A number of times during the ensuing years, Abigail would affirm her affectionate admiration for the First Lady, describing her as a friend "whom I both Love and respect."[108]

By early August, Abigail was doing her best to meet her myriad social obligations and host guests regularly. She reported to Mary that "I have never been before in a situation in which morning noon & afternoon I have been half as much exposed to company . . . at Richmond Hill it is expected that I am at Home both to Gentlemen & Ladies when ever they come out which is almost every day since I have been here. . . . I propose to fix a Levey day soon. I have waited for Mrs. Washington to begin and she has fixd on every fryday 8 oclock." Abigail was indeed kept very busy returning calls, and she noted that over a period of only three or four days she had paid more than sixty brief visits to local society women and the wives of politicians, including the First Lady. Entertaining and visiting became central elements in the sociopolitical lifestyle of the early nation, and Abigail's letters provide us with insight into the evolving social rituals. On one day, accompanied by her daughter, Nabby, and son, Charles, Abigail joined one of Martha's receptions, at which "Ice creems & Lemonade" were served. She then described the protocol, which included a formal presentation and curtsey to the First Lady. With obvious approval she related that "The President then comes up and speaks to the Lady, which he does with a grace dignity & ease that leaves Royal George [King George of England] far behind."[109]

Abigail ended up hosting dinners on Wednesday evenings and receptions on Mondays, where guests dropped in for short bursts of informal conversation and beverages, and "fixing" the Adams levees on Thursdays, which helped in some degree to reduce her often overwhelming visiting and receiving obligations. "I have been fully employed in entertaining company," she told Mary, and the guests included members of the Senate and their families and later members of the House of Representatives as well. John and Abigail were able to entertain all the politicians through a rotation process that included "24 persons at a Time" for dinner once a week at their Richmond Hill home, but she lamented that "I shall not get through them all, together with the publick Ministers for a month to come."[110] Although the social events were more frequent, more formal, and larger than those she had encountered back home in Massachusetts, she had her experience in Europe to draw upon, and Abigail undoubtedly realized the political importance of dinners and receptions as vehicles for cementing political alliances and building political capital. If it was not her natural milieu, as she claimed to prefer her more simple life back in Quincy, she was obviously determined to utilize the occasions to bolster her husband's position and satisfy her appetite for political news, and she had learned to be a welcoming hostess even as a girl.

In their official positions, John and Abigail were also besieged with patronage requests, including some from old friends like the Warrens and even from relatives such as Abigail's sister Mary, who lobbied (in the end unsuccessfully) for a government post for her husband Richard. Abigail had been especially close to her mentor Mercy Otis Warren during the Revolutionary War, but the two couples had parted ways over the new Constitution, which the Warrens rejected and Abigail and John so strongly supported because they considered it as an essential ingredient to the success of the future of American unity and progress. In the end, Abigail thought it best not to use whatever influence she had on behalf of her brother-in-law, but she discreetly assisted her sisters with financial gifts from her own funds.

In spite of the time devoted to entertaining public figures, Abigail still avidly followed official political developments both through newspaper reports, which she often complained were partisan and inaccurate, as well as through her insider position as the wife of the vice president. At dinner parties and levees, she may have been focused on social niceties, but she kept her ears open to details about government, financial matters, and diplomacy. She also noted with obvious dismay the increasing political jockeying for power and her husband's growing unpopularity, particularly among the southern politicians. Unsurprisingly, she bristled when John was criticized for his initial suggestion that the new president be addressed as "Your Highness." Still, in those early days in New York, Abigail tended to take public criticism of the president and vice president more philosophically than she would as time passed, and she concluded with resignation, "Thus it is to be seated high."[111]

Abigail helped John navigate social interaction and appears to have been much more adept than John at appreciating political nuances. For example, she quickly realized that John was committing a political misstep when he declined to accompany President Washington on his famous tour through the thirteen states soon after he took office in an effort to bolster support for the federal union. Abigail understood that accompanying Washington would have both enhanced John's public image and improved his relationship with Washington, and she encouraged him to later join Washington on his journey from Boston to Portsmouth.[112]

Political compromises in 1790 involving funding for Hamilton's new financial program for the nation resulted in a change of venue for the American capital. Philadelphia was to become the new interim capital of the United States, and ultimately, after a ten-year-period, the capital would move permanently to a new site on the Potomac River, what would become known as Washington, DC. The relocation to Philadelphia meant that, once again, Abigail and John were forced to move. It was not an undertaking Abigail took lightly, and she complained to Mary, "Do you not pitty me my dear Sister to be so soon all in a Bustle, and weary of removing again. . . . I feel low spirited and Heartless. I am going amongst an other new set of company, to form new acquaintances, to make and receive a hundred ceremonious visits not one of ten from which I shall derive and pleasure and satisfaction."[113] Still, as it had in the past and would in the future, duty prevailed, and Abigail set to making the best of the situation.

In those halcyon days after the American Revolution and during the early nascent republic, overall support had been strong for the new president and vice president in New York. In Philadelphia, the administration would come under increased assault, and Abigail also fretted about the personal high economic costs of moving and renting another house. She also had to contend with the fact that some of their shipped household items and clothing arrived damaged. Moreover, with its frigid winters and hot, humid summers, Philadelphia exhibited a climate that proved a threat to Abigail's often fragile health. It also resulted in a lamented separation from her grandchildren and Nabby, which she regarded "painful to me on many accounts,"[114] especially since William Smith's unwise economic schemes threatened to undermine the stability of Nabby's marriage and growing family. To make matters worse, Abigail's son Thomas and her cook sickened soon after their arrival, and Abigail's health suffered in Philadelphia as well. Yellow fever would also descend on the city on several occasions, including the infamous epidemic of 1793, which brought death and devastation to thousands and virtually closed down the government.[115]

Once settled in Philadelphia, where John would continue to preside over the Senate, Abigail told her daughter Nabby that, while the site of their new house at Bush Hill was "a very beautiful place," it did not compare with "the grand and sublime I left behind at Richmond Hill." The following year, in October 1791, they would move to a more modest sized, but more convenient, house at Fourth and Arch Streets in the center of the city. Still, despite inconveniences in settling in and the more lavish social life that existed in Philadelphia, which promised the unwelcome prospect of increased expenses, Abigail was, as always, determined to make the best of circumstances. Overall, she was actually pleased with the state of the American government, especially after her son-in-law William Smith received an appointment as the New York state supervisor for the federal excise, bringing some financial stability to Nabby's household. Abigail also counted her blessings after Polly Lear, the wife of Washington's aide and right-hand man Tobias Lear, informed her that "I am much better off than Mrs. Washington will be when she arrives, for their house is not likely to be completed this year." The week after the Adamses arrived in Philadelphia, the Washingtons made their appearance, but owing to inclement weather and illness in her household, Abigail did not have the opportunity to immediately visit with her close friend Martha.[116] She did not make her first "public" appearance at the First Lady's drawing room until late December, accompanied by her son Charles.[117]

During the first full year that Philadelphia served as the nation's capital, Abigail was largely optimistic about the future of the United States. In March, she told her sister Mary that Washington was set to tour Georgia and North Carolina the following week. She noted that "Our publick affairs never looked more prosperous. The people feel the beneficial effects of the New Government by an increasing credit both at Home and abroad and a confidence in their Rulers." She concluded with a reference to her strong religious beliefs and observed that realistically "Some grumbling we must always expect, but we have as a people the greatest cause for Gratitude and thankfulness to the Supreme Ruler of the Universe for our present happy and prosperous circumstances as a Nation."[118]

But as time went on, political life in Philadelphia was characterized by more discord. Many leaders had been divided about support for the

French Revolution, with Jefferson viewing it rather benignly as a step forward for liberty in France, while others like Abigail and John were aghast at the violent overthrow of the monarchy, which they felt had provided at least some measure of stability to the country. It drove a growing wedge between the two formerly friendly comrades that became further exacerbated by political essays written by Adams and his son John Quincy. As Jefferson continued his assault on Federalist policies, primarily directed at his political foe Alexander Hamilton, the Republican and Federalist parties drew further apart, and countless former friendships and alliances fractured.

Regardless of the political strife, Abigail was required to keep up the myriad social events expected of her as the vice president's wife. She grumbled to Mary that in Philadelphia she had "little Time that I can call my own." Her schedule was clearly full and demanding: "On Monday Evenings Our House is open to all who please to visit me." Not only did she have to arrange the events and supervise servants, but because of the frequent and often well-attended occasions, she also had to physically labor in the preparation of the "Wednesdays dinners which we give every week to the amount of sixteen & 18 persons which are as many as we can accommodate in our Thousand Dollars House. On Thursdays the replacing & restoring to order occupies my attention." Returning calls and "dining abroad" further cut into her precious personal time, and she clearly was aghast at the expenses that were incurred (including high rent) out of the Adamses' modest funds.[119]

According to Abigail, there was an excess of social activities in Philadelphia, many of which she would have to decline or "spend a very dissipated winter, if I were to accept one half of the invitations." Still, for the most part, she found the upper-class women of Philadelphia better educated and more genteel than those in New York. She also noted to Nabby that she and John had joined President and Mrs. Washington at an enjoyable assemblage, where the company was "of the best kind," as well as at a performance of the Richard Brinsley Sheridan's popular play, *The School for Scandal*. Despite the plethora of events, Abigail managed to meet her social responsibilities, at first entertaining visitors from late morning until midafternoon in the only room in the house that was suitable.[120] As visible members of Philadelphia's elite, Abigail and Martha attended many theatrical performances, which sometimes took on a political aspect, for they often revolved around ideas that were deemed too contentious to discuss in more conventional social settings. When the Washingtons or Adamses graced an auditorium, it was often seen as partisan gesture, and it was common for members of the general audience to exuberantly shout out their opinions of the production, especially when the plots contained any references to national or international political affairs.[121]

Despite her complaints about her increased social activities, Abigail appears to have cultivated acquaintances with many Philadelphia women she found very congenial. When she later returned to Braintree in 1792, John informed Abigail that her absence was "much regretted in Words and in reality" among the leaders of Philadelphia's social set. "You have many Sincere friends in this Town," John wrote flatteringly. "Mrs. Washington, Mrs. Powell, Mrs. Morris, Mrs. Dalton and many other Ladies have Spoken to me upon the Subject of your Absence, with a respect I am sure came from the heart."[122] Moreover, throughout Abigail's prolonged absence from the capital, Martha Washington repeatedly inquired after her health and asked John to send the First Lady's affectionate best wishes to his wife. As John put it once, "Mrs. Washington is here [in Philadelphia] and never fails to make the kindest Inquiries and to send the most cordial Regards."[123]

While Abigail resided in Philadelphia she continued to closely follow political issues. She had been pleased, for example, when Congress chartered the Bank of the United States in February 1791, viewing it along with John as a positive step for national economic growth and federal stability. In her last letter to Mary before she set out for Massachusetts in late April 1792, Abigail observed with some alarm that, owing to political intrigue, not only Henry Knox and Alexander Hamilton but also Washington and Jefferson had come under increased criticism. But she was relieved that her husband, the vice president, "they have permitted to sleep in peace this winter." Abigail was fearful that the fragile American government was already unraveling and that a "civil war" was on the near horizon. She presciently, if somewhat prematurely, declared to Mary that "I firmly believe that if I live Ten Years longer, I shall see a division of the Southern & Northern States."[124]

Despite his professed reluctance to continue in office, Washington was unanimously elected to a second term as president, and it was a period marked by increasing political division over the future path of the government and growing concern about the impact of European wars on the American economy, which was so dependent on undisturbed international shipping. Once again, John Adams served as Washington's vice president, but this time he was elected to what he had earlier famously termed as the "most insignificant office that ever the Invention of Man Contrived," by a somewhat wider margin.[125] Although John cast a number of important tie-breaking votes in his role as president of the Senate, overall his influence in the government was modest, and he was often marginalized by Washington's cabinet. Still, driven by duty and political ambition, John gave his best efforts to fulfill his circumscribed role. For Adams was preparing to step into what he hoped would be his natural selection as the nation's next President. As he would later confide to Abigail in January 1796, "I am heir apparent, you know, and a succession is soon to take place . . . all these hints must be Secrets. It is not a subject of Conversation as yet."[126]

During Washington's second term, after April 1792, owing to her uncertain health as well as the desire to live more frugally, Abigail spent most of the remainder of John's term in Quincy (as that part of Braintree had been renamed in honor of Abigail's illustrious grandfather, John Quincy). The cost to the vice president and his wife for the entertainment of so many political guests and the expense of renting a suitable house had taxed their income and left the frugal couple with an unwelcome debt. Back at home, Abigail would lend her significant economic abilities to putting their finances back on firm footing. Without Abigail at his side, John could rent a room in a boarding house and therefore not be expected to host large social gatherings. John joined Abigail in Massachusetts during the summer months, when his political duties were less pressing, and he even spent almost six months by her side in Quincy in 1793 during the period of one of her most serious health challenges. Thus they both fortuitously missed the infamous Yellow Fever epidemic that year in Philadelphia, a health crisis that for all practical purposes shut down the American government.

Back at their home in Quincy, Abigail kept abreast of policy issues and watched and commented as the second Washington administration was assailed by British interference in American shipping and the largely ineffective Jay Treaty, which had been created to address the problem. She also learned about the new popular rebellion against a whiskey tax and the scandal surrounding the French foreign minister Edmond-Charles Genêt, which served as an embarrassment to the American government. She complained bitterly to her daughter that their esteemed president, George Washington, was unfairly abused in the press for a variety of behaviors, including his supposed "ape of royalty" in hosting his regular levees, and that Mrs. Washington endured similar insults as a result of her popular weekly drawing rooms. Abigail was, however, pleased that, at the same time, "the bitterest party-writer has never dared to impeach neither the honor, the honesty, or the integrity of the Vice-President [her husband John] or fix a blemish upon his character."[127] Little did Abigail know that was to come later, when John Adams was elected president, and she would react even more vehemently to any criticism directed against her beloved spouse.

In the meantime, Abigail continued her role as "a Female politician," as she described herself, a description that during the era referred to a woman who gave serious and deep thought to the public issues of her time. At the end of 1793, she justified her ongoing active interest in public affairs to John. She wrote that "You know my mind is much occupied with the affairs of our Country. If as a Female I may be called an Idle, I never can be an uninterested Spectator of what is transacting upon the great Theater, when the welfare and happiness of my Children and the rising generation is involved in the present counsel and conduct of the principle [political] Actors." She also offered subtle praise to John in regard to his "political Character," which she professed herself happy to report had lost its only fault, his tendency to have sometimes displayed "irritability" to fellow politicians who held unwise opinions. Toward the end of the letter, she moved briefly from world affairs to the family finances, noting that "Having spun a thread out with respect to politicks I Will think a little of our own private affairs.[128]

Abigail was certainly familiar with Mary Wollstonecraft's influential publication *A Vindication of the Rights of Woman*, published in England in 1792, and it may have influenced her thinking about women's role in politics. Wollstonecraft's arguments concerning the capabilities of women and their right to political and civil rights certainly resonated strongly with Abigail. Although she may have dreamed of a time when American women could hold office, it is highly unlikely Abigail saw it as an attainable goal during her lifetime or in the foreseeable future. But she certainly felt women could and should follow political developments and voice their opinions, at least privately in correspondence and in lively and thoughtful discussions at appropriate social gatherings.

Increasingly conservative in her political outlook, she viewed with apprehension "the mighty [European] Revolutions which are revolving round us—in which kingdoms Principalities & powers are shaken to their center." Moreover, she deeply feared that "the shocks of the old world extend their agitations even to our peaceful Shoars" through immigrants and what she perceived to be dangerous foreign influences. As she staunchly observed to a Massachusetts senator in regard to her justification for female interest in public political discourse, "At such an Aeon as the present who can be an unconcern'd spectator?"[129] Of course, Abigail was, and would always remain, far from a dispassionate American observer.

As time passed and his political star waxed and waned, John was not confident that he would be elected to the nation's highest office over his rival, Thomas Jefferson, and Abigail expressed her mixed feelings about possibly ascending to the role of First Lady. Accustomed to sharing her frank opinions, Abigail also worried that, if John were elected, she would not be able to live up to the example of Martha Washington, whom she considered a model for proper decorous behavior as the wife of the president. Although Abigail possessed both charm and wit, she often found it a challenge to tamp down her strong opinions and accustomed "freedom of sentiment." Moreover, she fretted about whether she had the "patience, prudence, discretion sufficient to fill a Station so unexceptionably as the Worthy Lady who now holds it, I fear I have not."[130] Yet a descendant of Washington's secretary Tobias Lear, who was a great admirer of the Washingtons, later observed that "Abigail Adams was unquestionably the most brilliant conversationalist among the ladies of her day and an extremely intelligent and fascinating woman."[131] Clearly, Abigail could hold her own in conversations with even the most astute and successful politicians.

It appears that Abigail sometimes saw herself as being above the norms of society, particularly in regard to the laws of coverture. Certainly, she quite assertively expanded her economic role in the Adams family, despite formal legal restraints.[132] But her increasing confidence in her capabilities went beyond the economic realm and sent ripples into the unfolding of American Revolution and later the new nation. Although she unquestionably valued her role as a wife and mother, at the same time she also thought of herself as a successful entrepreneur, a prominent founding mother, and an influential political figure as the wife of the first vice president of the United States. She would continue to assert herself as she carved out her role as the country's second First Lady. Abigail's many years as the wife of a man in public life prepared her, better than Martha Washington before her and Dolly Madison after her, for her new role. Moreover, the relationship between Abigail and John Adams arguably reflected the most robust political marital partnership the country had ever witnessed up to that time.

THREE

Abigail Adams

THE SECOND FIRST LADY

I Shall esteem myself peculiarly fortunate, if at the close of my Publick Life, I can retire, esteemed beloved and equally respected with my predecessor [Martha Washington].

ABIGAIL ADAMS *to Mercy Otis Warren, March 4, 1797*

The task of the President is very arduous, very perplexing and very hazardous. I do not wonder Washington wished to retire from it, or rejoiced at seeing an old oak [John Adams] in his place.

ABIGAIL ADAMS *to Mary Cranch, June 23, 1797*

Abigail Adams became the second First Lady of the United States on February 8, 1797, when, at the age of sixty-one, John Adams was formally elected president, although he did not officially assume office until March 4. Abigail felt keenly the heightened degree of responsibility and increased level of public duty that would now fall on both herself and particularly her husband, and she observed, "My feelings are not that of pride, or ostentation upon the occasion. They are solemnized by a sense of the obligations, the important Trusts and Numerous Duties connected with it."[1] Abigail's words reflect the unwavering commitment to the public good that she and John had long internalized. Moreover, she fully understood the strong partnership the position would require, and Abigail soon declared to John that she was "always willing to be a fellow Labourer with you in all those Relations and departments to which my abilities are competent."[2]

John called upon Abigail's support almost immediately. As he put it so dramatically, "I never wanted your Advice and assistance more in my Life."[3] That he relied on the new First Lady for *advice* is most significant, as he obviously realized that, despite his intellectual brilliance and political acumen, he often lacked the requisite skills to navigate the political/social *culture* surrounding his presidency and that he would ascend to the nation's highest office in an exceptionally fraught period for the young republic. In December 1796, even before his inauguration, and with his typical dry wit, John summarized the challenges that would assail him as president: "John Adams must be an intrepid to encounter the open Assaults of France and the Secret Plotts of England, in concert with all his treacherous Friends and open Enemies in his own Country." In the same letter he referred to Abigail as the incumbent "Presidante" and assured her that, despite the rough road that was sure to unfold ahead, he was more than prepared to carry out his duties. Rather surprisingly, John also maintained that "he never felt more Serene in his Life."[4]

For both Abigail and John, the presidency capped long years of devoted sacrifice and service on behalf of the new nation. Yet John had received only three more electoral votes that his major opponent, Thomas
Jefferson. Despite the fact that Adams and Jefferson headed opposing
parties, because of the peculiarities of the early election system, Jefferson
then became Adams's vice president. From Quincy, Massachusetts, Abigail sent her heartfelt best wishes and prayers for providential guidance
as well as her assurances of John's worthiness for the position. At the
same time, she informed her husband that, owing to her professed responsibility for the family farm and her ailing mother-in-law, she would
have to be excused from the inauguration on March 4. In the end, Abigail did not join John in Philadelphia until May 6, and of his four years
as president, largely due to issues surrounding her often fragile health,
she spent only a year and a half at his side.

Abigail had good reason to approach the news of her husband's ascension to the presidency with trepidation and mixed feelings. When
John and Thomas Jefferson had first vied for the presidency, with John
often vilified in the press as an advocate of monarchy and hereditary
government (most unfairly, in Abigail's opinion), Abigail had shared
her fears with her son Thomas: "I feel anxious for the fate of my country," she confessed. "If the administration should get into hands which
would depart from the system under which we have enjoyed so great a
share of peace, prosperity, and happiness, we should soon be involved in
the wars and calamities which have deluged other countries. We should
soon become a divided and miserable people." Moreover, criticism of her
husband and the weaknesses she perceived in the new and often contentious two-party system sometimes led her to despair of America's political future, and she astutely understood that the first president of the
United States had occupied a singular position in the America psyche. "I
feel perhaps too keenly the abuse of party," she observed. "Washington
endured it, but he had the support of the people and their undiminished
confidence to the hour of his resignation, and a combination of circumstances which no other man can look for."[5]

As early as 1793, Abigail had observed that even the woman she personally admired so much, America's esteemed inaugural First Lady, had in her opinion come under unfair public scrutiny, for "Mrs. Washington [was] abused for her drawing rooms."[6] And at a time of political upheaval as the time of the election drew closer in late 1796, Abigail confessed to John how "anxious I am at the events passing before me." In the same letter, she asked her husband to extend her "sincerely affectionate Regards to the President and Mrs. Washington," a missive that also reflected her worry about what the future held for her family if John did become president. Reflecting upon Washington's imminent retirement, she observed, "If any people on earth are to be envyd they [the Washingtons] are the ones. Not for what they have been in power and Authority but for their transit."[7]

But when John's election appeared to be secure, Abigail allowed herself a moment of pride in his accomplishment and, once more, reflected on her admiration for the nation's original First Lady. Upon hearing that Martha Washington had extended her felicitous congratulations to John, Abigail voiced her opinion that "Mrs. Washingtons congratulation to you I believe perfectly sincere. Who would not wish for a successor that would not disgrace her predecessor." Clearly Abigail believed her husband was at least the equal of President Washington in his competence and commitment to the public good of the nation. As to her own role as the incoming First Lady, Abigail maintained that "I shall think myself the most fortunate among women if I can glide on for four Years with as spotless a Reputation, beloved and esteemed by all as that Good and amiable Lady [Martha] has done."[8]

Nearly all of Abigail's many biographers have titled their chapter relating to the period in which she served as the presidential spouse as "splendid misery."[9] That assessment had originally been offered by a friend, but it was one that Abigail initially felt was at least partly accurate. Yet, as Abigail's many successors would learn, no presidential couple was immune from intense public scrutiny, harsh criticism, and multiple challenges, and she would find that her position of First Lady held many positive moments as well. She certainly felt John was deserving of, and well qualified for, the nation's highest position, and her own proximity to the vortex of political life was often exhilarating for her. For example, Abigail appears to have been highly gratified after an Indian chief who later visited President Adams also paid his respects to Abigail as the "mother" of the country and when a volunteer infantry company named themselves "Lady Adams Rangers" in her honor.[10] Sometimes ceremonial roles were enjoyable as well, such as the time she reviewed a troop of New Jersey army soldiers on her trip back to Quincy in May 1800. She reported back to John that "I regretted exceedingly that you could not see them. . . . Major Tousard will tell you how well they performed. I acted . . . as your proxy praised and admired."[11]

Moreover, Abigail's remarks about "splendid misery" were written to her sister just a short time after she had arrived in Philadelphia, not long after the death of her mother-in-law and a favored niece and anxious about her daughter's precarious financial family situation, as well tired and drained after a long tedious journey. Still, the new position appears to have been daunting for her before she even left Quincy. She had not only delayed joining John because of her aging mother-in-law's ill health, but, even before he was formally named president, she also tested the waters surrounding her likely job as First Lady by insisting that a government committee and not she should chose and provide furnishings for a presidential residence, for which Congress had allotted only $14,000.

It was not a surprising response from a woman who was known for her frugality and economic sense, and Abigail certainly did not want to put the Adams's personal savings, for which she had labored so long, into jeopardy. She declared, however, that she would be willing to undertake the task of hiring of new servants and staff. After the election, and left to his own devices, John decided to rent the Philadelphia Georgian-style house that the Washingtons had occupied for the sum of $2,700, which put a strain on the modest Adams family income. Abigail also offered her mixed political opinion about John's rival, Thomas Jefferson, in the letter: "Tho wrong in politicks . . . and tho frequently mistaken in Men and Measures, I do not think him an insincere or coruptable Man. My Friendship for him has ever been unshaken," an outlook that Abigail would revise before long as the country moved closer to the next election, what became known as the "Revolution of 1800."[12]

Despite her reservations and ambivalence about returning to active public life and relocating again to Philadelphia, in reality Abigail had long hoped that her husband's talent, intelligence, and commitment to the nation would be widely recognized. But advancing age, ill health, family challenges, and the bitter party partisanship she had witnessed firsthand in Philadelphia had somewhat diminished her desire to see John in the prestigious but often precarious presidential position. Federalists generally called for a strong centralized government, with a robust fiscal base that supported the governing elite as well as commercial interests and economic development, and they also advocated improved ties with England, whereas, for the most part, Republicans favored an agrarian republic that stressed a limited federal government, enlarged voting rights for a broader group of white men, and support of France. Abigail was a fervent Federalist, perhaps even more so than her more moderate husband. Often, she railed against American Republicans as having aligned themselves with the most radical French "Jacobin" factions, and it appears that she feared they might even have supported a working-class "revolution" in the United States, for in her mind an excess of democracy promoted disaffection among the lower classes.

In response to the congratulations for John's election from the Adams family's longtime friend, the Massachusetts politician Elbridge Gerry, Abigail reviewed the "bitter Cup of Calumny and abuse" that even the nation's beloved Washington had endured as president. She confided that she feared that John, "who has near half the Country opposed to his Election," could look forward to even greater challenges. It gave her great pause, and as she put it so eloquently to Gerry, "At my time of life, the desire to shine in Publick life is wholly extinguishd."[13] It was not a new feeling for Abigail. Years before in 1790, when President Washington had endured a serious health crisis to the degree that many felt he was on the verge of death, Abigail had expressed a similar outlook to her sister Mary Cranch. Apprehension that as vice president John might be called on to take Washington's place had prompted Abigail to assert "most assuredly I do not wish for the highest Post [as First Lady].[14]

Still, John remained desperate for Abigail to join him. Uncertain and often overwhelmed by the challenging political climate and surrounding intrigue, he repeatedly entreated her to travel to Philadelphia. Abigail's emotional support, political loyalty and acumen, and social skills had long made her John's most trusted adviser. As was her pattern, despite her misgivings, she was determined to be a supportive, loyal, and hard-working wife who tried not to complain about her own anxieties and physical infirmities. In response to John's fervent pleas, she saw no choice but to put their domestic affairs in order as quickly as possible to return to his side. From a stop along the journey, she reflected on her upcoming new position as First Lady to her closest confidante aside from John, her sister, Mary. Indeed, it is through her correspondence with Mary that we learn the most about Abigail's experiences during the presidential years. Abigail reiterated her trepidation about her move to Philadelphia and confided to Mary that her upcoming role was "enviable no doubt in the Eyes of some, but never envy'd or coveted by me."[15]

As a prominent and affluent elite Virginia planter family, the Washingtons had long been accustomed to hosting lavish social events at Mount Vernon. When George ascended to the presidency, he placed great emphasis on official protocol and ceremony, which certainly by the time of his second term evoked outrage from the Republican faction, which accused him of incorporating rituals that had been practiced in European royal courts. In contrast, John and Abigail Adams stemmed from a far more modest economic background, and both came from New England Puritan stock, a group that emphasized greater material restraint and moral rectitude. In addition, when he embarked on the presidency, at first John often stressed virtues of republican simplicity, no doubt in part to deflect increasing unfair criticism that he was a supporter of a monarchical government.

It is ironic that a number of John's contemporaries criticized him for having been influenced by the European aristocracy. Yet, after having been exposed firsthand to European high society while they resided in Europe, both John and Abigail had found the aristocratic culture of France and England morally lacking when compared to the virtues of American life, and they continued to hold those fervent beliefs back in the United States. Not only John but also Abigail worried about the danger to the fledgling republic of aristocratic power wielded by unscrupulous politicians, and they also shared the belief in the need for a strong executive as a counterforce.[16] For Abigail, her husband embodied all the ideal traits of the best type of leader for the nation.

Indeed, when Adams arrived in Philadelphia as the new president, one local Republican newspaper scathingly noted the "Triumphal Entry of his Serene Highness of Braintree into the Capital."[17] John smarted under the attacks, but as one historian has observed, he was also often "tone deaf" to social nuances. It was often left to Abigail to step into the breach, further develop the appropriate style and protocol for the Republican Court, and assume the primary responsibility for the required presidential sponsored social events, including the innumerable dinners and levees.[18] Although Abigail always handled those types of occasions capably, her personal preference was for smaller, more intimate social interactions, where female involvement in national politics occurred through lively discussions in which elite men and women participated, exchanged views, and discussed ideas in the private sphere.[19]

After a five-year absence, and a trip through bad weather and harrowing roads, Abigail returned to Philadelphia in the spring of 1797, and she was almost immediately plunged into her duties as First Lady. Despite fatigue and compromised health, she spent two full, draining days dealing with the disarray she encountered in the former Washington house and putting the mansion back into at least minimal order. Abigail then promptly began the first round of social events that would come to define the Adams Republican Court, which would be conducted in a more frugal and somewhat more austere style than that exhibited by George and Martha Washington. She soon described her new role as presidential hostess to her sister Mary: "Yesterday being Monday, from 12 to half past two I received 32 ladies and near as many Gentlemen. I shall have the same ceremony to pass through to day and the rest part of the week . . . [today] Strangers &C[ongress] making near one Hundred asked permission to visit me, so that from half past 12 to near 4, I was rising up & sitting down." Despite her obvious weariness, Abigail noted approvingly that "Mr. A[dams] will never be too big to have his Friends."[20]

Not only was Abigail involved in orchestrating social events for her husband's administration, but she also closely followed unfolding government developments, including the president's May 16 address to Congress concerning relations with France. Clearly, Abigail viewed keeping abreast of details about political events and offering advice as part of her purview as First Lady. What is highly telling is Abigail's comment to her sister that, not only was she forwarding a copy of John's speech to Mary, but that also she actively sought feedback to discover the popular reaction to his remarks, what she termed "the Temper and Sentiments of the publick mind." The letter demonstrates that Abigail was acutely sensitive to the public relations component of political life and that she felt that, if she could gauge popular opinion about the question of war with France, it might help guide John's path.[21] But for the most part she worked behind the scenes privately, probably fearful— and justifiably so, as it turned out—that she would be accused of improper meddling.

Abigail also understood the political value of social events to garner support for her husband's administrative agenda. Eventually, Abigail settled on a formal Friday evening drawing room for women, and John hosted men on regular Monday afternoon levees, but there were many other occasions that included both men and women, most of whom were often members of Congress or diplomats and their wives. As time went on, increasing numbers of Philadelphia's elite citizens also joined the Adams family orchestrated events. That especially brought satisfaction to Abigail, who viewed it as a positive sign that Americans had begun to better appreciate John's positive qualities and accord him the respect she believed he deserved as president.

Like Martha Washington before her, and her later successor Dolley Madison, Abigail clearly understood the symbolic importance of her position and her role as an advocate for her husband's political party, in this case the Federalist faction headed by John as president. Martha had certainly been cognizant of how the events she and President Washington hosted helped strengthen the position of the fledgling federal government. However, Abigail brought a more sophisticated understanding of the ways in which she and other elite women could influence public opinion and political culture. Not only was she a valued adviser to John, but she realized that she could use her considerable intellectual and writing talents to also become a quasi–public relations envoy and help shape public opinion.

Abigail often conveyed information about government affairs and John's perspective to the increasingly influential print outlets by writing letters to newspaper editors and others who were in a position to disseminate what she considered more accurate assessments and who could dispel negative and incorrect information. In addition, she was popularly known to have the ear of President Adams and was thus often approached as a broker of patronage to use her perceived, sometimes real, influence to help persuade John to support various political interests. The result was that Abigail Adams forged a new role not only for herself as First Lady but also for her successors and other women who became key players in the Republican Court.[22]

During her tenure as First Lady, with a limited budget and only a small staff of servants to assist her, Abigail hosted numerous regular events. She normally began her busy days at 5 o'clock in the morning. Just a week after arriving in Philadelphia, Abigail shared details of her crowded schedule with Mary, which included mornings spent largely in family "arrangements," followed by the near daily rituals of receiving company and often hosting dinners for politicians. Still, Abigail began to feel more confident in her role as First Lady, and she confided that "I begin to feel a little more at Home, and less anxiety about the ceremonious part of my duty."[23]

In the summer of 1797, following a precedent set by Washington, the Adamses somewhat reluctantly hosted a reception for over one hundred and fifty political and military dignitaries to celebrate the Fourth of July, and Abigail complained to Mary that the cost of cake and beverages, including wine, came to $500, which not only taxed Abigail's energy but the family purse. But despite her continuing fatigue and receiving numerous visits from guests who came upstairs to her drawing room to pay their personal compliments after first greeting the president and toasting his health downstairs, Abigail came through the day much better than she had anticipated.[24] She clearly preferred the more intimate setting of the President's House for dinners or salons, which she found more conducive to genteel conversation and intelligent, intellectual discourse between both the male and female movers and shakers of republican politics and society. The new First Lady also recognized the events as opportunities to develop broader support for the presidency as well as the wider federal government. Although she had great respect for Martha Washington and her entertainment style as First Lady, Abigail had a different perspective on how best to shape the Republican Court. She astutely realized that her salon domain allowed her an important venue in which to promote significant "conversation among the various actors in public life."[25]

Abigail's years in the ostentatious European courts in Paris and London, where John had served as a minister on behalf of the new nation, had left her with a profound distaste for many of the outer trappings and elaborate ceremonies surrounding royal life, and she hoped to emphasize a more restrained, modest, but elegant approach to entertainment and dress that fit her ideal of proper American behavior. She also clearly utilized the many social events she hosted to try to mend fences and mitigate the increasingly political factionalism that surfaced to bolster the Federalist Party position. One nineteenth-century writer (who often tended to paint a rosy picture) chronicled the story of the early Republican Court and approvingly noted that Abigail, through her "grace and elegance" and "charms of conversation," was able to mitigate at least some of that divisiveness.[26]

Yet in reality Abigail was far from universally appreciated in her role as First Lady by Philadelphia society. Although Dolley Madison and Abigail Adams never met in person, when James Madison temporarily retired from politics, Dolley apparently still took an interest in the Adams administration from afar. While living at the Madison plantation at Montpelier in the summer of 1797, Dolley asked for news about the president as well as the First Lady's drawing room style from her close friend Sally McKean. The daughter of the prominent Philadelphia attorney and politician Thomas McKean, Sally was at the time being courted by the Spanish minister to the United States, Carlos Fernando Martinez de Yrujo, and both men had become adversaries of the Federalist administration. In reply to Dolley's inquiry, Sally sent her a catty report that maintained that "we have none [no drawing rooms] at all— for that old what shall I call her [Abigail] with her hawk's eyes, gave out that the weather was too warm, and it would affect her nerves, they must be very delicate of course, but I suppose we shall have in full splendor in the fall."[27] Obviously, Sally had little appreciation for Abigail's real health challenges or the fact that many political figures, including Republican leaders Thomas Jefferson and James Madison, often removed themselves from the capitals of Philadelphia and later Washington during the hot humid summers because of health concerns.

The letter from Sally to Dolley demonstrates that political gossip was rife at the time among the elite women, who almost universally aligned their political outlooks with that of their male family members, and it also reflected the increasingly deep schism that had developed between the Federalists and Republicans. Thomas McKean and John Adams had begun their relationship many years before as amiable friends, but by the time John became president, Thomas viewed him as a proponent of monarchical practices and the head of a party that threatened liberty.

Unsurprisingly then, in her letter to Dolley, Sally also had negative re-marks to make about the lack of elegance in the president's manners, very condescendingly comparing John unfavorably to George Washington, whom she asserted had at least known how to conduct himself properly in high society. Moreover, Sally accused the Adamses of exceeding the ceremonial customs of the European courts and referred to Abigail sarcastically as "*his Right Honorable Lady.*" McKean's vituperative, biting descriptions reflect the increasing political partisanship among women as well as men in the early nation and also the chasm that often divided Philadelphia's established elite from the Adams administration. The McKeans and Madisons were, of course, by then leading committed Republicans. Fearing the possibility of reprisals for the "treasonous" gossip she had transmitted in the letter, Sally signed her missive to Dolley with a pen name.[28]

In the end, the Adamses left the sweltering capital in the latter part of July 1797 to spend the rest of the summer in Quincy, eager to escape political life in Philadelphia, where John was already feeling assailed on all sides from personal criticism and threats to the nation ranging from possible Indian wars to diplomatic fractures with Spain. They were, however, ultimately pleased, albeit rather surprised, to hear of their son John Quincy's marriage to Louisa Catherine Johnson in London. Although Abigail sometimes proved to be a demanding and challenging mother-in-law to Louisa, John developed a warm, supportive relationship with his intellectual and cultured daughter-in-law, especially in his later years. The presidential couple was also gratified to be feted along their journey and similarly celebrated once in Boston, as well as on their return trip to the capital. Dutifully, Abigail returned with John to Philadelphia in October.

Abigail was incensed on John's behalf when a group of Philadelphians hosted a celebration on February 22, 1798, to mark George Washington's birthday. Washington was now a private citizen, and Abigail felt that, despite his many past worthy contributions, it was an insult to the current president—who incidentally happened to be her husband. It is interesting to note that the radical Republicans had complained about Washington's gala birthday celebrations (which they found distastefully similar to those that had once been given in honor of the British monarch) for some time. In this instance, Abigail was more closely aligned with the Republicans, who felt that the Fourth of July, rather than a presidential birthday, was the most appropriate time for a celebration in the American republic. Neither John nor Abigail attended the party in honor of the first president. Abigail justified her stance to her sister, Mary, asserting that John Adams deserved more respect and appreciation since "They have had & now have a Head, who will not knowingly Prostrate their dignity & character, neither to foreign nations nor the American People."[29]

Despite his sometimes public unpopularity and noticeable disloyalty and dissension from the cabinet members he had inherited from Washington, many of whom remained under Alexander Hamilton's sway, John's longtime experience with negotiation and his generally level-headed pragmatism enabled him to assert America's status as an independent nation and to ward off war with European powers. In retrospect, it was probably the greatest achievement of his term in office. Like Washington, who in his farewell address advised Americans to "steer clear of permanent alliances with any portion of the foreign world," Adams worked resolutely to avoid war with France and end the Quasi-War on the seas.

The French Revolution had left a memory of radicalism and bloody terror in the minds of many Americans, heightening disagreements between political factions. Republicans were regularly accused by Federalists of attempting to import the radicalism and mob rule of the French Revolution to the United States and allowing dangerous foreign emissaries to enter the country. During Washington's second term, the signing of the 1795 Jay Treaty with Great Britain convinced the French that the United States had abandoned its avowed neutral stance in European affairs. In the light of provocative French seizures of American merchant ships and sailors, Adams stood firm about American neutrality but at the same time left the door open for compromise. At first he was accused by some of being unduly harsh with France and too forgiving of England. This was a particular challenge as many of his policies were criticized by a number of prominent Republicans. These included John's own vice president, Thomas Jefferson, who had been a staunch supporter of the French Revolution, as well as John's fellow Federalist Alexander Hamilton, who became an even greater foe. Overall, Jefferson, who generally exhibited an optimistic nature, viewed the French Revolution favorably because he believed it possessed the power to oust the detested monarchy and bring progressive republican ideals of freedom and liberty to the oppressed common people. He, therefore, tolerated its excesses long after John and Abigail became horrified by the ensuing violence.

Once again, Abigail, who could certainly be a stinging critic, was an astute judge of human nature and politically sophisticated. She listened to her husband's concerns and frequently offered counsel and advice. Her support was crucial in guiding John through one of the most difficult periods in his life, and it is clear that the couple *together* reviewed in great detail and frankly discussed political events, many of which she shared in her private correspondence with her confidante, her favorite sister Mary Cranch. Often, when writing to her sister, Abigail simply vented her deepest feelings and neglected to be discreet. Indeed, Abigail had confided in Mary so often during John's presidency that she once wrote contritely, "I believe I have wearied you with politics."[30] When it appeared that war with France was inevitable, Abigail revealed her anxieties to Mary, but in concert with John's views she asserted, "Is it possible that any person can suppose this Country wish for war by which nothing is obtained. . . . But in *self defense*, we may be involved in war; and for that we ought to be prepared, and that is what the President means . . . [if] "we are involved in war, we must & we ought to meet it, with firmness, with Resolution & with union of Sentiment."[31]

Still President Adams held out hope for negotiation when he sent three commissioners—John Marshall, Elbridge Gerry, and Charles Pickney—to Paris to try to help improve relations. But probably the most infamous crisis of the Adams administration, the XYZ Affair, occurred when three French government agents, denoted by the letters X, Y, and Z in later documents, refused to recognize these envoys before a number of preconditions were met—namely, a $10 million loan and a bribe of $240,000 before normal diplomatic relations would be resumed. These demands were met with fury by the president, who firmly told Congress on March 19, 1798, that the underhanded offer was not compatible with the best interests of the United States. Adams then asked Congress to keep the information in the dispatches confidential; instead, 1,200 copies were printed and distributed, fueling both public patriotism as well as more contention between Federalists and Republicans. Soon Abigail, who appears to have been privy to all the details of the behind-the-scenes diplomatic negotiations, became more strident in her antipathy for France. Now that the XYZ revelations had become public, she expressed her hope that "the people be united now they have before them such proof of the base views and designs of France to Plunder us of all we hold dear & valuable, our Religion, our Liberty, our Government and our Property."[32]

As time passed, Abigail increasingly feared what she regarded as French subversion and repeatedly raised the specter of French revolutionary "Jacobins" infiltrating the American government. She asserted to her sister that Jacobin allies (by then she counted Jefferson in the latter category) in the Senate and House exerted misguided and undue influence. By mid-April she was able to report with satisfaction that "The publick opinion is changeing here very fast, and the people beginning to see who have been their firm unshaken friends and defenders of their Rights and Liberties. The Merchants of this city have had a meeting to prepare an address of thanks to the President for his firm and steady conduct. . . . I am told that the French Cockade so frequent in the streets here, is not now to be seen, and the Common People say if J[efferson] had been our President and Madison & Burr our Negotiators, we should all have been sold to the French."[33] Later, in a letter to Mercy Warren, she defended John's policies and praised him "for his

Labourious and hazardous exertions in the public Service." She also observed to Mercy approvingly that "We have seen our Country rise superior to oppression, and despotism and take its Rank and among the Nations, presenting at this period, the *only spectacle* of a Free Republic."[34]

As voiced publicly by the influential conservative British statesman and political philosopher Edmund Burke, who stressed the context of specific circumstances, and whom Abigail admired, the excesses of the French Revolution had represented the demise of the steadying order of political balance and religion, which in her eyes were the underpinning of national stability. She refused to even consider France as a republic after the revolution but simply regarded it, as did Burke, as an anarchic, godless, and violent entity. War fever became rampant among many Americans, and the real concern about a possible clash with France motivated John to ask George Washington to serve as commander in chief of a new American army in the event it became necessary to go to war. Abigail viewed this as a wise step on John's part, for she astutely recognized the powerful image of the former president that was embedded in the American psyche. She declared that Washington's appointment would "unite all Parties in the country. It will give weight, force and energy to the People, & it will dismay our Enemies."[35]

With growing support for war among many Americans, John and Abigail's reputations rose considerably, and for a time the president was feted lavishly wherever he traveled. In 1797, he was celebrated at especially festive dinners in Boston and New York. When John arrived back in Philadelphia, he was met by a cheering crowd, and a gratified Abigail informed her sister with satisfaction that John's popularity was demonstrated by the great respect he was shown in every city and town through which he passed. Although Benjamin Bache, a strong Republican party supporter, continued his jibes at the presidential couple unabated, Abigail vigorously voiced her defense of John's steadfast adherence to republican values: "Every person who is acquainted with the Republican manners and habits of the president can witness for him, that every kind of show and parade are contrary to his taste and inclination and that they can be agreeable on no other ground, than as the Will of the people." Abigail's remarks were clearly a reposte to Bache, as well as to Jefferson, who viewed himself as the upholder of the principles of liberty that were fought for during the Revolutionary War. Abigail also snuck in a backhanded personal jibe at Jefferson when she praised John as never having given his descendants any cause to "Blush for any illegitimate offspring."[36]

Anti-French sentiment continued to increase. In early 1798, as many as 1,100 Philadelphian filed through John's weekly levee sporting the patriotic black cockades of the American Revolution, a clear rejection of the French symbol. For a time, Abigail supported war against what she considered French subversion. However, despite the popular cry for a belligerent response and significant preparation for possible hostilities, by the end of 1798 Adams, who knew that he lacked strong congressional support, was determined to pursue good relations with France if the opportunity presented itself. He appointed a minister to France who was able to successfully negotiate with the French, and eventually peace appeared on the horizon. President Adams later counted his peace efforts among the greatest successes of his administration.

During the impending crisis, Abigail commented candidly on the strain the threat of war imposed on John and fretted to her sister that "I am affraid the President will be overwhelmed. Business thickens upon him. Officering all the frigates, contemplating what can be done at this critical period, *knowing what he thinks ought to be done*, yet not certain whether the people are sufficiently determined to second the Government, is a situation very painfull as well as responsible."[37] Abigail clearly understood that without a strong national will and unified political support for war the situation was fraught with potential disaster. Yet she continued to rail against the French, whom she felt continued depredations on American commerce while approaching possible peace negotiations with nefarious ulterior motives.[38] She remained skeptical that American diplomats could reach any agreement with the French leader Talleyrand, whom she considered underhanded, and she confided to Mary that "I expect Congress will decare [*sic*] war before they Rise."[39]

In the end, John and Abigail were not able to return to Quincy until the height of summer in late July. Then when Abigail became critically ill, John remained by her side as she hovered near death during one of the worst health crises of her life. In the end, he did not return to Philadelphia on his own until November. Ironically, even as she was still recuperating, and before she received John's letter from the capital about the possibility of reconciliation with France, Abigail had already heard the news through circulating rumors via friends in Boston. In the midst of the political turmoil, John Adams shocked his own Federalist Party members by successfully negotiating a peace with France. It caused a split among the Federalists, and was a factor in his defeat for a second term.

Although many Americans including Abigail were surprised by John's overtures, she loyally backed John's new path and soon reversed her earlier vehement support for war. She wrote John that, if she had indeed been in Philadelphia, "the old woman"—as Abigail was sometime referred to derogatorily in the Republican press—would not have tried to dissuade him, as she viewed John's appointment of William Vans Murray as an envoy as "a master Stroke of policy" and a test of French sincerity. After a lengthy discourse on the future of the negotiations, she looked to John for approval of her analysis and concluded, "Pray am I a good politician?"[40]

From the day that Martha Washington became the first presidential spouse, the American public as well as politicians were concerned about the possibility of an unelected First Lady wielding too much power. For many, European queens and other women who were a part of the royal courts had indulged in deplorable intrigue and power struggles to promote their personal and family interests. That was one reason both Martha and Abigail tried to distance themselves from the taint of ostentatious manners. Abigail rather disingenuously insisted to John that she never "pretended to the weight" of influence that some had suggested, referring perhaps obliquely to newspaper editorials that claimed the president never made an appointment without her approval.[41] Nevertheless, the controversy surrounding the entire diplomatic episode demonstrated that at least in the arena of public opinion, Abigail had been perceived as wielding direct significant influence on the president and, therefore, indirectly on political policy. Certainly, Abigail regarded one of her responsibilities as First Lady and as a patriotic republican wife as defending her husband from his detractors by any means available to her.

An area that left John especially vulnerable to criticism was the diplomatic appointments he made during his administration, and one of his most controversial acts was the naming of his own son, John Quincy, who had been President Washington's minister to the Netherlands, as the new foreign minister to Prussia. By then the Adamses had become a prominent and visible American political family, and from his youth, when John Quincy had first accompanied his diplomat father to Paris, he been groomed by his parents for political greatness. Abigail appears to have viewed herself as the matriarch of the family unit, who needed to look out for the best interests of not only her husband but also her son, son-in-law, and even more distant relatives.

Abigail insisted that John only took "Merit, virtue & Talents" into consideration when he conferred appointments, but even though his son John Quincy was in reality eminently qualified for the position, the president's choices often left him open to accusation of inappropriate acts of patronage characterized by nepotism and favoritism.[42] These included the hiring of one of Abigail's nephews as John's secretary and another nephew who was appointed a judge. It is noteworthy that when Adams served as vice president back in 1789, Abigail had already conveyed what she considered her husband's principled outlook about patronage. She quoted him as affirming that, although he possessed no patronage privileges at the time, even if he had, he would never betray his "clear conviction of the public Good, and all the maxims of his Life," by ever making the authority entrusted to him "subservient to his private views & those of his Family and Friends."[43]

But even a Boston newspaper jumped into the fray and inaccurately accused John Adams of reaping an exorbitant presidential salary and intimated that his son John Quincy had received a generous windfall salary with his appointment as minister to Prussia. Once again, Abigail was incensed at the press and infuriated at what she considered the lies the editor had printed. She went to great pains to tell her sister that John's salary was the same as Washington's had been but worth less during John's tenure because of inflation. Moreover, not only did all the expenditures have to be accounted for, but the salary was also to be used to cover all presidential-related expenses.[44] A year later, Abigail was still defending John as a virtuous president who made appointments based on neither "Love [nor] fear." She compared her husband favorably to President Washington, who she felt had often been motivated by the desire to promote harmony over seeking competence, and complained that "You did not hear at that day so much Noise of *Executive Patronage.*"[45]

Abigail became an activist and quasi–public relations manager, defending her husband through letters she sent to family and friends, in the hopes that her arguments would be transmitted in some form to contemporary newspapers. Indeed, her grasp of politics, strong opinions about political issues, and staunch Federalist views were widely recognized, and, of course, she was herself at times personally attacked for her alleged pivotal influence on John's actions. Abigail's first major target was the press. Many years earlier during John's first term as vice president, she had already formed a negative opinion about journalists when she commented that "the News writers will fib, to answer particular purposes." As John's most ardent defender, she often made the point that her husband was a visibly honorable and virtuous man, whose "Rule through life has been to vote and act, independent of Party agreeable [only] to the dictates of his conscience."[46]

Abigail was particularly incensed with the Republican journalist James Callendar, who frequently criticized Adams, and she was especially furious with Benjamin Franklin's grandson, Benjamin Franklin

Bache. In a high temper, she characterized the editorials of Bache, who was once a classmate of John Quincy Adams in Paris and later became the well-known editor of the Philadelphia newspaper, the Republican supported *Aurora*, as full of "batterys of abuse and scurility."[47] Still Abigail insisted resignedly that "I expected to be vilified and abused, with my whole family when I came into this situation [as First Lady]."[48] Abigail's intense ire over Bache's missives are particularly interesting because early on, Henrietta Liston, wife of the British ambassador, had suggested that Abigail was somewhat impervious to the criticisms of her husband in the press. In the summer of 1797, Mrs. Liston reported to her uncle that "I believe I told you how pleased I am with Mrs. Adams, she has spirit enough to laugh at Baches abuse of her Husband, which poor Mrs. Washington could not." Clearly the diplomat's wife admired Abigail's plucky and confident demeanor as she concluded, "I hope to acquire that sort of spirit in time,"[49] but Henrietta apparently did not realize that privately Abigail was seething.

Henrietta also had expressed her appreciation for John Adams earlier in the year after she and her husband had dined at the president's mansion while Washington still held office. As Mrs. Liston put it, she "sat between the rising and setting sun," in the company of both "Great Men," and found Adams to be a man of "wit and humor" in his manner of conversation.[50] No doubt the increasing rapprochement between England and the United States influenced her favorable opinion of both Federalist presidents.

But Abigail's patience for Bache's frequent barbs grew thin, and she ceased to be amused. Less than a year later, Abigail reported to her sister that Bache had unfairly cast negative aspersions on the president and sarcastically referred to her as "the Excellent Lady of the Excellent President." Bache later died during a yellow fever epidemic in Philadelphia in 1798, and Abigail probably felt little regret at his loss. She especially blamed foreigners, particularly French emissaries, for providing what she considered blatantly false information to the American press and their efforts to "calumniate the President, his family, his administration."

But just a month later Abigail was pleased to report that with the exception of "Bache & CO who in his paper calls the President old, querulous, Bald, blind crippled, Toothless Adams," the presidential couple had now become "wonderfully popular" with Philadelphia citizens.[51]

Fear and anger combined to push Abigail to conflate the excesses of the press and "alien" influence in the guise of Republican politicians and their allies. She raged to Mary Cranch that "There is no end to their audaciousness, and you will see that French emissaries are in every corner of the union sowing and spreading their Sedition. We have *renewed information* that their System is to calumniate the President, his family, his administration, until they oblige him to resign, and then they will Reign triumphant, headed by the *Man of the People* [Jefferson]."[52] Moreover, she was moved to assert to Mary that, not only did her husband, as president, not seek glory, but that he had, in fact, been studiously neutral in the conflict between England and France. Abigail made it very clear that John only contemplated a strong response to the French out of justified self-defense. She went so far as to declare rather histrionically that the critics of John's measured policies were people who "would gladly see their Government prostrate, Religion banished . . . and our Country Shared by France."[53]

Indeed, Abigail became such a staunch and vocal supporter of the Alien and Sedition Acts, in part, because her husband had so often been vilified (in her opinion always unfairly and unconscionably) in the press. At one point she lashed out in anger at "the vile incendiaries" who "keep up in Baches paper the most wicked and base, violent & caluminiating abuse" and averred that "nothing will have an Effect until congress pass a Sedition Bill." Just weeks later Abigail offered additional factors to justify her support and maintained that passage of new laws would help squelch unfounded libelous criticism of the president and Congress and "contribute as much to the Peace and harmony of our Country as any measure."[54]

It became Abigail's fervent hope that the four congressional acts passed in the summer of 1798, collectively known as the Alien and Sedition Acts, would not only provide the president with the means of re-moving potentially treasonous foreigners—especially those whom she had frequently referred to derogatorily as "French Jacobins," who she believed might be a potential threat to the American government—but also help curtail the unfettered freedom of the press, which in her mind had promoted so much falsehood and dissent against her hus-band's beleaguered presidency. Both Abigail and John had always been extremely sensitive to public criticism of any kind, and the heightened public reaction prompted her to assert that "I wish the Laws of our Country were competant to punish the stirrer up of sedition, the writer and Printer of base and unfounded calumny. This would contribute as much to the peace and Harmony of our Country as any measure, and in times like the present, a more careful and attentive watch ought to be kept over foreigners. This will be done in the future if the Alien Bill passes."[55]

Irritated by the oppositional element in the press and influenced by what he saw as legitimate concerns about foreign threats and the divi-sion and agitation produced about the debate over war with France, John signed the bills, which carried potential fines and jail time for offending journalists and other writers. Unfortunately, despite his best intentions, the legislation had the opposite effect than that John and Abigail de-sired. Its unpopularity as a visible curtailment of republican notions of American liberty, free speech, and the right of assembly played a nega-tive role in John's unsuccessful bid for a second term. In the eyes of Re-publican Party popular public opinion, even moderate Federalists such as John Adams had always been elitists, reactionary leaders who had no respect for ordinary citizens.

Abigail herself was far from immune to public criticism, and some of her detractors referred to her derogatorily as "Her Majesty." She appears to have especially aroused the ire of her personal foe, the influential con-gressman and vocal anti-Federalist Albert Gallatin, later secretary of the treasury under President Madison. Gallatin once reported to his wife that one of his friends who had visited the Adams "court" told him that

Abigail had requested the names of all the congressional visitors so she could identify which were "our people" [Adams's Federalist supporters]. He concluded sarcastically that "She is Mrs. President not of the United States . . . but of a faction."[56] Abigail, in turn, regarded the Swiss-born Gallatin as an underhanded Republican enemy who used his position to insinuate French influence into the American government. Others complained that Abigail used her influence to request that John offer patronage appointments to friends and family, such as Nabby's wayward, often erratic husband, William Smith, whom the Senate reluctantly confirmed for a military post. Later Smith occupied the position of surveyor-general of New York.

In the summer of 1798, Abigail became deathly ill, and John spent long months by her side at their home in Quincy, where she was confined to bed for eleven weeks. Abigail suffered from severe headaches, fever, insomnia, and rheumatism and was officially diagnosed with dysentery, some form of diabetes, and the usual vague "bilious" fevers, which may have been a recurrence of malaria. In November, when she finally began to recover, John returned to Philadelphia, and Abigail remained in Massachusetts, but she still cared avidly about politics in the nation's capital. It is telling that Abigail entreated John to keep her abreast of all that was "proper to be communicated" about public affairs, since, owing to her weakened state, she could be only "a half way politician this winter."[57]

The overtures toward peace negotiations with France had angered many of Adams's more radical Federalist detractors, who perhaps exaggerated Abigail's influence when they complained that her absence from Philadelphia may have been a primary factor in the president's decision to change course. John captured the sentiment perfectly when he caustically reported to Abigail, still recovering her health back in Quincy: "How they [his Hamilton faction opponents] lament Mrs. Adams's Absence! She is a good Counsellor! If she had been here Murray would never have been named [an envoy to France] nor his Mission instituted."[58] Certainly Hamilton viewed John Adams as a rival and had long sought to derail his political aspirations on several occasions.

John joined Abigail in Massachusetts in April, and he conducted government business by correspondence from his home while he waited out the results of the peace overtures to France. With her health improved, Abigail resumed her extensive correspondence and continued to air her outspoken social and political opinions, including lobbying for a treaty with the Dutch. Another area that occupied Abigail's thoughts was the subject of taxes, as both she and John realized it would become a significant issue for Americans in the future. In a letter written in July 1799 to her younger sister, Elizabeth Peabody, she referred to a book she had sent to Elizabeth's daughter. Some of the condescending views in the volume about women prompted Abigail to voice her refutation: "I will never consent to have our sex considered in an inferior point of light. Let each planet shine in their own orbit. God and nature desgnd it so—If man is Lord, woman is *Lordess*." Although that had long been her position on the roles of men and women in society, now that she held the most visible female position in the United States as First Lady, her assessment about political participation for women was even more telling: "If a woman does not hold the Reigns of Government, I see no reason for her not judging how they are conducted," she declared.[59] Her words intimate that she perhaps saw a time on the horizon when women would become more formally involved in government, but they also reflect that she believed women had a responsibility in the interim to follow political issues and make their opinions known through informal avenues.

John returned to Philadelphia in October 1799, and Abigail followed shortly in November, when she quickly resumed her duties as First Lady, including making and returning visits and hosting her drawing rooms when Congress resumed. In fact, shortly after she arrived she was obliged to receive so many visitors that she complained she was unable to leave the presidential mansion to engage in any physical exercise because of her onerous schedule. One of several female visitors who did not meet her exacting standards for proper dress for American women appearing at the Adams court was Madame Maria Bingham de Tilly, the daughter of the Philadelphia society leader Anne Bingham, whom Abigail had earlier admired. The teenaged Maria had eloped with an expatriate French count, and according to Abigail, she exhibited "all the appearance and dress of a Real French woman." This was not meant as a compliment, as by that time, Abigail largely disdained French politics, culture, and fashion.[60]

Although Abigail had been a staunch early supporter of the proposed war with France, she reversed course in support of her husband. Now an advocate of the peace mission to France spearheaded by President Adams, Abigail observed to her sister that whatever the final outcome and despite the criticism engendered by some members of the Senate and a member of his own cabinet, "the President will have the satisfaction of knowing: That he has done every thing Encumbent upon him to preserve Peace and restore harmony." Later in the month, she reiterated her firm belief that, despite objections from the Republican opposition, as well as from Hamilton, John's Federalist rival, and some remonstrations from the British minister, John, as president, was entirely correct in his decision to send envoys to France. Abigail forthrightly summed up her political view on the rightful place of the United States in the world when she asserted, "As an independent Nation, no other has a Right to complain, or dictate to us, with whom we shall form connections, provided those connections are not contrary to treaties already made."[61] The President's efforts to avoid war were eventually fruitful, and a formal peace treaty with France was signed in October 1800, with the approval of the Senate.

Just two days after George Washington's death in mid-December 1799, Abigail hosted a memorial event for the late president. It was one of her most well attended drawing rooms as First Lady, attracting over a hundred guests, who embellished their clothing with touches of black to reflect their state of mourning. Although she felt that Washington was being lionized to a greater degree than was warranted, she genuinely sympathized with the terrible loss her good friend, Martha, had suffered. Abigail had witnessed firsthand the deep affection between the nation's first president and his wife. Abigail's note to the former First Lady conveyed her heartfelt condolences: "I intreat Madam, that You would permit a heart deeply penetrated with your loss, and sharing personally in your Grief, to mingle with You, the Tears which flow for the partner of all Your joys and Sorrows." Later, Abigail confided to her sister Mary that, although Washington was unquestionably a worthy figure, "To no one Man in America, belongs the Epithet of *Saviour* of his Country . . . at no time, did the fate of America rest upon the Breast of even a Washington, and those who assert these things, are Ignorant of the spirit of their countrymen."[62] Although Abigail had initially been one of George's greatest admirers, by the time of his demise, she regretted the cult of personality that had developed around him, something many of his Republican detractors had often decried. It is clear that Abigail felt John's central role in the birth and political development of the nation had been unappreciated.

That last season in Philadelphia before the nation's capital moved to the banks of the Potomac was probably Abigail's most enjoyable period as First Lady. With her daughter Nabby and son Thomas by her side, Abigail took evident pride in her acknowledged role as the female leader of the local political/social set. She received an inordinate number of visits before she left Philadelphia and ably hosted several dinners a week and her regular drawing rooms for members of Congress and their families as well as other guests from the city's upper social strata. The executive mansion was often filled with lively discussion, and meals for thirty to forty guests were common. In January 1800, Abigail observed that she had hosted more "Congress Ladies" than she ever had previously in Philadelphia, which she attributed to the women's low expectations for being entertained once the capital moved to the "new city" of Washington.[63]

Now that Abigail was comfortable in her role, the prospect of a second term for John did not seem quite as daunting to her. In February 1800, Abigail informed her sister that, "If his country calls him to continue longer in Her Service, I doubt not that he will be obedient to her voice, in which case I certainly should consider it my duty to accompany him." Although Abigail emphasized duty, her willingness to continue on for another possible term was a far cry from her initial, at least professed, reluctance to follow in Martha Washington's footsteps as the second First Lady.

Ironically, now that Abigail appeared to have been more enthusiastic about her husband's presidency, he was destined not to win reelection. As a result, Abigail became increasingly pessimistic about the potential success of regular popular elections and the vicious factions that had swept her husband out of office. In her eyes, John had steered a steady and admirable course for the United States: "3 years are now past, and we have enjoyd as much peace, quiet, Security and happiness as any people can boast of in the same period of time. . . . Our National Character has risen in the public estimation, and the public confidence has in no way been diminished. Faction has not been so turbulent nor malice so active. [But] The Electioneering campaign I presume will bring all their forces into action."[64]

In April, Abigail hosted a dinner followed by tea in her drawing room and dancing for a group of young people, including her son Thomas. Obviously in a festive mood, Abigail observed that the guests, who numbered twenty-eight, had all appreciated the evening, and some had even remarked that it was one of the most enjoyable times of their lives. Even the president spent a pleasant hour with the group. Abigail also folded in some political analysis concerning potential interference in American affairs by European nations and commented that she believe the United States government had "quite as much to Guard against from that quarter [England], as from the Great nation [France]."[65] Abigail hosted her last drawing room in Philadelphia on May 2, 1800, when she entertained nearly two hundred men and women, and the following week she gave her last formal dinner.

Abigail set out for Quincy on May 19. John joined her in Massachusetts after a journey to Washington to view the site of the new capital,

FIGURE 3.1. Engraving of Abigail Adams from an original painting by
Gilbert Stuart. (Courtesy Library of Congress.)

which he observed with approval. During that trip, John visited Mount
Vernon and told Abigail that "Mrs. Washington and her whole Family
very kindly enquired after your health. . . . I like the Seat of Government
very well and shall Sleep, or lie awake next Winter in the President's
House."[66] After summering in Quincy, John returned to Washington in
October to occupy the new President's House for his remaining days as

president. Abigail arrived in November, after a sad and wrenching final visit to New York to meet with her dying son Charles, who passed away not long after she joined John in the new capital.

Charles Adams died at the age of thirty, apparently owing to alcoholism and a life of dissipation. Abigail sadly noted that she had found her son "laid upon a Bed of sickness, destitute of home. A distressing cough, and affection of the liver and a dropsy will soon terminate a Life, which might have been made valuable to himself and others." Like Martha Washington before her and Dolley Madison, who would later follow as First Lady, Abigail experienced the pain of having a son who had as a child shown great promise, a future that was never fulfilled. Still, despite deep sorrow, Abigail was determined to do her duty as First Lady and continued on to the capital. When she stopped in Philadelphia on her journey south, she stayed temporarily at the former presidential mansion there before departing for Washington City with some trepidation about her new temporary residence, what she referred to as "an unseen & unknown abode."[67] John was also shaken by his son's death, especially pained by the self-inflicted ignominious cause of Charles's demise. Months later, John confided to Thomas Jefferson that Charles "was once the delight of my Eyes and a darling of my heart, cut off in the flower of his days, amidst very flattering Prospects by causes which have been the greatest grief of my Life."[68]

John lost the election of 1800 to Jefferson only by a narrow margin, demonstrating that at least a good number of American citizens had appreciated his policies. Despite John's professed desire to rise above politics and Abigail's initial reluctance to serve as First Lady, it was a severe blow to the couple who had for so many years stood at the center of American political life. But in the end, both John and Abigail became philosophical and were gratified that the negotiations he initiated with France had concluded with a peaceful settlement. Owing to John's defeat, Abigail spent only one brief season of three months in Washington, DC. But the Adamses held the distinction of being the first presidential family to occupy the President's House, what would before long become known as the White House. It was an edifice Abigail almost immediately realized would become a pivotal historic space and national symbol and, as she so felicitously put it, a foundation "for the ages."[69]

Although George Washington had laid the cornerstone for the building, he left office long before its completion. Washington and Thomas Jefferson had helped plan the edifice that would house the home and office of the president and become an enduring symbol of liberty for the republican nation. Ironically, it was a site that had been built, in part, by enslaved black African Americans who had been denied their own liberty, another demonstration of the inherent conflict between the ideals of the Declaration of Independence and the institution of slavery.[70] John had preceded Abigail to the new capital on November 1, and on his first full day in residence, he wrote to Abigail, bestowing his famous hope for the future home of all American presidents: "I pray heaven to bestow the best of blessings on this House and all that shall hereafter inhabit it. May none but honest and wise men ever rule under this roof."[71] Undoubtedly, the thought of a future female or African American president never crossed his mind.

When she arrived to join John in Washington on November 16, 1800, to Abigail's dismay, the capital city was at the time little more than a rough frontier outpost. Soon after her arrival she observed that "this place known by the name of the city, and the Name is all that you can call so," but she asserted that "I am determined to be satisfied and content." She also was pleased that, despite what she considered many false dispersions cast against John by Hamilton and his supporters, the president remained popular in his own state of Massachusetts, and John's birthday was celebrated with due honor in his hometown of Quincy. With her typical tart humor, Abigail also informed Mary that she and the president were well, and although the newspapers had falsely reported that John suffered from "Ague and fever," she rejoiced "that it was only in the paper he had it." She also proudly noted that on November

21, the president would deliver his first address in the new capital city to both houses of Congress.[72]

When Abigail and John Adams resided in Washington, half-finished buildings sprouted in the midst of swampy ground and a tree-filled forest, and a population of only about five hundred resident families was augmented by three hundred government members. The future White House, then called the President's House, featured only six rooms. It commanded a beautiful view of the Potomac but was essentially set in a wilderness. The accommodations in the unfinished presidential home were rudimentary, famously forcing Abigail to entertain dignitaries in very modest quarters and to hang the wash in the empty East Room. Fires were lit in all the rooms to keep the cold and damp at bay. She reported to her sister that "Not one room or chamber is finished in the whole." Yet Abigail realized that, despite the rough nature of the new capital, social occasions were still extremely important to the local women, and Abigail informed her daughter Nabby that "the ladies are impatient for a drawing room."[73]

Because the capital lacked many of the amenities found in the more established American urban centers, in the beginning most of the wives and other family members of those men who were involved in government typically stayed at home. But even in early Washington, Republican Court events continued to offer the modest number of elite women living there an avenue for public and political influence through social venues. Those types of ceremonial occasions had originated with the Washingtons in New York. They then followed in the new nation's second temporary capital in Philadelphia and were first overseen by Martha Washington and then by Abigail after her husband became president. By the time Dolley Madison became First Lady, increasing numbers of wives and daughters of male politicians would travel to Washington to take an active part in societal life.

Abigail was one of dozens of Washington women who entered the public sphere as they filled the galleries and overflowed onto the floor of the Senate when John made his first speech to both houses of Congress that November. A number of the capital's elite society women attended congressional debates. Despite overwhelming personal concerns for her family, including the fate of Charles's widow and daughters and her own daughter Nabby's erratic and unreliable spouse, as well as the increasing unpopularity of John's administration, Abigail carried out her social duties as the First Lady conscientiously. It was Abigail, who in 1800 first began the tradition of opening the presidential mansion to visitors in Washington City on New Year's Day. It was a custom that continued until the early 1930s. Her predecessor, Martha Washington, had hosted similar receptions for crowds of ordinary citizens when she served as First Lady in New York and Philadelphia. Outwardly gracious and charming, as the first hostess in the new President's House, Abigail was tormented by inner anxiety and stress about the future of both the nation and her own extended family members.

Shortly after she arrived in Washington, Abigail wrote Mary about the upcoming election and proclaimed philosophically: "As to politics; they are at present such a mere turn penny, that I believe it is best to leave all calculations to those who daily occupy themselves with them, and say from the Sincerity of my Heart I do: That I hope the termination of the present contests will be such as will be most productive of the Peace, Liberty and happiness of our common country, let who will be at the Head of the Government."[74] If we take Abigail at her word, it appears she decided she could live with the uncertainty of the upcoming election results and had attempted to make peace with the possible outcome that John would not serve a second term. Nevertheless, John's defeat, coupled with the death of her beloved son, Charles, capped a dark period for the First Lady. Yet the resilient partnership that Abigail and John had developed helped them both endure the personal tragedy and the painful political blow, and they stood poised with regret, tempered by some measure of relief, to "retire from public life."[75]

Moreover, Abigail maintained that when it was clear John would not be reelected, she made up her mind to retire with dignity without wishing any of her husband's political detractors ill. Obviously conscious of her responsibility in the visible role as First Lady during her last days in Washington, she stressed that "I would strive to act my part well. . . . I wish for the preservation of the Government, and a wise administration of it. In the best situation, with the wisest head and firmest Heart, it will be surrounded with perplexities, dangers, and troubles, that are little conceived of by those into whose Hands it is like to fall." She had certainly been referring to Thomas Jefferson, and she also confided to her sister Mary that "The President [John] had frequently contemplated resigning" during some of his most challenging days and that she herself had at times thought "It would be best for him to leave the people to act for themselves."[76] She was determined to remain in Washington until the final outcome of the election, which was then tied between Aaron Burr and Thomas Jefferson, was decided.

It is noteworthy that, before Abigail departed in February 1801 for Quincy, where she would remain for the rest of her life, she first visited her old friend, Martha Washington, in December 1800 at Mount Vernon. Although she was pleased to have been able to spend time with the original First Lady, whom she still admired, Mount Vernon failed to impress Abigail, and she deplored the institution of slavery that was still very much in evidence on the plantation after George Washington's death. We can only speculate about what Abigail thought about the skilled and unskilled work of the black slave labor that had been essential to the building of the President's House on the Potomac that she and John had so briefly occupied. In the waning days of the Adams administration, in January 1801, Thomas Jefferson joined the Adamses for dinner at the President's House, and he stopped to bid Abigail farewell in early February before she took her final leave of the capital. The longtime close ties between Jefferson and the Adamses had not yet been entirely severed, and Jefferson would not officially become the new president until the thirty-sixth ballot broke the election loggerhead on February 17. Although outwardly civil, the old, deep friendship had frayed, and John pointedly left Washington surreptitiously before daylight on the day of Jefferson's inauguration.

Even after John left office, Abigail remained politically informed and opinionated. One of her biographers maintained that "most women [of her era] had little opportunity to acquire political knowledge; she conversed with statesmen in Europe and the United States and wrote long letters of political commentary. Few if any of her countrywomen matched her experience."[77] As a fiercely staunch supporter of the Federalist Party, Abigail viewed Jefferson's election as a Republican to the presidency in 1801 as a tragic disaster that threatened the stability and future of the fragile American republic. Moreover, by then she increasingly regarded Jefferson, who had defeated her beloved husband for a second term as president, as a traitor and a duplicitous and underhanded foe who would bring the country to ruin along with his godless party. As a widower, Jefferson was not accompanied to the White House by a First Lady, but Dolley Madison would often serve as hostess when women were present at his generally austere social functions.

A dispirited and perhaps understandably somewhat bitter John and Abigail Adams escaped Washington shortly before Jefferson's formal inauguration. To mitigate at least some of what he considered potential Republican mismanagement, John hastily conferred a few midnight appointments before he left office, naming John Marshall as chief justice of the Supreme Court and bestowing a federal judgeship on his nephew, which again prompted accusations of nepotism. These final actions confirmed Jefferson's suspicions about the Federalist agenda. Ultimately, Jefferson would come to regard his election to the presidency as the "Revolution of 1800," a period in which he felt he had demonstrated his overarching commitment to the American republic by wresting control of government from the Federalists and returning power to the common man and "the people." According to the historian Brian Steele, Jefferson always insisted that his underlying political goal had been not to restrict governance but to better "align the state with the will of the nation."[78]

Abigail could never bring herself to appreciate Jefferson's argument about his devotion to the public good because the personal pain she experienced on behalf of John was too deep. In Abigail's mind, she and

John had formed an unshakeable family unit, and the disappointment experienced by one partner in the marriage was felt equally by both. Yet in the mid-1780s, when both John Adams and Jefferson had been stationed as diplomats in France on behalf of the new United States, Abigail had enjoyed a close mutual friendship with Jefferson, whom she regarded as a kindred spirit, and the two had often discussed political and social subjects of import. Indeed, at one point, Abigail and Thomas had shared political information about "Mr. Madison's honour and integrity."[79] And when Madison ran for president, although she would have far preferred a Federalist candidate, she realized that Charles Cotesworth Pickney was not an electable choice. She, therefore, echoed her son John Quincy Adams's judgment that Madison was "the fittest and one of the most sensible and candid of the Virginians, a moral man," and the "best . . . on the other side [the Republicans]."[80]

In part, Abigail's tolerance for Madison was connected with the political career of John Quincy, who had sided with Jefferson and Madison in support of the Embargo Act of 1807, the only Federalist senator at the time to do so. The legislation was aimed at forcing France and England to respect American rights during the Napoleonic Wars in Europe and allowing the United States to remain neutral and allow trade with both sides. But the embargo, which banned the export of American goods, was highly unpopular with many United States citizens from merchants to farmers, as it put serious pressure on the American economy. While most Federalists had denounced the embargo, Abigail steered a more neutral political course and diverged from the official party line. She clearly understood the wider implications of the embargo and even defended it when she wrote to her daughter Nabby in March 1808. She maintained that, although "the Embargo distresses us all. Yet is it a measure that I am convinced was the best calculated to avert the horrors of war . . . hard as it is to be borne, we had better suffer temporary privations."[81]

Abigail was incensed at the "calumny" and "bitter spirit of party" to which John Quincy was subjected in the Boston newspapers over his political actions, and he ultimately resigned his senate position as a Federalist and became a Republican. Although she may have privately been appalled that her son had officially switched parties, Abigail defended what she considered his honorable actions as fiercely as she had her husband's policies during his political career. She even shared with Nabby John Quincy's assessment that Madison's conduct as secretary of state during the European conflict was exemplary as well as John Quincy's opinion that "the neutrality of the present administration has been as fair and impartial as it was under with of those which preceeded and during the former War." Moreover, Abigail was clearly highly distressed at the divisive public discourse that increasingly categorized American politics. She astutely observed that, "in the present state of our country, union is essentially necessary to our very existence," certainly a situation that Abigail's successor Dolley Madison understood and would later devote her considerable efforts to mitigate.[82]

In May, Abigail was still smarting from the unfair abuse she believed John Quincy continued to endure, and as a result, she longed for more civility in the public sphere. In a lengthy letter filled with political references, she told Nabby that she felt the "great object of the honest men of both parties should be to unite for the common good, and to cultivate a spirit of candour liberality and harmony . . . until that can be effected our country will be torn alternately by contending factions." She ended her missive with an apology to her daughter for having penned such a "political rig that I have little room left" and concluded with praise of her husband's wise conduct during his presidency.[83] Later, she would refer nostalgically to John's administration as the "Halcion [*sic*] days of America."[84]

As time passed, Abigail continued to use what public influence she had retained through her reputation as the matriarch of a prominent political family. When Dolley Madison reigned as First Lady and wielded considerable powers of patronage during her husband's administration, Abigail was not above writing Mrs. Madison to secure a good job for one of her grandsons. Abigail was obviously familiar with Dolley's reputation as an unofficial power broker and for, at times, successfully filling government positions with family members and supporters, something Abigail had indulged in during her own years as a presidential spouse. Abigail had not only been an active partner in her husband's political life, but she had also sometimes meddled in her son's career as well.

When Madison became president of the United States, Abigail was not above lobbying him on behalf of her eldest son. Driven by ingrained family and Puritan notions of duty, John Quincy had followed his father's example of national service. Accompanied by his wife Louisa and their young children, John was at the time stationed in Russia as the American ambassador in St. Petersburg, a reward for his support of Jefferson's Louisiana Purchase and Embargo Act, in which Madison had played a pivotal role. Despite a good salary for the time, the high cost of living in Russia in 1810 taxed the younger Adams family's modest income. Abigail (without her son's knowledge) rather brazenly interfered in American politics by entreating Madison to bring her son back before he became virtually bankrupted. Using her most charming manner, Abigail informed the president that she appreciated "the honor done to Mr. Adams, by your repeated nomination of him to this Embassy" and "that I entertain a high respect for your person and Character and to add my best wishes for the success and prosperity of your administration."[85]

Madison's reply demonstrated his sometimes unappreciated diplomatic skill. He assured Abigail she had his "highest esteem and very respectful consideration."[86] At the same time, Madison sent his secretary of state a missive that assured him that if financial constraints forced him to return to America, he was free to do so without any criticism from the president. Reading between the lines, however, it was clear that Madison's preference was that John Quincy stay in Russia to act on behalf of the best interests of the American government, a position Madison reversed when a sudden opening on the Supreme Court made the younger Adams an ideal candidate as a loyal Madison supporter. In the end, despite her intervention in political affairs through the back door, to Abigail's bitter disappointment and Madison's at least mild consternation, John Quincy declined the Supreme Court position and remained in St. Petersburg.

Well after John and Abigail had left the White House, Abigail kept abreast of politics and continued to speak her mind without reservation. She studiously followed congressional debates that appeared in print form in the newspapers of the day. Even when corresponding with family members, she freely mixed family updates with political commentary. As she wrote her daughter Nabby in the fall of 1808, after a detailed description of family and friends who had been laid low by a variety of illnesses, Abigail concluded, "So much for domestick affairs. now for a seasoning of politicks."[87]

Old age and frequent poor health did not diminish Abigail's interest in American affairs. She remained sharp witted and introspective, followed international political developments, and stayed a staunch advocate of a strong and united national government. But her elitist inclinations were evident. In the Spring of 1808, during the Napoleonic Wars, she complained to Nabby that "English partizens and French partizens (tho they are fewer in number) divide our country." Without any sense of irony, she declared that at the same time "the pure and Native Americans can scarcely find a spot upon which he may place his foot, and make a firm stand against these encroachments."[88] When Abigail referred to "Native Americans," she was not discussing American Indians but, rather, old-stock families such as the Quincys and Adamses, who were among the earliest British colonial residents. Despite the ideals she had espoused during the American Revolution, she remained in some ways a social snob, a believer in the traditional social hierarchy that separated the elite from more ordinary or even poor citizens.

As Abigail once wrote to her daughter-in-law Louisa's mother, Catherine Johnson, "I cannot wean myself from the subject of politics." She later asked Catherine for updates on Napoleon and what she perceived as the "disunion of the cabinet" under Madison.[89] Even though Madison was a Republican, she again broke party ranks and supported his position in the War of 1812, reminiscent of her spirited anti-British patriotism during the Revolutionary War. Abigail justified the right of females to take a firm political stand in public affairs, maintaining that women had a responsibility to interest themselves in an area "which some suppose exclusively belongs to your [male] sex," when "the future destiny of their Country" hung in the balance.[90] Later, in the spring of 1814, she wrote her sister Elizabeth Peabody Shaw in support of Madison's embargo and assured her that the president had the nation's best interests at heart. Obviously referring to John's political experiences, she asserted that often challenges arose that interfered with the "wisest plans which are Sugested by the Rulers of a Nation," and with a bit of self-mocking humor she concluded that she had a tendency to run on when discussing politics.[91] Perhaps politics were a welcome distraction from personal tragedies. Abigail reveled in being surrounded by family and friends back in Quincy, but all was not idyllic. In 1813, Abigail was devastated by the deaths of both her sister Mary and brother-in-law Richard Cranch. Then, even more painfully, the Adamses' beloved daughter Nabby died of breast cancer. Abigail experienced some consolation as Nabby's daughter, Caroline, became a treasured part of Abigail's household until the young woman married.

Still, despite the wrenching losses, daily life went on, and with it Abigail's continued interest in public affairs. Abigail and John met President James Monroe in July 1818, when he stopped to visit them at their home in Quincy during a tour of the northern states. The Adamses hosted a well-attended private dinner for Monroe in their home for forty friends. Abigail found the fifth president agreeably affable and possessing "unassuming manners." Although she was less charitable about life in the White House, which she noted was filled with too much ceremony, and which in her day would have been denounced with "The Cry of Monarchy . . . from Georgia to Maine," she clearly viewed the Monroe administration as an improvement over Jefferson's and Madison's tenures.[92] Abigail could certainly be highly partisan in her opinions, and her positive outlook about Monroe was no doubt enhanced by his choice of her son John Quincy as secretary of state.

Abigail Adams was a woman of her era, but in some significant ways she was ahead of her times. During the late eighteenth century, it was unusual for women to discuss, think, and write as knowledgeably and frankly as Abigail did about political issues. One historian has even recently suggested that she had more insight into political nuance than her husband John.[93] Her ever-present taste for her "dish of politics" was the result of a combination of factors that inclined her toward a life-long interest in public issues. They included her own keen intellect and ever-curious mind; the fact that her father William Smith had been a prominent Congregationalist minister and her maternal grandfather, John Quincy, an active politician; her own deep-seated religious faith; and her committed support of the American Revolution. She was also influenced by her later proximity to the centers of political power in the new republic through her husband's key role in the revolution, as an American minister in Europe, and subsequent election as vice president and president. The Adamses were indeed a political family, and Abigail also took deep pride in her eldest son's pivotal role in national American politics. Although she did not live to see him follow in his father's footsteps as the sixth president of the United States, she witnessed John Quincy's distinguished diplomatic career and was honored when, in 1814, he was one of the American emissaries who signed the Treaty of Ghent to end the War of 1812. She also reveled in his appointment as the secretary of state under Monroe.

Attended by her life partner, her husband John, and surrounded by family members, Abigail died quietly at home from typhoid on October 28, 1818, just a few weeks short of her seventy-fourth birthday. Despite severe illness, she remained alert until the end. From the first time she stepped on the national stage, she had understood that the private elevated circles in which she and some of her elite contemporaries moved could exert influence that reverberated into the public arena of politics as well. She had particularly taken her role as the second First Lady seriously and had been determined from the start to make the position both respected and of consequence. During the days of the Revolution and throughout John's long public career, particularly during her tenure as First Lady, Abigail consistently viewed herself as an essential part of political family unit. Underlying all these complicated threads of her long and event-filled life was her unfailing love and fierce loyalty for her husband, John. His political allies became her friends, and his detractors became her enemies. Politics became not only a frequent source of conversation and debate but another essential tie that bound Abigail and John Adams together.

FOUR

Dolley Madison

THE FIRST LADY AS "QUEEN OF AMERICA"

We have all, a great hand in the formation of our own destiny.

DOLLEY MADISON *to Mary E. E. Cutts, August 1, 1833*

The nation's third First Lady, born Dolley Payne, drew upon elements her predecessors had introduced, but she made the position uniquely her own by astutely expanding her sphere of influence through intentional social interactions. Dolley Payne Todd Madison appears to have exhibited a charismatic personality almost from birth and was known for the ability to make friends easily. She was born on May 20, 1768, in North Carolina to committed Virginia Quakers John and Mary Coles Payne, who transplanted their growing family to that southern colony before returning after a year to Virginia, where Dolley grew up. Dolley was fifteen when the Paynes and their eight children moved again, this time north to Philadelphia. Influenced by his principles as a man who had enthusiastically converted to Quakerism, Dolley's father emancipated the family's slaves before he left the South. Financial success, however, eluded John Payne in the bustling commercial urban center of Philadelphia, which boasted a population of about thirty-nine thousand at the time. His laundry starch business failed, he was shunned by his fellow Quakers for questionable business practices, and he died virtually bankrupt and in a depressed state in 1792. All four of Dolley's brothers suffered a similar lack of success in their personal lives and commercial ventures, and the eldest three died before they reached the age of thirty. Her youngest brother, John, became an alcoholic, and he led a troubled life despite the generous financial assistance and unfailing moral support and concern from Dolley and her second husband, James Madison. Dolley's mother, Mary Payne, was forced to take in boarders after her husband's death to help sustain the family, and her elite establishment attracted many young men who were active in politics and sought respectable lodging.[1]

Although Dolley may have had only a rudimentary education at a small country school in Virginia, her vivid and compelling correspondence suggests that somewhere along the way, perhaps later in a Quaker school, or simply as a voracious reader, she became a knowledgeable and articulate young woman, as well as a lively conversationalist with a vivacious manner. In her later years, Dolley provided her first biographer only with the vague information that she "was educated in Philadelphia."[2] Even as a teenager, her warm personality and attractive appearance seems to have made her popular with her Quaker peers. In 1790, Dolley made a good match when, propelled in large part by her father's insistence, she married a rising young attorney, fellow Quaker John Todd. The young couple moved into a comfortable home in a good Philadelphia neighborhood, and in short order the Todds became the parents of two sons. However, illness soon tragically affected Dolley as a young wife and mother. The notorious yellow fever epidemic of 1793 swept away in one fell swoop what had, by then, become a beloved husband, as well as her sickly six-week-old infant baby boy, William Temple, and her in-laws, leaving her ill and weak from complications following childbirth and with her young remaining son, John Payne, to care for.[3]

Dolley's correspondence and the details of her harrowing days in the midst of the epidemic offer a graphic glimpse into the anguish and uncertainty experienced by the victims of yellow fever as well as the broader health challenges faced by early Americans, regardless of social and economic status. As the epidemic spread, Dolley's husband sent her and the children away to a safer area in the countryside at a farm near Gray's Ferry, Pennsylvania. However, John Todd remained in Philadelphia to care for his parents and conduct his law practice, and he visited his wife and children when circumstances allowed. As the sad events unfolded, Dolley poured out her heart to her brother-in-law: "A reveared Father in the Jaws of Death, & a Love'd Husband in perpetual danger. . . . I am almost destracted with distress & apprehension—is it too late for their removal. . . . I wish much to see you, but my Child is sick & I have no way of getting to you."[4]

Fortunately, the twenty-six-year old Dolley recovered, although as many as five thousand other Philadelphians, including her husband and baby, died before cooler weather finally brought an end to the mysterious "plague," which no one at the time understood was spread by infected mosquitoes. Her mother, brothers, and sisters also survived the epidemic. Unsurprisingly, Dolley was left with a lifelong heightened sense of anxiety over health issues and remained very close to the remaining members of her immediate family, especially her mother Mary and her three sisters, Lucy, Anna, and Mary.

In 1794, less than a year after the death of John Todd, the captivating Dolley captured the heart of forty-three-year-old Episcopalian Virginia planter and the future American president, James Madison, seventeen years her senior. By then, after two failed courtships, most of Madison's friends had considered him a confirmed bachelor. James was a brilliant rising Republican politician and the wealthy heir to large southern plantation worked by African American slaves when he was introduced to Dolley by fellow politician Aaron Burr, who had boarded in Mary Payne's household. The couple married on September 15, 1794, effectively pivoting Dolley onto the national stage and placing her in close proximity to those who possessed significant political power in the fledgling nation.

The Madisons resided in Philadelphia for the next few years, and Dolley appears to have had little regret about leaving her Quaker upbringing behind. She turned from the simpler lifestyle, and typically modest Quaker type of dress of her childhood and first marriage, to the whirl of elite society and more flamboyant costumes, which she adopted when entertaining after she wed James. Her rather quiet earlier life in Philadelphia faded away as she became part of the active political and social life of the temporary national capital. Her days and evenings were soon filled with celebrations, dinners, and drawing rooms, and as the wife of a prominent congressman, she likely attended President Washington's birthday celebration and similar high-profile events, which provided her with the opportunity to educate herself about the intricacies of protocol surrounding United States governmental ceremonial practices.

Yet, despite her new immersion in political life, she retained lifelong friendships with several of her early Quaker friends, including the

FIGURE 4.1. Portrait of Dolley Payne (Todd) Madison by Gilbert Stuart. (Courtesy Library of Congress.)

leading Philadelphia businessman, and later minister to Spain, Anthony Morris, who recalled that, when Dolley first arrived in the city as a teenager, she brought with her "the delightful influences of a summer sun."[5] She was especially close to Elizabeth (Eliza) Collins Lee, who like Dolley married out of the Quaker faith, also to a politician. In fact, Eliza was present at Dolley's bedside every day of the former First Lady's last illness. On her deathbed, Dolley expressed her abiding affection for her oldest and dearest friend.[6]

Although she and James never had any children together, Dolley not only brought her young son Payne to the marriage but also her twelve-year-old sister Anna, who became a surrogate daughter to Dolley. When a decade later, Anna married prominent Maine congressman Richard Cutts in 1804, Dolley felt almost as if she had, once more, lost a child. Earlier in 1800, Dolley's youngest sister Mary also married a politician, the Virginia congressman John G. Jackson. The other Payne daughter, Lucy, was married first to George Washington's nephew, George Steptoe Washington, and then, after his death in 1808, she later wed Supreme Court Justice Thomas Todd in 1812, so all of the Payne daughters became part of the preeminent American political circle of the era. In fact, the Madisons' wedding took place at Harewood, the estate that belonged to George Steptoe and Lucy Payne Washington, and Dolley's brother-in-law was the nephew of nation's first president. Like Martha Washington and Abigail Adams, Dolley became a key figure in an extended political family unit, and it was an era in which claims of blood and kinship mattered. In Dolley's case, not only her Coles and Payne relatives but also some of James Madison's relations were drawn into the emerging network that connected the developing political elite class of the time.

After their marriage, the Madisons rented a fine, spacious house in Philadelphia, which became the first site of Dolley's growing political sphere. Although Dolley may have been gregarious and friendly by nature, that did not mean that she did not *intentionally* use her sociability to help achieve her husband's political goals or as a means of cultivating her own political power, particularly her patronage efforts on behalf of her friends and relatives. Dolley's good friend, the prominent politician Henry Clay, was famously reputed to have asserted that "Everybody loves Mrs. Madison," which, in turn, was said to have prompted Dolley's response that that was because "Mrs. Madison loves everybody."[7] Dolley's popularity and ability to smooth over contention became legendary, but at the same time she at least privately voiced her dislike for some of James's critics, and she had her own detractors as well. These included a number of elite men and women (generally Federalists) who found her lacking in sophistication and elegance, as well as disgruntled Virginia neighbors who lived near the Madisons' Montpelier estate and members of the extended Madison family whom she failed to charm.[8]

Many influential politicians came into Dolley's orbit after her second marriage, and she became especially skilled at using her personal and political friendships to her husband's advantage. During her two years as the wife of a prominent congressman in the temporary capital of Philadelphia, her dinners and parties became a popular gathering place for both the city's political and social elite. In February 1796, while Vice President and future president John Adams resided in Philadelphia, he was invited to dine with James Madison and his personable spouse. John described the evening in a letter to his wife, Abigail, who was then living at their home in Quincy, Massachusetts, owing to her delicate health. Although John was an avowed Federalist, who later fell out with the Republican congressman from Virginia over their markedly different political views, at the time he still had a good relationship with James and admiringly pronounced the charming Mrs. Madison "a fine Woman."[9] Adams's remarks serve as an example of Dolley's reputed ability to transcend party ties and to work with her husband's enemies as well as his friends.

Dolley's experience as a congressional wife served as a training ground for the future as James became even more politically prominent. She learned to project an image that for the most part pleased Federalists as well as Republicans, and her innate sociability served to draw people from all walks of life into amiable conversation. John Adams also noted that two of Dolley's sisters were also present at the dinner he attended at the Madison's home and that one of them (Lucy) was married to President Washington's nephew, whom Abigail had met personally when the young man had once visited the Adams's home.[10] Indeed, as the Payne sisters were married to political men, like members of the

Washington and Adams families, Dolley, her husband James, and her sisters, and their spouses interacted frequently with one another and formed an extended political family unit.

John Adams's enthusiastic early appreciation of Mrs. Madison also lends support to the notion that, as domestic ideology became more firmly embedded in the United States in the nineteenth century, Dolley represented the new "feminine ideal," a woman who reflected pure virtues and appeared to be above party politics and partisanship, as well as one who had the ability to foster a more conciliatory and amiable political spirit in the contentious environment of the early nation.[11] Certainly, like Martha Washington and Abigail Adams before her, Dolley served as a model of the republican wife, but at the same time she was able to use that image to her advantage to support James's political goals. Dolley was known for her fondness for fashionable French styles, both in furnishings and fashion, but she was even able to use that traditionally feminine area of interest purposely to foster a unique American consciousness. As the historian Holly C. Shulman contends, Mrs. Madison "interpreted European dress, manners, and food through a purely American filter," an approach that melded the Federalist desire for high style and the Republican emphasis on simplicity.[12]

Although John Adams did not report any information about Dolley's manner of dress when he visited the Madison household, it is unlikely that Abigail would have approved of the riot of colors, ostentatious turbans, sparkling jewelry, and low-cut gowns Dolley increasingly favored as time passed. Dolley became known for her resplendent finery, but like the original First Lady, Martha Washington, Abigail had always adopted a more sedate, austere, but still elegant manner of dress. Although both Abigail and especially Martha, whose fortune allowed her more leeway, appreciated fine clothes and had collected some lovely jewelry of their own, they never approached the degree of attention that Dolley displayed toward fashion. Unsurprisingly, Abigail's Puritan roots and her deep anti-French feelings as a committed Federalist often extended to the subject of proper standards for dress. Her outlook was revealed by

the displeasure she had earlier expressed when the daughter of Philadelphia society leader Anne Bingham arrived at a drawing room reception
rouged and decked out in an elaborate French-designed gown.[13]

Dolley and Abigail never met in person, but they clearly knew each
other by reputation. Nearly twenty years after John described his dinner at the Madisons, Abigail wrote Dolley to request that she use her
reputed patronage skills to influence her husband, President Madison,
to secure a political appointment for one of Abigail's grandsons as a secretary of the American legation to England. She also expressed her "esteem for your [Dolley's] Character."[14] The following year, Dolley penned
a letter to Abigail in which she apologized for not writing sooner and, in
turn, conveyed her "high respect and regard" for the former First Lady.[15]
Abigail, in return, thanked Dolley for her efforts and noted that owing
to ill health she had the "misfortune to have but a slight personal acquaintance" with James Madison during the years they had both passed
in and out of Philadelphia. However, with deep political disagreements
between John and James apparently long forgotten, she assured Dolley
that "There is not any one who entertains a higher Respect for [Madi-
son's] publick and private Character" than Abigail had.[16]

After experiencing increased demonstrations of partisan political sentiment during his congressional years, James decided it was time to retire.
With the election of Federalist president John Adams in 1797, the Madisons left Philadelphia and retreated to Virginia, where James returned
to farming and Dolley took a leading role in local society and honed
her organizational and social skills, although her aging mother-in-law,
Nelly Conway Madison, still remained the mistress of the impressive
Montpelier plantation home. Even as he ascended to the presidency,
a disgruntled John Adams predicted that James would be drawn back
into politics before long, observing caustically to Abigail that "Madison,
I supposed, after a retirement of a few years is to become President or
V.P. . . . It is marvelous how political Plants grow in the shade."[17]

John was correct in his assessment, and he had presciently sketched
out the trajectory of Madison's future career. During Adams's presi-

dential term, Thomas Jefferson, Madison, and he became increasingly divided over political ideology and the development of John's administration, when he served as the titular leader of the Federalists. The three founders, who had earlier considered themselves comrades and even friends, especially fell out over the Alien and Sedition Acts, which both Madison and Jefferson regarded as an unconstitutional assault on the free press. However, later, after Madison became president, as private citizens, both John and Abigail largely supported "Madison's War" of 1812.

With Thomas Jefferson's ascension to the presidency in 1800, control of the national government and policy was transferred to the Republicans. That political party emphasized what they considered a more open, democratic type of political popular culture, which they insisted harkened back to the true and genuine ideology of the American Revolution. As Jefferson's protégé, James Madison came on board as the new administration's secretary of state—a highly visible position that he held from 1801 to 1809, and one that Dolley realized held the potential for great influence and the opportunity to burnish his reputation. James served in Jefferson's cabinet for eight years during a period when he was mainly occupied with negotiating often delicate foreign relations with the European powers of Great Britain, France, and Spain. Delayed by family responsibilities and James's poor health, the Madisons did not actually move to the new capital of Washington, DC, until May 1801, and it is there that Dolley emerged as a prominent figure in her own right.

At times, as Jefferson had lost his wife in 1782, Dolley served as hostess, especially when women were present at White House events. But during those early years, relatively few politicians brought their wives to the nascent city during the months Congress was in session, so Dolley's main interactions with females were with those women who were established local residents and who formed part of the social rather than political elite. Certainly, her exceptional talents were evident even during Jefferson's administration, when she began to take on a more public role. The Madisons began their life in Washington as guests in the President's

FIGURE 4.2. Engraving of Thomas Jefferson, president of
the United States, c. 1801, from a painting by Rembrandt
Peale. (Courtesy Library of Congress.)

House and then moved to an interim row house in Washington's Six
Buildings development. They finally occupied a large, welcoming home
at 1333 F Street, just a few blocks from Jefferson's presidential residence.

Yet, for all her visibility, Dolley's social undertakings *alongside* Jefferson were rather modest, for as president, in contrast to the heads of the
two previous administrations, he continued to downplay the political

value of formal social interaction and instead studiously emphasized republican simplicity at his small gatherings. Indeed, some scholars who have studied his new Republican "court" found Jefferson's antipathy toward the earlier social rituals of the Washington and Adams administrations, with their attendant public spaces in which women could influence manners and civilize interaction, as a key factor in the increased political animosity that developed during the third president's administration. In contrast, a number of earlier Federalists had viewed American women as valuable participants in the contentious political arena, for they felt females could serve as civilizing agents and as "buffers between clashing men" and thus help build a more virtuous civil society. Jefferson, however, was often influenced by his memories of Parisian women, whom he had encountered while he had been stationed in France. In his opinion, many of them had interested themselves inappropriately and far too vocally in political matters, to the detriment of French society.[18]

Moreover, although Jefferson admired many aspects of French culture, including art, literature, and cuisine, he detested the institution of monarchy and the court practices he had been exposed to during his residence in Europe. He especially viewed the complex and intricate court rituals under Louis XVI as corrupt, dissipated, and rife with political intrigue. In line with his long-held republican ideals, during his presidency Jefferson introduced what he considered the more democratic, unpretentious ceremonial style of "pell-mell." In practice, that meant he tended to host only modest-sized and homogenous groups at his informal dinners, where he controlled the social style and substance of the conversation. Throughout his lifetime, Jefferson almost pathologically abhorred contention, so it is unsurprising that he rarely brought politicians who held differing ideas together, ironically fueling more bipartisan divisiveness between the two political parties. As a result, political players had no safe platform in which to air their diverse opinions and work toward compromise. In Jefferson's vision, the family unit formed the bedrock of the American republic, and he maintained that females should confine themselves largely to the domestic realm and have no active functional role in politics. As Jefferson had informed George Washington even before he became the nation's first president, women best served America by remaining in their "natural" domestic sphere as supportive and capable wives and mothers, who did not involve themselves in men's "political work."[19]

Thus, under Jefferson, ceremonial practices and rituals were decidedly toned down from the previous Washington and Adams administrations, which Jefferson and many others in his Republican party had criticized as veering dangerously toward monarchy, a system in which they warned social and political undertakings were dangerously intertwined. Jefferson consciously adopted a ceremonial style that sought to remove any royalist connections and one that he hoped would reflect the democratic republican principles he espoused. For example, according to Congressman Samuel Taggart of Massachusetts, Jefferson traveled through Washington on horseback rather than by a showy expensive carriage, as the Washingtons had, and he was highly informal and idiosyncratic in his dress, famously sometimes greeting guests in his slippers. Both the Washingtons and Adamses had often been criticized by Republicans as exhibiting a royal-like demeanor, but Taggart, a staunch Federalist, instead derogatorily dubbed Jefferson's style "Democratic Majesty."[20] Jefferson's gestures were meant to convey that he was fundamentally simply a citizen of the United States, a man of the people, who served at the will of the people.[21] No matter that Jefferson was an astute politician who skillfully manipulated events behind the scenes and privately appreciated gourmet dining and purchased exquisite furnishings and expensive fine wines associated with elite society. When he returned from France (where he had dressed himself in high fashion) in 1789, he was said to have shipped 680 bottles of French wine to Monticello.[22]

During its early years as the nation's capital, Washington was still a nascent city and society in formation, which provided Dolley with unprecedented opportunity to help shape its social development. In other words, she was "present at creation," and in essence the government served as both Washington City's political as well as its social center. In that new environment "the president, or, as would happen next, the president's lady [Dolley Madison], was king."[23] In the absence of a flesh and blood visible First Lady during Jefferson's administration, Dolley became arguably the leading woman of local Washington society at the time, a position that continued and grew during her own husband's terms in office. Her real focus while Jefferson was president was to quietly but determinedly build a political base to support James, both when they were at home at Montpelier and at their welcoming F Street residence, which by then included two of Dolley's attractive sisters, Anna and the widowed Lucy. Tactfully ignoring Jefferson's rather truncated established social protocol, as the wife of the secretary of state, Dolley often initiated valuable contacts with other important Washington families, reaching out not only to those who were connected to government work (in reality the real leaders of society in the new capital) but also to foreign diplomats and the local social elite who operated outside of official circles. She particularly established alliances with other "political" women, which ultimately would bear fruit, for the quest for future unity in the young nation could best be accomplished, not in the rancorous political arena, but through the social sphere.

Moreover, through Dolley's efforts, the Madison home became known for convivial dinners that brought politicians and their female family members from *both* parties together for civil conversation, which helped develop a workable political culture for the country.[24] The Madison residence often served as a counterpoint for social faux pas, which on occasion resulted from Jefferson's attempt to foster an egalitarian style. One notorious occasion was the time when he, and by extension James, allegedly insulted Elizabeth Merry, the wife of England's minister to England Anthony Merry, at a dinner Jefferson hosted at the President's House. The incident would be referred to notoriously as "The Merry Affair," and it caused a significant diplomatic uproar, as Anthony Merry claimed that the behavior of the president and secretary of state had reflected underlying partisan American support of France over England. Madison worked to smooth over the tensions officially through correspondence with Merry and his diplomatic predecessor, and Merry and Madison actually developed a good working relationship. Although privately Dolley may not have cared much for Mrs. Merry's prickly and haughty personality, she was able to help facilitate a rapprochement and carry on relatively cordial relations with the British couple. Perhaps because of the initial embarrassing encounter with Jefferson and James, Elizabeth never became one of Dolley's many staunch admirers, and according to the Washington writer Margaret Bayard Smith, she later condescendingly pronounced one of Dolley's F Street hearty dinners a mere unsophisticated "harvest home" affair.[25]

As an aside, it is interesting to note, that, although Jefferson's remarks to George Washington in 1788 about women's natural domestic role were made well over a decade before he assumed the presidency, it reinforces the notion that after the Revolution the ideology of separate spheres had already begun to gain more widespread support. Popular ideology emphasized that in the new republican order, women held separate but equal roles in society. Increasingly in print, ostensibly for the well-being of the polity, females were frequently encouraged to limit their political participation to smoothing over party friction rather than indulging in active political involvement. Prescriptive advice in contemporary magazines and newspapers exhorted women to use their considerable feminine talents to focus on the vital base of home and family and raising future good citizens, and they were advised to leave the arenas of politics and business, which lacked "purity," to men. In other words, "men would be responsible for politics; women would be responsible for society." Yet, even through the first decades of the nineteenth century, many middle-class and elite women continued to keep abreast of political issues and write about political affairs, at least privately to friends and family members.[26]

Dolley Madison was probably the most prominent woman at the time to adeptly sidestep that societal prescription to her political advantage, as well to her husband's. At all times, she kept an eye out for opportunities to further James's political career. She very visibly appropriated normative female roles by smoothing over sharp differences and worked to appear to be above politics, but at the same time she was able to influence and manipulate public opinion and support for her husband James, both through her social activities as well as through her extensive networks of correspondence. When Jefferson retired from the presidency, Madison stepped in as the heir apparent. The campaign between James and the Federalist candidate, Charles Cotesworth Pickney, was often bitter, and even the popular Dolley was subject to frequent, very personal, derogatory coverage in the partisan press. Federalists and Republicans continued to berate one another and to divide along party lines, especially on foreign policy issues. In the increasingly fraught European clashes between France and England, as an ostensibly neutral observer, the United States became a pawn during the Napoleonic Wars.

Although James carried negative political baggage owing to his cosponsorship with Jefferson of the controversial Embargo Act of 1807, which had failed to bring about the desired results in regard to European relations, he was able to triumph over his political opponents to head the American government. He was elected the nation's fourth president by an impressive margin in the Electoral College and officially began his first term on March 4, 1809. James Madison's success was due, in no small part, to Dolley's political savvy and acknowledged exceptional charm, as well the powerful political connections that she forged in the unofficial spheres that allowed space for women to exercise political influence. She had also served as an unofficial but essential and pivotal campaign manager for her husband.

Dolley's years as, first, the wife of a congressman and, then, as the spouse of the secretary of state, had prepared her well to assume the role of First Lady. She had acquired not only an air of sophistication and style but also a keen understanding of the workings of the political world and countless ties to the most important political players of the day. As one historian observed, Dolley's "understanding that entertainment was a venue for political lobbying, her creation of the President's

House as a stage from which to convey an image of power, cultivate political loyalties and project dignity and authority, and her shaping of the
hostess's role as a powerful position for women, set precedents for . . .
the political influence of women." In essence, Dolley Madison "stood at
the juncture where public and private life meet,"[27] what another Madison scholar has termed a "kind of third world," in which she helped not
only define the public social space for the federal government's executive
branch but also to create the appropriate etiquette customs best suited
for a new republic through her talent as a hostess and her imprint on
the remodeled White House, located at 1600 Pennsylvania Avenue.[28]

Dolley's influence was recognized not only by female society figures,
such as her old friend Eliza Collins Lee, who pronounced Dolley "peculiarly fitted to the station" of First Lady,"[29] but also by the prominent
male politicians of her time. The eldest son of John and Abigail Adams,
John Quincy, then a senator from Massachusetts, observed that Dolley had been overtly involved in political electioneering on behalf of
her husband.[30] Senator Samuel Latham Mitchell of New York, one of
the most astute political observers of the day, dubbed her the "Queen
of Hearts" and noted Dolley's potential impact on Madison's election
against his rival, the Federalist candidate Charles Coatesworth Pickney.
Mitchell declared that "The Secretary of State has a wife to aid in his
pretentions," and because of this advantage, "Mr. M. is going greatly
ahead of him."[31] Pickney himself was reputed to have later observed
ruefully that he "was beaten by Mr. and Mrs. Madison. I might have had
a better chance had I faced Mr. Madison alone."[32]

All through the years that Dolley was a part of the public political
world, her family members hovered in the background. As time passed,
with palpably increasing concern, she followed their illnesses and financial challenges, particularly those of her sister Mary, her youngest
brother John, and her own son Payne. When Mary's husband, Richard
Cutts, went bankrupt, the Madisons came to their rescue by buying
their Washington residence and allowing them to remain there at no expense. Sadly, a number of Dolley's close relatives, including her beloved

mother Mary, also died during the periods she was most involved in political life, but Dolley still managed to maintain especially strong ties to her remaining siblings and their offspring. They often visited her or stayed with the Madisons for extended periods of time after James was elected president, both in Washington and during the summers when the Madisons retreated to the family estate at Montpelier. During her marriage to Madison, Dolley suffered many personal loses that often left her bereft, but at the same time she became more publicly visible as a social and political force. As a leading member of Congress at the time later recalled, by her marriage to a fellow southerner, Dolley had "become the wife of one of the first men of the nation, enjoying all the responsibility and *éclat* of such a position."[33] At her husband's side, Dolley became a formidable political player in her own right and a consummate hostess. Whether living in Philadelphia, or later in Washington, or at the family estate in Virginia at Montpelier, the effervescent Dolley dazzled and sparkled.

Dolley's very capable but subtle and consciously feminine style of political lobbying began even before James became president, and she aided him in making the job of secretary of state both a powerful position and a stepping stone to the presidency. Her popular social gatherings on F Street had allowed James to remain outwardly committed to the republican ideal of the public good and seemingly above the sordid sphere of active campaigning and politics. Unquestionably, Dolley proved supremely successful at her public/private undertaking, and she particularly excelled at one-on-one interactions, to which she apparently brought just the right degree of social sensibility. Foreign diplomats as well as American politicians from opposing parties were welcomed in the Madison home, and she was able to build an extensive network that included many influential political players. Just two months after Mitchell commented on the politically valuable advantages that Dolley brought to James, he predicted that "Mrs. Madison has a bright prospect of being Lady Presidentess, and of being mistress of the sumptuous mansion on Palatine Hill for four years."[34]

Unlike her predecessors Martha Washington and Abigail Adams, Dolley appears to have basked in public attention, at least when she was the subject of admiration and praise, and she seems to have very much enjoyed her admittedly supportive role to James. Her more flamboyant fashion style was a marked contrast to her husband, who was always clad in black from head to toe, and it would probably have displeased and even shocked her considerably more staid predecessor Abigail Adams. Back in Massachusetts, the former First Lady, who continued to follow political developments, predicted Madison's election, observing that "Mr. Madison I think will be our next president." Abigail made no comments about Dolley, whom she had never met in person, but concerns about the future of the increasingly fragile republic prompted Abigail to confide to her daughter Nabby that, "if Mr. Madison can, he will perform wonders the people are so divided that it is like a House which cannot stand."[35]

If the formation of the United States was a grand republican experiment, the new capital of Washington offered a dynamic woman like Dolley the unprecedented chance to play a visible role in building the burgeoning city as the new heart of the nation's body politic, complete with a more fluid social structure than had existed in either New York or Philadelphia. It was certainly an environment that allowed for innovation. As the first presidential wife to reside in Washington, albeit briefly, Abigail Adams immediately recognized the hunger for gatherings and ceremonial rituals among the nascent city's residents, most of them connected in some way with the United States government. Shortly after she arrived for her short tenure in Washington City, Abigail Adams realized that, despite the rudimentary nature of the new capital city, and especially the unfinished President's House, social occasions were still extremely important to the locals. Abigail informed her daughter Nabby that "the ladies are impatient for a drawing room"—or a salon, as it might have more accurately been termed—and she turned her hand to providing a few appropriate events during her short stay in Washington as the city's First Lady.[36]

But by the time Dolley became First Lady, the burgeoning city of Washington had already experienced significant growth, and compared to Martha Washington and Abigail Adams, she brought comparative youth, significant energy and optimism, and especially more enthusiasm to her position than her two predecessors. Dolley was not technically the initial First Lady in the new capital of Washington, as that distinction belonged to Mrs. Adams, but as a result of personality and her length of time in the position, she became regarded as the city's pioneer presidential spouse. Although Martha Washington joined George in Philadelphia for the festive inauguration of his second presidential term, neither Martha nor Abigail attended their husbands' first swearing-in ceremonies. Dolley, however, ensured the day of James's inauguration on March 4, 1809, was filled with highly visible celebratory events, which began with a military escorted parade to the beautifully decorated, impressive chamber of the House of Representatives within the Capitol Building. The rather austere formal inauguration ceremony itself was a far cry from the investiture of European monarchs, who wore elaborately ostentatious costumes and jeweled crowns. Madison, like George Washington before him, took the oath of office dressed simply in a dark, well-made American-manufactured suit, but an excited throng of over ten thousand people assembled in the streets surrounding the Capitol Building to cheer him as he was paraded home. In the evening, a much-anticipated gala ball was scheduled.

The events later in the day surrounding James's inauguration as the fourth president of the United States were a representative beginning for Dolley's more exuberant style, but it was one that delighted many of the couples' supporters in the capital. At the same time, Dolley also appears to have made a studious effort to bring dignity to the presidency and her position as First Lady, and for the inauguration ceremony she wore an elegantly simple cambric gown, but one embellished with a long train. She also wore an eye-catching bonnet topped with a white plume. The *National Intelligencer*, Washington's leading political newspaper, was moved to admiringly refer to Dolley as "The Presidentess."[37] The publication was founded and edited by Samuel Harrison Smith, the husband of Dolley's friend and admirer, the writer and social journalist Margaret Bayard Smith. Both the Smiths were committed Jeffersonian Republicans, and as the editor of the newspaper, Samuel supported both the Jefferson and Madison administrations until he sold the enterprise in 1810.[38]

Although the newly elected president and his First Lady greeted several hundred guests at their home in a rather modest manner after the official ceremony, the evening affair was more extravagant. The glittering inaugural ball at Long's Hotel on Capitol Hill was attended by over four hundred members of Washington's elite, including politicians and their wives as well as local social leaders and visiting dignitaries. None of the Madisons' predecessors had hosted a ball on the same evening as the presidential inauguration, and it became exceedingly popular and established a precedent. Still, James Madison may have been somewhat lost in the

FIGURE 4.3. Lithograph of James Madison from a painting by Gilbert Stuart. (Courtesy Library of Congress.)

Figure 4.4. An engraving of Mrs. Madison. (Courtesy Library of Congress.)

throng, as he tended to shrink and become awkward in crowds, but the new First Lady was in her element. Dolley appeared as a colorful presidential spouse, draped in an elegant French buff-colored velvet gown, wearing stunning pearls and "crowned" with what became her signature type of headgear, a turban, in this case sewn of velvet and silk and decorated with tall bird-of-paradise feather adornments. Tall and statuesque, Dolley was easily visible in the throng as the feathers bobbed on her plumed hat. Margaret Bayard Smith remarked that "she looked a Queen,"[39] but it is also clear that Dolley had aimed at an aura of restrained elegance, when she eschewed the diamonds long favored by European royalty for more modest pearls. Mrs. Smith later collaborated with Dolley on the first biographical sketch of her as a First Lady, a celebratory piece that praised Dolley's social talents.

During the entire eight years of her husband's administration, Dolley managed to combine a regal presence with a spirit of social inclusiveness and down-to-earth accessibility, which exuded the well-known southern hospitality. Moreover, she was able to successfully bring back some of the popular ceremonies that Jefferson had curtailed, such as the drawing rooms presided over earlier by Martha Washington and Abigail Adams. Dolley's preeminent biographer, Catherine Allgor, asserts that Dolley's political strategy reflected genius, that it was an enterprise that successfully melded "her connection to local community and her strength in diplomatic relations, her blending of democracy and aristocracy to invent an American political style, her creation of a persona larger than life and in contrast to her husband."[40] All these elements combined to make Dolley Madison symbolically as well as functionally one of the most visible, effective, and powerful First Ladies in the history of the United States. Moreover, as Shulman observes, "Through her conduct she defined republican manners and created republican rituals that affirmed the political legitimacy of her husband."[41] Dolley succeeded in helping to elevate the broader role of the presidential executive, but she did so with the particular intent of bolstering James's position as president.

The numerous ensembles and distinctive jewelry Dolley wore during the presidential years, including her dress at Madison's inauguration, were far more elaborate than either of her predecessors had displayed at any time during their tenure as First Ladies. Dolley's extravagance not only made a vivid social impression but also placed a serious strain on the Madison finances, as did the exploits of Dolley's son, Payne, who flitted from one personal and economic disaster to another. But her easy, welcoming demeanor and French-inspired fashion style made her popular with many Americans, and the often-sparkling and courtly clothing she donned on social occasions conveyed the importance of her privileged position to the public. Margaret Bayard Smith noted admiringly that at the inauguration ball, "She looked like a queen," one who exuded "dignity" and "grace." Smith further maintained that "It would be *absolutely impossible* for any one to behave with more perfect propriety than she did. . . . It seems to me that such manners would disarm envy itself and conciliate even enemies."[42]

Dolley's old friend, Anthony Morris, later concurred with Margaret's assessment. In a letter to Dolley's niece he once noted that the First Lady exhibited "the peculiar power she always possessed of making and preserving friends and of disarming enemies, for even ladies . . . will have enemies when they come into conspicuous stations in society."[43] As Anthony suggested, of course even a woman as popular as Dolley had her detractors. During James's first campaign, the partisan press hurled derogatory sexual slurs at Dolley. And some of her contemporaries regarded her as lacking in sophistication, while others maintained that dressing like a European royal contradicted good taste and the ideals of republican simplicity. But even her critics had to acknowledge her innate charisma, social charm, and astute understanding of political currents.[44] It is telling that at James's presidential celebration, all eyes were on the distinctively dressed First Lady, with her queenly but accessible demeanor. Dolley was by far the star of the political show and a social powerhouse. The "Lady Presidentress" had clearly arrived and would soon serve as symbolic "Republican Queen" for the nation.

Abigail Adams had looked to Martha Washington as the exemplar of a First Lady, but Dolley likely viewed both Martha and Abigail's styles as overly formal and staid. She planned and executed both her manner of dress and large-scale social gatherings, which included dinners and drawing rooms, with an eye for the symbolic value they could contribute to both her husband's presidency and the emerging political structure. The appellation of "levee," which during the Federalist administrations had carried an often perceived elitist connotation, was dropped from Dolley's lexicon for the preferred title adopted for the more informal gatherings known as the "drawing room." She appears to have reveled in her high visibility, and robust social interactions and nightly dinners at the White House were common. Yet her "dove parties" for the wives of cabinet members and diplomats, held while the men engaged in more overtly official dinners, gave Dolley the opportunity to build even broader alliances with the political families of the elite ruling class.

Moreover, Dolley clearly enjoyed interacting with people and serving as a leading force in local society. Her beautifully decorated carriage, drawn by four handsome matched horses, was a common sight in Washington City, as she rode about town to pay frequent visits to friends, relatives, officials, and dignitaries. Ironically, despite Republican emphasis on simplicity, Dolley's fashionable "Chariot"—as the noted architect and engineer Benjamin Henry Latrobe, who helped the Madisons procure the carriage, described it—rivaled the conveyance in which Martha Washington had traveled. During Martha's tenure as First Lady, the distinctive Washington carriages had been denounced soundly by critics of the Federalist Party as unseemly and royalist.[45] The Madison carriage also transported Dolley to congressional debates, where she kept her finger on the national political pulse so she could report back to the president.

Dolley became a skilled and discreet diplomat as well. At the inaugural ball, she was observed to be "equally gracious to both French and English, and so affable to all."[46] As Margaret Bayard Smith later noted, Dolley became a "neutralizing" force, helping to smooth over the political differences and growing pains of an emerging two-party system and often converting potential personal enemies of her husband, if not to political allies, at least to amiable and civil colleagues.[47] Although avowed Federalists had at first boycotted Dolley's social events, before long even they began to attend, as they rapidly realized the occasions presented opportunities for both enjoyable entertainment and an avenue to bolster their own social positions, as well as venues to lobby other prominent politicians and potentially make their voices heard. Moreover, as Margaret noted, Dolley was also a leader in encouraging local women to attend congressional debates and Supreme Court discussions and other politically related occasions, which served as robust sources of interaction in a city that was dominated by government but did not yet have the longtime traditions of elite society that had developed in older locations like New York and Philadelphia. In fact, Margaret maintained that Dolley and her female Washington contemporaries were treated with palpable respect by the male political elite: "On every public occasion a launch, an oration, an inauguration, in the court, in the representative hall, as well as the drawing room, they are treated with marked distinction."[48]

Once in office, President Madison largely delegated the remodeling supervision of the presidential mansion to Dolley. She worked in close consultation with Latrobe, who redesigned what by the spring of 1809 began to be referred to as the "White House," rather than the "President's Palace,"[49] by the approving American public. Latrobe's wife, Mary, who was also a Philadelphia Quaker, had been acquainted with Dolley for many years. Together, utilizing the sum of $26,000 authorized by Congress, Dolley and Benjamin, with the assistance of Mary, turned the building into a magnificent American version of a European palace filled with furnishings mostly created in the United States. It was an edifice that was aimed at commanding foreign respect, one that would serve as a symbol of power but that would also consciously exude the republican virtues that informed the nation.

The Madisons moved into the White House on March 11, and after initial redecoration, Dolley was ready to host her first glittering drawing room at the end of May in one of the smaller finished parlors at the White House, one decorated in sunny yellow, which featured elegant drapes. The more impressive Oval Room, where Abigail Adams had famously hung her wash in her brief tenure in Washington, would not be completed until New Year's Day of 1810. The presidential mansion was at first popularly known as the "Palace," an impressive edifice but one that a journalist later maintained featured no "regal pomp."[50]

Still, the founders—and, indeed, most early Americans—had been raised as British subjects, and English culture and some royal customs still seeped into White House ceremony, for even Dolley's drawing rooms exhibited an air of British gentility. However, in graciously welcoming guests from across the social strata to her highly popular events, such

FIGURE 4.5. Cartoon drawing of "The Reign of Dolly Madison," which appeared in *Puck Magazine*, 1901. The drawing depicted a welcoming First Lady Dolley Madison serving wine to a guest, in contrast to later, less welcoming presidential administrations.

as her "Wednesday Nights," the affable, social Dolley took a more open and "democratic" approach than had her predecessors, Martha Washington and Abigail Adams, who had both focused almost exclusively on members of the political and social elite. And through Dolley's concerted social efforts, politicians, elite men and women, and, indeed, citizens of all stripes had far more access to James Madison as president than had occurred during the previous administrations with the chief executive.

Benjamin Latrobe, among others, was not always pleased with the result. Although he observed that the first drawing room hosted by Dolley as First Lady drew a crowd of "respectable people," by the third round, it was attracting "a perfect rabble in beards and boots."[51] Both Martha and Abigail had tried to incorporate republican simplicity into their affairs by serving a simple fare of light refreshments such as ice cream, cake, and lemonade at their summer gatherings. Dolley offered a similar array of modest desserts but also encouraged attendance by guests from wider, more inclusive social strata. Large crowds of several hundred became common at her glittering White House "squeezes," so called because attendees were often literally jammed into the reception room. In 1816, Mary Boardman Crowninshield, the wife of the secretary of the navy, observed of one of Dolley's events that she attended, "Such a crowd I was never in. It took us ten minutes to push and shove ourselves through the dining room." Instead of being formally seated, as the Washingtons had customarily been, James and Dolly stood at one end of the room and interacted with guests as they continued "moving in and out." Ironically, despite Dolley's efforts to rename her social occasion, Mrs. Crowninshield still referred to the event as "the President's levee."[52]

But whether those outwardly more egalitarian events served as the significant foundation for the transformation of the early republic into a republican democracy is questionable. Latrobe may have summed it up best when he observed, "We are jammed between our republican principles and our aristocratic wishes."[53] Like her predecessors as First Lady, Dolley Madison still had to navigate a path between a decorative social style that satisfied both those who longed for the trappings of royal authority and those who insisted on a more modest American version. Dolley, who served as First Lady from 1809 to 1817, largely succeeded, at least initially, in straddling both elements. Certainly she was a force to be reckoned with, and even at more intimate, smaller-sized political dinners, she was able to win many a politician over to her husband's outlook. Her influence and even political presence became so well accepted that over time she was given an honorary chair on the floor of Congress. And like Martha Washington, Dolley received free postage franking for her mail during her lifetime. Dolley became so widely well known that crowds would later throng to her state funeral in Washington in 1849.

Although both Martha and Abigail had tried to instill their respective "courts" with the proper combination of elements of American republicanism and desirable and appropriate aspects of more courtly European customs, Dolley became the most successful of the three in developing a distinctly American style that resonated with both political players and members of the broader population. When elite members of society or foreign dignitaries dined with the Madisons, the unflappable

Dolley could exude elegance, but she also could reflect a more down-home, warm, and welcoming persona to ordinary citizens. For the most part, at official events, Martha and Abigail had welcomed their guests in a courtly manner, seated in the focal point of the room as visitors approached them to formally pay their respects, although at smaller dinners they engaged in lively conversation. At her drawing rooms, Dolley was almost always on the move, mingling congenially with both male and female guests, and stopping to talk with everyone. According to Margaret Bayard Smith, who was a perceptive if biased observer, the result was "more ease, freedom and equality."[54]

Like the Washingtons and Adamses before them, the Madisons announced some of their more open public events in local newspapers to attract a wider crowd. The more formal levees hosted by George Washington and John Adams had been transformed into more welcoming occasions by Dolley, who took charge of the entertainments and often offered more modest but hearty-type menu choices at dinner occasions, while James devoted himself with more focus to the affairs of state. Unlike George Washington, James seems to have had only moderate interest in the details of furnishings and decorations at the presidential mansion. But he did understand that Dolley's social functions provided a platform that helped to build and coalesce Washington City's governing class and that her drawing rooms, in particular, served as a communications base that facilitated the exchange of ideas and valuable political information as well as a testing ground for proposed policies.

Dolley also astutely understood the deep potential of the White House as a national symbol. Therefore her efforts, together with Latrobe, in designing and redecorating the public space were planned with an eye for ensuring a federal legacy for posterity. George Washington had envisioned Washington as a city that could eventually take its place as one of the leading capitals in the world, and he hoped that the United States would become recognized as major player on the world scene. Over time, his plan took root. When the executive mansion was later completed under the Madisons, it featured twenty-three beautifully furnished rooms contained in three spacious stories, and the president's home commanded a magnificent view of the Potomac River and lush surrounding foliage. Under Dolley's talented hand, once remodeling and decorations were completed, in the American mind the impressive structure compared favorably in its elegance, sophistication, and beauty to the famed palaces of Europe. In her own personal fashion and in the design of the White House, Dolley adroitly incorporated a French-inspired style that balanced the Federalist desire for courtly flourishes with emphasis on emerging American traditions. Her French chef, for example, used his acclaimed Continental talents to prepare many American dishes. As Shulman maintains, Dolley created "a kind of third world between public and private."[55] Thus she could manage to appear both queenly and accessibly inclusive of people from all walks of life.

According to Allgor, although the founders of the American republic, including James Madison, were responsible for conceiving and planning the grand idea for a federal union, it was Dolley who "built it brick by brick, one cup of tea, one favor, one connection at a time." Allgor also posits that Dolley created the American version of the salon, which in its focus on politics differed from its artistic-centered French counterpart. Moreover, she argues that Dolley "created an American ruling style" that "would evolve over the centuries." It was an American version that combined courtly European manners with the "refined republican morals of the new United States."[56] But Allgor either overlooks or minimizes the fact that political discussion and lobbying were present to at least some degree even at Martha Washington's drawing rooms and certainly at those overseen by Abigail Adams, who was an accomplished political player in her own right. And the two First Ladies also sought, if not always as successfully as Dolley, to combine European refinement and manners with the new republican ideals in a manner that helped bring people from disparate regions and political factions into a shared national vision.

Whether Dolley was in reality *quite* the "powerful political player" Allgor maintains is somewhat debatable,[57] but it is clear that, as First

Lady, Dolley built significant support for James's presidency through her extensive social circle, helped ameliorate a significant degree of the vituperative divisiveness that characterized American politics at the time, experienced widespread popularity, and likely played at least a modest part, if not a deciding factor, in making Washington and the White House the political center of the United States.[58] Margaret Bayard Smith famously declared years later that under Dolley's skillful guidance at her events, "*party* was lost in social *spirit*."[59] And in the broad sociopolitical arena, Dolley imprinted a template that emphasized civility in the development of public manners in the nascent capital, a cooperative ideal that worked to minimize regional differences for the larger national purpose. If she was irritated by political events or politicians, she expressed those feelings only privately, at times in somewhat indiscreet letters to her close relatives, such as her favored sister, Anna.

In addition to her sociopolitical influence, Dolley was also a "principal actor" in the events surrounding the War of 1812 and became regarded as a heroine for remaining in the White House as the British approached.[60] Certainly, she followed the developments leading up to its outbreak closely, and half a year before war was formally declared, Dolley confided to her sister Anna that "I believe there will be War as M[adison] sees no end to our perplexities without it—they are going on with the preparations to [g]reat extent."[61]

Moreover, by utilizing her strong friendships with the politically powerful, most visibly when her husband was president, her own powers of patronage became well known. There were, after all, many positions that needed to be filled, from judgeships and diplomatic posts to more modest staff positions in the early United States. Prominent women such as Thomas Jefferson's daughter, Martha Jefferson Randolph; Catherine Johnson, the mother-in-law of John Quincy Adams; and even the former First Lady, Abigail Adams, at various times over the ensuing years begged for employment favors on behalf of their relatives. Dolley did not always succeed in placing friends and relatives, and she certainly was not able to dispense patronage on the levels queens had in Europe.

But on a personal level, among her successes, she managed to secure a diplomatic assignment to Spain for her dear friend, Anthony Morris, as well as a position for a nephew from her first marriage. In the spring of 1809, for example, Dolley told her nephew Samuel Todd that she would "make every exertion to procure you some eligible employment," an effort that came to fruition as he received a clerkship that year in the Madison administration.[62] Allgor has observed that, despite the avowed philosophical republican aversion to the practice of bestowing positions to relatives and supporters that had flourished in the European courts, American leaders soon realized that patronage rewards often made practical sense. Soon nearly "everyone acknowledged Dolley's power of appointment," and she became an important cog in the female Washington City "patronage machine."[63] Moreover, in the emerging democracy, patronage appointments contributed to rising social mobility for young men of ability as a first step up the social ladder.

Like her predecessor, Abigail Adams, Dolley was not above using her personal political influence with her presidential husband to secure positions for friends and family members, and her patronage skills far exceeded that of Martha and Abigail before her. Dolley was frequently successful as a patronage broker, and among the many appointees she was reputed to have sponsored was the writer and businessman Joel Barlow, who became the American minister to France and carried on ultimately unsuccessful negotiations with Napoleon. The Barlows moved to Washington in 1804 and quickly became part of the Madison political circle.

As a reflection of their close friendship, after arriving in Paris, Joel and his wife Ruth frequently fulfilled Dolley's requests for the purchase of French goods. Dolley often asked Ruth to send her "large Headresses" and other decorative fashion items and, in an attempt to curtail the high bills Dolley had run up, "any other pretty thing, suitable to an Economist & draw on my Husband for the Amt."[64] Even as the War of 1812 approached, Ruth Barlow continued to send Dolley stylish fashions from Paris mixed with political news. She confided to Dolley that "we hope that things will yet go right here & that good may come out of evil." Ruth reaffirmed that she and her husband Joel would continue to "serve our country & do anything which may add to the honor & prosperity of the present Administration."[65] Through her efforts, Dolley had also been able to secure a job for her often unpredictable brother, John, as Barlow's official secretary, but he never actually accepted the position. Like Abigail Adams's brother, Dolley's sibling also descended into alcoholism, and the two First Ladies both attempted to reform their close relations, with little success.

One of the Madisons' recent biographers has observed that, in private, James often listened closely to Dolley's opinions on appointments and contemporary issues and that "behind the closed doors of the White House, Dolley was a full participant in national politics."[66] Certainly, James regarded his wife as his full partner in politics as well as marriage. In August 1809, for example, when Dolley remained behind at Montpelier while James returned to Washington to attend to critical international matters, not only did James plaintively inform her that "Every thing around and within remind me that you are absent" and assure her of his "constant affection," but he also sent her intelligence updates and newspaper reports on "foreign" developments.[67]

In addition to her social and decorating skills, Dolley also garnered public approval for her charitable work. With her overt support of the Washington City Orphan Asylum, Dolley modeled philanthropic volunteerism for future generations of First Ladies.[68] Both Martha Washington and Abigail Adams had supported benevolent work, but Dolley, with her talent for publicity, made it a more visible undertaking. Not only was she a prominent founder of, and a fundraiser for, the orphanage, but she was named its "First Directress," in effect, chair of the board of overseers, and she presided over the organization's meetings. Although undoubtedly Dolley supported the children's home, in part, out of genuine altruism, it was also a media coup in an era when early print culture in the United States was developing rapidly. Her active participation in the work of the orphanage added to her celebrity and popularity and helped attract the active participation of other prominent women such as her friend Margaret Bayard Smith.

Dolley certainly worked on behalf of her husband to help him deal with the greatest challenges of his administration, including a visibly divided and contentious Congress, the growing assaults from France and England that threated American integrity as a nation, and later an unpopular war, for which the country was ill prepared. Like his presidential predecessors before him, James Madison tried to avoid an overt confrontation and steer a neutral course between the great and warring European powers. Many United States citizens, however, were turning fiercely anti-British because of continued impressment of American seamen and the attendant violation of United States rights at sea, as well as the loss of business because of the closing of European ports to American trade. Despite his best efforts, James could not avert United States involvement in open hostilities. At the beginning of 1812, formal preparations began for war, and many "War Hawks" and expansionists in Congress—such as Dolley's close friend Kentuckian Henry Clay, who served as Speaker of the House, and South Carolina Congressman John C. Calhoun—felt the country's very honor was at stake.

Still, Dolley tried to bring Federalist politicians into the fold through her dinners and drawing rooms, and she was successful to a degree. In late March, she told her sister Anna that "The Feds. As I told you, ware all affronted with M, refused to dine or come but they have changed their *tack*—last *night* & the *night* before, our rooms are crouded with republicans, & such a ralying of our party has alm'd them [Federalists] into a *return*."[69] The nemesis of both the Madisons, Congressman John Randolph, continued to be especially virulent in his criticisms of the presidential couple politically as well as personally. As Dolley put it, "Randolph has been firing away at the House, this morning against the declaration of War, but we suppose it will have little effect."[70] Madison's vice president, George Clinton, died in office in April 1812, and he was replaced by the seasoned politician Elbridge Gerry of Massachusetts. The War of 1812 was formally declared on June 19 with the support of a majority in both houses of Congress, although the president was very reluctant to engage in a battle with such a small and underprepared American army and due to his ever-present preference for conciliation.

While political developments played out, at the same time Dolley also continued to foster close ties with her family members, and during the entire period as First Lady, she worried about her son, sisters, and extended kin. Dolley's relatives were always welcome in her home, even during the years at the White House. Her sister Lucy and her sons visited frequently, and Anna Payne Cutts, her husband Congressman Richard Cutts, and their children even spent winters with the Madisons during both James's terms in offices. Dolley's favorite cousin, Edward Coles, became an official part of the household as James Madison's personal secretary. Edward and the Madisons developed an extremely close relationship, although Edward, a fervent abolitionist, often disagreed vociferously with his relatives over the institution of slavery. In the spring of 1813, Edward became ill, and Dolley was forced to take over many of his duties. Dolley had sometimes assisted her first husband, John Todd, with office tasks in his legal practice and had proved both efficient and competent. Through the end of the summer, Dolley became, in essence, the president's chief assistant, fielding letters and visits with politicians, and she became James's most trusted confidante about the progress of the war. She also penned letters on his behalf in her distinctive, elegant handwriting.

Through all the strains of war, Dolley still managed to serve as a vivacious hostess in the evenings, consciously working to boost morale and encourage support based on patriotic sentiment. In May 1813, she described the "fears & alarms, that circulate around me. For the last week all the City & G. Toun [general town] (except the Cabinet) have expected a visit from the Enimy & ware not lacking in their expression of terror & reproach." At the same time, she asserted that "we are making considerable efforts for defense" and put on a brave face, including when James became seriously ill.[71] Even in 1814, during the height of hostilities, social life in Washington went on. In fact, Dolley informed Martha

Jefferson Randolph that "we have Ladies from almost every State in the Union, & the City was never known so thronged with strangers."[72] Harriet Martineau, the influential English writer, who many years later visited with the Madisons at Montpelier in 1835 after James retired, observed of Dolley, "there is little doubt that he owed to her intellectual companionship, as well as her ability in sustaining the outward dignity of office."[73]

In the meantime, the course of the war seemed to go from bad to worse, and the country became deeply divided over the wisdom of "Mr. Madison's War." The weak American forces suffered many discouraging, humiliating defeats at the hands of the formidable British army and navy, and the tide did not turn until the victory at Baltimore in 1814, when the British were forced to withdraw from the city. Ironically, owing to poor communication, the morale-raising American victory at the 1815 Battle of New Orleans, which made Andrew Jackson a national hero, did not occur until after the peace treaty had already been signed. In the meantime, even as hostilities continued, peace negotiations were already under way in Europe, where John Quincy Adams played a central part in concluding the Treaty of Ghent to end the war. In attempt to give Dolley's feckless son, John Payne Todd, some chance to succeed in life, he was sent by the Madisons to Europe as part of the diplomatic mission. But following his usual pattern, the indulged young man only continued on his path of dissipation, as Dolley desperately searched for ways to assist him.

During Dolley's campaign for James's reelection, she had clearly understood that the ongoing hostilities between the United States and Great Britain would play a pivotal role in her husband's failure or success, but she still maintained, perhaps somewhat disingenuously, that she was "anxious for the fate of the war *only*—knowing that if success crowned our arms, prosperity and happiness would attend out country."[74] Although Americans increasingly worried over the war's outcome, Dolley continued to present a studiously optimistic and confident public image during the fraught period, insisting that a gala second presidential inauguration for James go forward and that her drawing rooms and other social occasions, like her lively Fourth of July gala, would continue unabated even in the face of the real threat of British invasion. In fact, her events were only sidelined by one of her husband's serious bouts with sickness.

In essence, Dolley became the nation's symbolic cheerleader during the war, raising public morale with her positive attitude. Despite serious threats to the nation, during the war Dolley's already well attended drawing rooms attracted as many as five hundred guests. And during the months leading up to the presidential election, Dolley continued politicking on behalf of her husband, allowing James to retain his reputation for republican virtue, which stressed that those running for office remain above stooping to campaigning and the machinations of party politics. In other words, Dolley did the hands-on "dirty" work for him, and with her active intervention, James Madison was reelected in December 1812, although only by only a narrow margin over his opponent DeWitt Clinton. Indeed, as a testimony to her political influence, the writer and prominent politician James G. Blaine later claimed that Dolley had "saved the administration of her husband. But for her, DeWitt Clinton would have been chosen President in 1812."[75]

Like George Washington before him, the fragile James Madison experienced a life-threatening illness during his presidency, but James was the first president to become seriously ill in the midst of a war. Undoubtedly, James was worn down by political challenges, which probably compromised his already weak immune system. In 1814, a virulent bilious fever, likely a flare-up of his chronic malaria, left him bedridden for weeks in retreat at Montpelier. Dolley, who always experienced heightened anxiety over the health of her family members, was both frantic and frazzled as she cared for him around the clock. Those who visited the president during his illness were alarmed by his appearance, and rumors of his impending death rippled through the capital. The *Federal Republican*, for example, maintained that Madison was in "a state of debility, so exhausted, as to render his chance of even a few more months at least precarious."[76]

Fortunately, Madison's health improved, and in early July, Dolley was able to report that her husband was recovering, and "for the last three days his fever has been so slight as to permit him to take bark [a form of quinine] every hour and with good effect." Dolley had devotedly "nursed him night & day—sometimes in despair."[77] A letter from former President Thomas Jefferson to James revealed the widespread concern that had been generated by the president's illness. Jefferson wrote that he hoped Madison was "entirely recovered. If the prayers of millions have been of avail, they have been poured forth with the deepest anxiety."[78] Later in the month, Dolley confided to one of her closest friends, Hannah Gallatin, wife of Swiss-born Secretary of the Treasury Albert Gallatin, that "You can . . . have no idea of its extent and the despair in which I attended his bed for nearly five weeks! Even now I watch over him as I would an infant, so precarious is his convalescence."[79] Dolley, too, was left worn out and exhausted by the ordeal.

As time passed, Dolley continued to forge alliances with powerful political players, such as Congressman Henry Clay. Allgor even goes so far as to credit Dolley and Henry for "setting the stage for the new democratic system" of the United States that incorporated popular participation within a strong federal government and party system.[80] That may be a bit of hyperbole, but Dolley's political strategies certainly paid off. James was elected to a second term, although he took only half of the popular vote. In the Electoral College, however, he trounced his rival opponent, DeWitt Clinton, a candidate fielded by a rebellious faction of James's own Republican Party. As a result of the tide of the war turning toward the American side, and with Dolley's decided influence, Madison's election was assured. Allgor maintains that Dolley played a major role—perhaps even a more central one that James Madison himself—in that successful outcome, despite the "disastrous war and domestic unrest" that plagued his administration.[81]

In the end, Madison's tenure became best known for the ill-advised War of 1812, one that Dolley supported faithfully. In a letter to her cousin Edward Coles, in the spring of 1813, Dolley maintained that she had "allways been an advocate for fighting when *assailed*, tho a *Quaker*."[82] By July 1814, the impending war situation had clearly become critical, with imminent assaults threatened both from Great Britain and by James's internal American political critics as well. Dolley reported to Hannah Gallatin that "We have been in a state of perturbation here, for a long time—The depredations of the Enemy approaching within 20 miles of the City & the disaffected, making incessant difficulties for the Government." Yet, at the same time, Dolley affirmed that, despite critics who insisted that they would "stop him" if James even contemplated removing from the White House, despite the possibility of real danger, she was not the least alarmed and was "determined to stay with him."[83]

The war, of course, had presented many serious challenges to the Madison presidency, the most infamous being the burning of the White House and the similar destruction by fire of the unfinished Capitol Building and the Treasury offices by the British forces. With James gone from the presidential mansion to review the troops and receive more updated military intelligence (which turned out to be inaccurate), Dolley was left in the White House with only a small retinue of servants. Most residents of Washington, even those troops who were supposed to be guarding the president's home, had abandoned the capital in fear of a British invasion. President Madison wrote Dolley that "The reports as to the enemy have varied every hour" and that he believed the British were "without cavalry and artillery" and not in a condition to strike Washington. Of course, his assessment turned out to be highly inaccurate and patently untrue.[84]

Dolley, in turn, told her sister Lucy that she had assured James that her only real fear was for his safety and that she had reaffirmed her determination to remain in the White House as long as she could. All the while, she continued collecting important government documents and packing them in trunks to take along in case, as James had suggested, she needed "at a moment's warning" to leave quickly. Dolley later reported that, as she waited, she had anxiously scanned the horizon with her spyglass, searching for her husband's approach as cannons sounded in the distance.[85] With no sign of James and the British clearly fast approaching, the next day Dolley was, indeed, forced to abandon her steadfast commitment to remain in the White House. Finally, she fled to safety ahead of the British invasion, leaving behind the meal she had prepared for forty American politicians for her uninvited English "guests."

Dolley and her sister Anna Cutts, along with Anna's three children and a servant, occupied one carriage, followed by her brother-in-law Richard Cutts in his own vehicle and the other household members, who commandeered their own makeshift conveyances. Ironically, the calamitous virtual destruction of the presidential mansion served as a boost for the Madisons' image, as it made Dolley a heroine in the popular American imagination for both the courage she displayed in the face of real danger, her legendary rescue of government documents, and most notably a large painting of George Washington. Although only a copy of the original famous Gilbert Stuart painting, the portrait held great symbolic value, and her conduct during the crisis elevated her popularity and public standing.

Understandably, the tension and shock of the desolation and severe level of destruction in the capital left the normally resilient Dolley in low spirits. But as she had done so many times before, she regrouped, and the presidential couple temporarily resided with the Cutts family in their home on F Street. The razing of the president's mansion forced the Madisons to find other more permanent accommodations. In September 1814, they moved into the impressive Octagon House, which had been graciously offered to them by the wealthy Federalist businessman John Tayloe. Under a year later, they moved yet again, this time to an unfurnished home in the Seven Buildings development at the corner of Pennsylvania Avenue and 19 Street. Dolley decorated the new residence with attractive used French furniture, some of which she purchased from her old friend Hannah Gallatin, for the Madisons tried to cut economic corners to meet their reduced personal financial circumstances. From 1816 to 1821, Gallatin served as the ambassador to France, and the couple had no need in the interim for the furniture they had accumulated in America. The Madisons remained until James's term was completed in the spring of 1817. It was in this mansion that, in February 1815, a rejuvenated and beaming Dolley Madison presided over a reception to celebrate the president's signing of the Treaty of Ghent, the document that would formally end the war.

It was a sad and frustrating irony that, although the treaty signaled peace, none of the thorny issues that had provoked America's involvement in the hostilities had in reality been resolved. The United States gained no territory, nor was the practice of impressment of seamen curtailed by the treaty; that issue would simply fade away as a result of the new political realities created once Napoleon had been defeated and ceased to present an existential threat to Great Britain. President Madison and the Senate officially ratified the peace treaty on February 18, 1815. Despite the shortcomings of the treaty, the War of 1812 fostered renewed American pride, and the Madisons emerged with their reputation enhanced. According to assessments at the time, Madison had been a measured, thoughtful statesman, and Dolley, a patriotic and brave marvel.

Although Congress ultimately voted to retain Washington as the nation's capital, the Madisons would retire to Montpelier before the White House was rebuilt. The final decision was close, with the House of Representatives passing the resolution to remain in Washington City by a modest margin in the fall of 1814, but it was not until February 1815 that the Senate finally approved a plan for appropriating funds to rebuild the capital's public buildings. Certainly, Dolley had lobbied tirelessly to keep a devastated Washington as the nation's capital following the war.

After the war, in the two different residences the Madisons occupied in Washington after the destruction of the White House, Dolley's presence grew even more visible, and her drawing rooms and other events continued unabated. If anything, the crowds at her parties grew as the residents of the capital searched for a path to revitalize their community. In one instance, Dolley reigned at a crowded reception in honor of the new British minister to the United States. She not only managed to impress all the high-level political guests, including Chief Justice John Marshall, but she also impressed the British minister, who took one look at her elegant rose-colored gown, which featured a long dramatic train, her glittering gold jewelry, and an impressive turban, embroidered with a gold crown, and declared, "She looked every inch a queen." According to another observer who visited the White House in 1811, "Her Majesty's appearance was truly regal, dressed in a robe of plain satin, trimmed elaborately with ermine, a white velvet and satin turban, with nodding ostrich plumes and a crescent in front, gold chains and clasps around the waist and wrists."[86]

James Madison retired from the presidency in March 1817 and lived out the rest of his life in relative peace and tranquility at Montpelier. After the war, James's reputation had risen considerably, and before the presidential couple left the capital, they were feted at numerous dinners and receptions. Dolley was singled out during those events for special praise for her charm, glamour, and social talents and especially for her ability to get along with people from all classes and political persuasions. Although far from being an unbiased observer, Dolley's lifelong friend Eliza Collins Lee summed up the sentiments of many of the First Lady's admirers when she observed: "On this day eight years ago I wrote . . . to congratulate you on the joyful event that placed you in the highest station our country can bestow. . . . How much greater cause have I to congratulate you, at this period for having it filled it as to render yourself more enviable this day, than your successor, as it is more difficult to deserve the gratitude and thanks of the community than their congratulations—*You* have deservedly received it all."[87]

As Dolley was poised to return to Montpelier, Eliza further noted that the former First Lady would "retire from the tumult and fatigue of public life to your favorite retreat in Orange, and will carry with you principles and manners not to be put off with the robe of state . . . talents such as yours were never intended to remain inactive on retiring from public life, you will form a more fortunate arrangement of your time."[88] Eliza's prediction was fulfilled. The Madisons entertained numerous visitors, including Dolley's family members as well as political leaders, during the retirement years. Famous for their gracious southern hospitality, the former presidential couple even hosted popular, well-attended Fourth of July celebrations replete with mounds of tasty dishes prepared and attractively displayed by hard-working domestic servants, who were part of the over one hundred enslaved people who lived on the Madison plantation.

Yet, compared to the glittering social life Dolley had enjoyed in Washington and the political network she had helped create, country life in Virginia must have appeared dull, and she undoubtedly felt isolated at times, especially during the winter seasons. Clearly her presence was missed in the nation's capital, for in 1819, Eliza Lee declared to Dolley that "your absence from this City is more and more lamented. That the urbanity, benevolence, and chearfullness that was defused through the circles over which *you* presided will be long sought for *in vain*."[89] In later years, James became housebound due to escalating ill health. However, during the first winter and for several years after their return to Montpelier, he was still agile, and assisted by Dolley and her remaining brother John C. Payne, James began to edit his political papers, with an eye toward publication, including materials from the pivotal 1787 Constitutional Convention, in which he had played so critical a role. It was a long and arduous project that was not completed in his lifetime.

For the first decade after leaving office, James remained active in supervising the Montpelier farm and took daily invigorating rides through the countryside. Yet, like many Virginia farmers, James faced increasing economic challenges. Poor harvests and declining commodity prices had combined to chip away at the Madison family fortune, as did the need to cover Dolley's son Payne's indiscriminate spending, for which he was even sent to debtor's prison for a time. Financial downturns for other family members also took a toll. The Madisons were said to have covered about $40,000 of Payne's debt, a good portion directed by James alone, to save Dolley anguish and protect her from full knowledge about her son's plight.[90] Another severe blow to Dolley was the death of her beloved sister Anna in 1832.

On a more positive note, during his retirement James also worked in tandem with Thomas Jefferson to help create the University of Virginia. But by the time James reached the age of eighty, his infirmities had made him a spectator rather than participant in public affairs, and letters to and from family members offered Dolley a limited lifeline to the outside world. Her devotion to James, however, remained steadfast, and as she told a niece, "I have never left him half an hour, for the last two years—so deep is the interest, & sympathy I feel for him."[91] Still, James enjoyed the company of friends and relatives at Montpelier. One famous visitor, the English writer Harriet Martineau, who met with James when he was nearly eighty-four, recalled that, although the former president complained of very poor eyesight and deafness in one ear, he remained an engaging and lively conversationalist.[92]

James's health only proceeded to decline as time passed. By the spring of 1835, Dolley told her niece that "My days are devoted to nursing and comforting my patient, who walks only from the bed in which he breakfasts, to one in the little chamber, where you left him.[93] After increasing weakness and disability, James Madison died peacefully on June 28, 1836, at the age of eighty-five. For over four decades their lives had been so intertwined through genuine deep affection, mutual interests, and a shared political life, that understandably Dolley was overcome with "grief and dejected spirit which could not at first be restrained."[94]

With the support of her close circle of relatives and friends Dolley moved determinedly forward to keeping the plantation on an even keel, settling James's estate, and—perhaps the most challenging of all— overseeing the project to publish his papers. James had struggled with the philosophical morality of slavery in his lifetime and attempted to operate as a "benevolent" slave master, but as a southerner who profited economically from slavery, he was never moved to personally free his enslaved workers and end the practice at Montpelier. Moreover, recent scholarship has suggested that James even supported constitutional protection for slavery.[95] If the hard fact that the Madisons owned many slaves had ever caused Dolley serious qualms, it was not recorded, and she was frequently criticized as a slaveholder by members of the antislavery movement. In the later years, she herself often sold slaves to raise much needed cash.[96]

In a letter written to her niece from Montpelier in 1831 while James was still alive, Dolley did make a brief reference to the infamous Nat Turner slave rebellion. But she did not comment on the immorality of the slavery system, only her concern for the safety of the slaveholders and not the plight of the enslaved people. She informed Mary Cutts that "I hope the bustle and alarm of Insurrections are over in the city—tho I hope all will be on guard ever after this. I am quiet, knowing little about it and that I cannot help myself if I am in danger. I believe there is none at present."[97] Still, officially the subject of slavery was ignored, and two days after James's passed away, President Andrew Jackson reported the former president's death to the American Congress, noting he had "departed this life . . . full of years and full of honors." Friends and relatives such as Dolley's cousin Isaac Coles attempted to assist Dolley with the publishing project, but when it became clear it would not proceed smoothly, the strain added to Dolley's constant anxiety about her troubled son, Payne. Literally worn out from years of tending to her sick husband and grief over his death, as well as her often taxing role as a primary support to her siblings, her own health declined precipitously, and she suffered a physical and emotional breakdown in 1836. As the normally cheerful Dolley herself later put it, "my health which supported me in his illness has forsaken me since his death."[98]

Yet Dolley made a heroic effort to preserve her husband's historical legacy. Nevertheless, she experienced great financial anxiety in her last years and worked diligently to compile her husband's papers for sale to Congress with the hope of keeping the family plantation afloat. However, she realized only about $25,000 from the transaction, and she was finally forced to sell Montpelier in 1844 in the face of mounting debt. By 1841, Dolley had confided to Richard Cutts that "I am sick and overwhelmed with business."[99] In 1837, Dolley moved back to Washington, occupying the Madison house on President's Square. As she had been in the past, once more, she became a revered personage in the capital.

But Dolley was often forced to depend on the kindness of friends such as Secretary of State Daniel Webster, who was reported to have regularly sent her baskets of food delivered by Paul Jennings, James's former valet. Short of funds, Dolley had sold the enslaved man to Webster, who eventually allowed Jennings to purchase his freedom. The spring of 1849 ushered in a period of increasing debility for Dolley. She died at the age of eighty-two, and shortly before her death on July 12, 1849, the once lively, optimistic First Lady despondently counseled a niece that "there is nothing in this world below worth caring for."[100]

Dolley Madison had conformed to the social ideal of her time by serving as an admirably loyal and supportive helpmate to her husband. But she also became a political force in her own right, and she had been befriended by eight American presidents. Although both Martha Washington and Abigail Adams became well known and even famous in their own time, as the leading female in Washington City, Dolley became both a legitimizing figure and one of the nation's first celebrities, as well as a force for conciliation between the warring political factions of her era. A contemporary magazine published a laudatory essay about her, written after she left "the exalted station" of First Lady, and the writer maintained that Dolley had pursued a path of "peace and good will." In the article, the story's author also made reference to Thomas Jefferson's declaration during his administration that "we are all federalists, we are all republicans," but claimed that Mrs. Madison had "reduced this sentiment to practice." Moreover, as a result of Dolley's charm, "the air of authority was softened by the smile of gayety."[101]

Indeed, Catherine Allgor suggests that, during James's presidency, Dolley "emerged as arguably the most famous and loved person in the

United States." She also maintained that Dolley, owing in part to her feminine sensibilities, which emphasized cooperation and harmony, was "not only a master politician, but also one of the few modern politicians of her era." Allgor observes that Dolley presided over the "psychological and emotional aspects of politics," which allowed James the latitude to appear above politics, but maintains that in the final analysis it is impossible to "separate the complex weave of Dolley and James that made up the political partnership."[102]

It is a reflection of her era, which by the 1830s emphasized domesticity within the parameters of acceptable "women's sphere," that, when the *Daily National Intelligencer* reported her death in 1849, Dolley was praised for her feminine charm and personality rather than for her ability to wield political influence. The newspaper obituary writer observed that "All of our country and thousands in other lands will need no language of eulogy to inspire a deep and sincere regret when they learn the demise of one who touched all hearts by her goodness and won the admiration of all by the charms of dignity and grace."[103] While Dolley was still alive, Congress had honored her with her own seat on the floor of the House of Representatives. And her funeral became a state affair attended by President John Tyler, a number of his cabinet members, United States senators, United States congressmen, and various other important members of the American government, for all official business had come to a halt in her honor. Thousands of Washington residents from all social strata packed the funeral, the most well attended for any female in the history of the capital up to that time. The memory of her diplomatic and political talents, her knack for congenial and welcoming social interaction, and her courage in the face of genuine personal and political challenges remained long after her passing. Dolley Madison had enlarged and solidified the unofficial position of First Lady and demonstrated that the presidential spouse had both a symbolic and real sociopolitical role to play.

As has been observed, history does not remember the First Lady as either a child who grew up in a troubled family or as a plantation mistress, who as James's grieving widow had an embattled relationship with the extended Madison family. Her largely self-promoted reputation rests primarily on her central social role as the popular hostess of the nation's capital in early Washington and the heroic part she played in the War of 1812, when the presidential mansion was burned down.[104] All three of the First Ladies of the United States had displayed physical and moral courage during war. Martha Washington had joined General Washington in his winter quarter army camps throughout the Revolutionary War, and the British were almost literally on Abigail Adams's doorstop during the hostilities, when she witnessed the Battle of Bunker Hill from a field near her home. But Dolley was the only one of the three presidential spouses who experienced war firsthand *while* she served as First Lady.

First Revolutionary comrades and then political enemies, John Adams and Thomas Jefferson reconciled in old age and carried out a marvelously sparkling correspondence that encompassed broad philosophical matters, including the fundamental meaning of life, and, of course, past political events. In 1817, as the Madison presidency came to an end, the two elder statesmen mused about its outcome. Even John, the former Federalist leader, acknowledged that James Madison's presidency, "despite a thousand Faults and Blunders . . . has acquired more glory and established more Union, than all his three Predecessors . . . put together."[105] But men of their times, neither Adams or Jefferson acknowledged the central role that Dolley Madison, as the nation's third First Lady, had played in that significant accomplishment.

However, Adams had become seemingly more sensitive to the nuances of human emotion as he aged. He shared with Jefferson his sense of sorrow for the Madisons, James and especially "his Lady," because they had had no children together and no grandchildren to comfort them in their retirement. John observed that he and Thomas had been fortunate because, although their offspring may "have cost us Grief, anxiety often Vexation, and sometimes Humiliation; Yet it has been cheering to have them hovering about Us; and I verily believe they have

FIGURE 4.6. Dolley Madison House, Washington, DC, 17 & H.
(Courtesy Library of Congress.)

contributed largely to keep Us alive."[106] Undoubtedly, both former presidents were aware of the disappointment experienced by the Madisons, who were both fond of children, and the anguish Dolley's son Payne had caused them.

Dolley Madison lived out her last years in Washington, DC, in her Lafayette Street row house not far from the nation's presidential mansion, what was by then referred to officially as the White House. The Madisons had purchased the house years earlier to help the Cutts family survive when they were so financially challenged. There Dolley was courted by members of local society, and she enjoyed visits from family members, old-time friends, and those who were then part of the politically powerful governing elite. It was a fitting location, as Dolley Madison had played a central role in creating the vision for the White House as an enduring national symbol of a democratic republic and making social occasions a central part of Washington life. By the time it was sold, Montpelier was left in ruins, but the private residence she and James had built in Washington in 1819, after he left office, for many years remained a welcoming haven and hub for a new generation of politicians who came to pay homage to the former "Queen of America."

Like her two predecessors, Martha Washington and Abigail Adams, Dolley also often had to walk a political and social tightrope. In the process, she helped shape a distinctively American and democratic style as the consort of the nation's leading male political figure in a role that has never been officially authorized. As was the case with Martha and Abigail, even while she worked to advance her husband's career, Dolley dared not appear too political or partisan or to simply imitate the manners and customs of European queens. To this day, despite the criticism she sometimes encountered in her time, Dolley Madison has retained a reputation for her enduring contributions to the role of First Lady, a testimony to her fundamental success in navigating a complicated and often daunting task.

Conclusion

THE FIRST LADYSHIP LAUNCHED

The unfolding lives of Martha Washington, Abigail Adams, and Dolley Madison during the early days of the fledgling United States vividly demonstrate that the republican experiment was not only a male enterprise. Although they possessed neither the vote nor the ability to hold office, the three women played important roles in the building of the nation, and albeit to varying degrees, they were active participants in a broadly conceived public sphere. It was an area where private people join together to form "a public," an intellectual construct first postulated and popularized by the influential German philosopher Jürgen Habermas in the 1970s. One significant outcome of Habermas's paradigm was to expand our thinking about what constituted political spaces and actions.

Yet, at the same time, we need to keep in mind that the three First Ladies entered that broad public space as part of a *family unit*, rather than through what today we would term the broad category of "women." Examining their experiences suggests that there was a fundamental and strong underlying relationship between family, politics, and governance during the early national period. The emerging concept of republican motherhood reflected that reality and attempted to recruit wives and mothers as moral exemplars of virtue to help create the active and responsible citizens that American leaders believed the new republic required in order to flourish.[1] Martha Washington, Abigail Adams, and Dolley Madison were all principled, capable women, but they adhered to the practices of the eighteenth century, a world considerably different from ours. Their supportive positions were seen as natural and correct, and they were not invested with modern notions of women's rights. Still, all three had to figure out how to blend their roles as women, wives, mothers, and public figures.

Even Thomas Jefferson, who espoused a very circumscribed apolitical role for women in the newly created United States, viewed the family as the *essential* underlying building block for sustaining a democratic nation and viewed family life and the political American world as closely intertwined. At the core of that participation was the marital partnership, which in some cases also fanned out to other family members, including, most notably, sons and daughters, siblings, and even more distant kin and relatives who had been acquired through marriage. Bushrod Washington, George Washington's nephew and residual heir to the Washington estate, for example, served as a Supreme Court associate justice until he died in 1829. Martha's widowed niece, Fanny, married widower Tobias Lear, Washington's personal secretary, and thus he became not only a political actor but also an extended family member. Although Lear was not an elected government politician, he was closely involved in governmental affairs and moved in official society. And Martha's great-granddaughter later married Robert E. Lee, who became the famous Civil War commander of the Confederate Army.

Certainly, all three initial First Ladies—whether Martha Washington, Abigail Adams, or Dolley Madison—used their sociopolitical positions to advance the interests of their families, and through their elite place in official society, they helped perpetuate a class of national political leaders. Abigail Adams was not only the mother of a future American president. Politics permeated Adams family discourse. Her daughter Nabby also became a "female politician," in the parlance of the era, as did her daughter-in-law Louisa Catherine Adams, a highly accomplished and articulate woman and a future First Lady in her own right. The Adams women all discussed political issues knowledgeably, both formally in the presence of male politicians and more informally in pointed conversation with family members and friends. In 1808, for example, Abigail Adams and her daughter Nabby Adams Smith carried on sophisticated correspondence in which they both discussed in great detail the pivotal political issues of the day, from local, to national, and even to international affairs, including Jefferson's infamous Embargo Act, party strife in the United States, and Napoleon's machinations in Europe—all interwoven with family news.[2]

In late eighteenth-century and early nineteenth-century America, society and politics were closely intertwined. As a result, social and ceremonial rituals and rules played a basic and integral role in the political development of the federal government within the new republic of the United States, certainly on a level more visible than we are accustomed to in our times. Whether in the temporary national capitals of New York and Philadelphia, or especially later in the permanent site at Washington, DC, the formation of social life surrounding the early political administrations "guaranteed the perpetuation of the values of the leading class."[3] That social development was significantly influenced by the three First Ladies owing to their leading elite roles as presidential spouses and their widely recognized prominence as members of official families who wielded great significant social and political power. As a result, their individual tastes and styles exerted influence on the manner in which the republican governing culture developed, and they helped establish acceptable social protocols for their day, some of which have endured to our times. In other words, they helped forge the rituals of American democracy.

Martha, Abigail, and Dolley became both political partners and, at times, their husband's political agents in facilitating relationships with key political players. All three, in tandem with their own husbands, were motivated, in part, by their underlying commitment to public service, but at the same time they desired to advance the personal reputations of their spouses and protect their own interests. As the historian Sophia Rosenfeld has suggested, we might best be served by focusing on "families as the key units in the new political order."[4]

Many recent historians have focused on social occasions in the early American republic, such as salons and state and unofficial diners, where women, including America's three First Ladies—who were themselves excluded from voting and holding official office—could and did engage in the discussion of political ideas and culture and even become political agents. One leading political historian has argued that, particularly during the early republic, "a wide variety of informal norms, processes, and symbolic action can be considered genuinely 'political' in the sense that they influenced the structure of power or the dynamics of political action" and that women specifically played a critical part in the development of the first two-party political system. At the same time, we need to acknowledge that there were indeed boundaries between formal and informal politics and that women by no means had unfettered access or influence in the "formal institutions of governance."[5]

In other words, patriotic grassroots celebrations—such as parades, fireworks, and balls—and especially elite social spaces—such as salons and drawing rooms, long associated with women—can be seen as sites for the development of a *national* political culture. However, we need to be cautious to not exaggerate the influence of upper-class women in the early United States. Nevertheless, as two prominent historians of the presidency point out, it is particularly in those informal public spaces where, "as partners in the presidency, first ladies have influenced, politics, policy, and the history of the country."[6] If women rarely, if ever, took a leading role in governmental decisions, it is still the case that the three First Ladies could and did influence the development of the nation's early political culture. It was a space where emerging politicians and their families, if they followed acceptable etiquette and displayed manners suitable to meet elite prescribed standards, could ascend to the national stage.

Because of their visible positions as wives of presidents, American First Ladies have had unparalleled and obviously more intimate personal access to their presidential husbands than any else in the broader administration. Their roles were unofficial and were dictated by developing custom rather than by law. As the first presidential couple, the Washingtons set a precedent for official social protocol when they hosted state and ceremonial occasions *together*. In effect, they established the role of

Lirst Lady as a partnership with the president, at least in the realm of ceremonial and social events, and those undertakings often carried political weight that enabled First Ladies to exhibit influence on political affairs.[7] As historians have come to an appreciation of the manner in which Habermas and many of his followers have expanded the concept of what constitutes public spaces—which includes areas associated with women, such as drawing rooms—social and cultural institutions have taken on a more nuanced political relevance.

Historically, over time each individual First Lady, of course within the constraints of their era, has had the opportunity to carve out for herself a specific role that has been located on a spectrum that has spanned involvement from nonpolitical, to quasi political, to overtly political. While none of the three First Ladies could *make* public policy, they often served as sounding boards for their husbands' political ideas, promoted and supported their spouse's political careers and presidential agenda through the social quasi-political networks they developed, and took the pulse of public opinion.[8] Certainly, Abigail Adams and Dolley Madison excelled in all three areas, and Martha Washington, despite her apparent reluctance to become more overtly and visibly politically active, undoubtedly served as George Washington's confidante and booster, in albeit a more unobtrusive manner. But the social customs of their era dictated that the actions of all three be carried on to a significant degree behind the scenes, in what one historian has termed an "intermediate zone" in which women involved themselves in "public concerns." In the Revolutionary era and the early republic, women's political influence and gatekeeping functions were often viewed as normative, as were their "indispensable role in cultivating the habits of civility, that were essential to the stability and independence of the new republic."[9]

In the early days of the United States, cultural symbols and events were especially critical to the success of the first presidential administrations, which operated in "the uncharted waters of American republican government." George Washington, John Adams, Thomas Jefferson, and James Madison all exhibited and experimented with competing visions of the ideal form of political culture, but it was Martha Washington, Abigail Adams, and Dolley Madison who actually played crucial roles in putting their presidential styles forward. Although charismatic and imposing, George could be stiff and unapproachable in public. John and James were both brilliant intellectuals, but they could be awkward in social situations, and John was known for his not-infrequent abrasiveness to political colleagues. Yet Martha, Abigail, and Dolley used what was perceived to be the female sphere as both a social and political tool to help develop their husband's presidential styles and even to help achieve their political goals.[10] As Catherine Allgor has pointed out, both male and female members of the cultural and political elite grappled with how they could best meld their elite status with republicanism.[11] The three First Ladies helped to integrate those often-opposing strains, and in the process, they often served to deflect criticism away from their respective husbands.

Enlightenment-inspired thought, particularly espoused by the Scottish philosophers, postulated significant new ideas about women and family that Americans adapted to their particular needs. As Rosemarie Zagarri has argued, writers like David Hume and Adam Smith "broke down the conceptual barrier between public and private spheres and defined a social, though not political role of importance for women." That articulated philosophy served as a foundation for a more "revolutionary" role that was articulated in the ideology of the republican mother.[12] Moreover, since wives and mothers were "shapers of morals and manners," women had an indirect although critical "political role to play" in a commonwealth like the United States.[13]

In other words, since women were central to the family unit and social development, and because the family served as the cornerstone of political culture and civilized society, the role of women came to be seen as crucial to the success of the early republic. George Washington, John Adams, and James Madison would have likely agreed with the American physician James Tilton, who wrote, "The men possess the more ostensible powers of making and executing the laws. The women, in every free country, have an absolute control of manners; and it is confessed, that in a republic, manners are of equal importance with laws."[14] Moreover, the vision of the republican mother and the republican wife dovetailed nicely with the role of First Lady, and the involvement of presidential wives like Martha, Abigail, and Dolly in benevolent charitable endeavors was appreciated as a proper role for women that both furthered republican ideals and was also tied closely to the nurturing women's sphere.

But at the same time, the idealized view of educated women holding social equality with men did not extend to political equality. In fact, they were often seen as being in conflict. As Zagarri puts it, "Social equality affirmed traditional gender roles while it disparaged the desirability or necessity of a direct political role for women," resulting in an intellectual compromise that was poised precariously between innovation and tradition.[15] The historian Carol Berkin has noted that, as a reflection of the accepted hierarchical ethos of the era, "the Revolution also left much undone. The eighteenth century embrace of freedom, liberty, and equality was not yet wide enough to encompass women, men without property, African Americans, or Indians."[16] This helps to explain why brilliant and often forward-thinking men like Adams were conflicted about the idea of women's direct political participation in American government. Moreover, despite the areas of political involvement for women that opened up with the American Revolution, "by the 1820s, firmer distinctions were made between women's social contributions, which were acceptable, and their political contributions, which were not."[17]

As has been noted, the ability of elite political women such as Martha Washington, Abigail Adams, and Dolley Madison to host and socialize with political players from both sides of the aisle in "quasi-public parlors" made them pivotal actors in the early republic political arena. They were often able to diffuse some of the significant polarization between opposing parties. Although it is an area often underrated today, during their era the roles of intermediaries and go-betweens were critically appreciated, and acknowledging their activities helps us gain a better grasp on the larger picture of how political life operated in their day.[18] As the historians David S. Shields and Fredrika J. Teute have observed, elite women such as Martha, Abigail, and Dolley "actively engaged in constructing a republican society of manners that moderated politics" and that, moreover, "once controlled behavior and the allocation of power." They helped construct the "political domain" of their era, while influencing public concerns.[19] Although it is now recognized that Shields and Teute perhaps too optimistically ascribe more political influence to the early First Ladies than is warranted, that does not mean that their agency was inconsequential. As Rosenfeld observes, although "republicanism closed some traditional avenues for women in public life, . . . [it] also opened up some promising new ones that we now associate with the birth of human rights."[20]

The influential writer Harriet Martineau observed in 1835, after she visited Dolley and James Madison in retirement at Montpelier, that "Mrs. M. is celebrated throughout the country for the grace and dignity with which she discharged the arduous duties which devolve upon the president's lady." The same could be said by extension of Martha Washington and Abigail Adams.[21] Today, we understand that a spouse's popularity has significant impact on a presidential public image, but it was Martha Washington, Abigail Adams, and especially Dolley Madison who demonstrated just how important a president's partner and family connections could be.

Moreover, all three First Ladies had worked alongside their husbands to help create a viable republic as part of a partnership that was political in nature; they could not have realized that in that in the process they were also laying the foundations for a democracy that would take clearer shape in the Jacksonian era and evolve through the nineteenth century. But from the beginning, Martha Washington, Abigail Adams, and Dolley Madison had demonstrated their deep commitment to the principles of independence and liberty that had first emerged in Revolutionary America and continued to develop in the early national period. The prominent American political families of modern times, such as the Roosevelts, Kennedys, the Bushes, and the Clintons, are not a new phenomenon. Family political influence took root at the dawn of our national history, and the stories of our initial First Ladies provide insight into the nature of political power in the early United States, both at its center and on the margins. In each of their own ways, Martha Washington, Abigail Adams, and Dolley Madison succeeded in putting their own distinctive stamp on the role of First Lady. That complicated position, pioneered by the trio, often served as a lightning rod for real influence as well as controversy, a phenomenon that endures even to this present day.

ACKNOWLEDGMENTS

One of my favorite things about completing a new book is the opportunity to express my appreciation to the many people who provided support, lively discussion, constructive criticism, and encouragement along the way. As always, I am indebted to numerous family members, friends, and colleagues, who have served as tireless "boosters." First, my gratitude to Clara Platter, my editor at New York University Press, for her unreserved enthusiasm for *First Ladies of the Republic* from its genesis as a mere glimmer of an idea to the final manuscript, and to Amy Klopfenstein, Clara's very capable editorial assistant, for her tireless efficiency and helpful attention to myriad details. I would also like to thank NYU Press Managing Editor Dorothea Stillman Halliday for her wise guidance and Jennifer Dropkin for her meticulous copyediting. At the University of Denver, Provost Gregg Kvistad, Dean of the University Libraries Michael Levine Clark, Director of the Center for Judaic Studies Sarah Pessin, and my faculty colleagues have for many years exhibited unwavering support for all my scholarly research and writing endeavors.

I am especially appreciative to many gracious historians around the country, including Catherine Allgor of the Bancroft Library, Alan Kraut at American University, Sophia Rosenfeld at Yale University, Holly C. Shulman at the University of Virginia, Rebecca Tannenbaum at Yale University, and Rosemarie Zagarri at George Mason University, for a number of stimulating and fruitful conversations and email exchanges, as well as valuable feedback. This respected group of historians not only helped me clarify my thinking on a number of important issues, but often offered helpful practical suggestions to improve the manuscript as well.

I have a special appreciation for archivists, who so devotedly assist historians in locating primary sources, which are, of course, the lifeblood of historical inquiry. My gratitude to the many archivists around the country who assisted me by tracking down elusive letters and sometimes hard-to-find related materials. They included the friendly and helpful professionals at the Massachusetts Historical Society; Mary Wigge, a research editor on the Martha Washington Papers Project; and several staff members associated with the University of Virginia Rotunda and the *Founders Online* primary source correspondence projects related to many pivotal American founders. I would also like to thank Peggy Keeran, humanities librarian and acting collections librarian, and Merisa Bissinger, acquisitions manager at the University of Denver, for their gracious willingness to add many helpful secondary sources for my research and writing project to the library collections. Thanks also to my colleague, Thyria Wilson, for her assistance with preparing for publication many of the photographs that appear in this book.

I have been blessed with an amazing family and loyal group of friends who enhance my life on a daily basis. I'd especially like to thank my husband, Lewis, and our children and grandchildren for their constant support and encouragement and their willingness to patiently hear stories (often multiple times!) about our remarkable inaugural First Ladies.

NOTES

PROLOGUE

1 Hedley, *Queen Charlotte*, 1–25.

2 Ibid., 51.

3 The Earl Marshal, "The Form of Proceeding to the Royal Coronation," 7.

4 Washington's suit is on display at Mount Vernon; see *George Washington's Mount Vernon*, www.mountvernon.org.

5 However, a gala ball in Washington's honor was celebrated a week after his inauguration. As time went on, particularly during his second administration, Washington was often criticized in the Republican press for allegedly mimicking royal procedures at the events he and his wife Martha hosted. The celebrations of his birthday around the country, which many found reminiscent of the manner in which King George's birthday had been honored, came under special virulent attack. For his second inauguration Washington donned a more impressive velvet suit. For a detailed account of the partisan struggle over ceremony and ritual during Washington's tenure, see Newman, "Principles or Men?"

6 *Gazette* (New York), May 27, 1789.

INTRODUCTION

1 Rosenfeld, "'Europe,' Women, and the American Political Imaginary," 272.

2 Ibid., 277.

3 I am indebted to Sophia Rosenfeld for a helpful conversation and her thoughtful essay, "'Europe,' Women, and the American Political Imaginary," for suggesting another promising paradigm for viewing the roles of early elite women in the early United States through the lens of family units.

4 Martha Washington to Fanny Bassett Washington, October 22, 1789, in Fields, *"Worthy Partner,"* 219.

5 Shields and Teute, "The Republican Court," 181.

6 Abigail Adams to Mary Cranch, June 24, 1785, in Abigail Adams, *The Letters of Mrs. Adams*, 256–257.

7 Allgor, *Parlor Politics*, 74.

8 See, e.g., "Signora Catoni" [Sarah McKean] to Dolley Madison, August 3, 1797, *Founders Online*.

9 See Allgor, *A Perfect Union*. Although she sometimes indulges in hyperbole, Allgor makes a convincing case for Madison's pivotal role in utilizing social gatherings to diffuse political dissension and help build national unity.

10 Abigail Adams to Martha Washington, February 9, 1797, in Hogan et al., *The Adams Papers*, 11:552–553.

11 Troy makes a similar point in "Mr. and Mrs. President?" 597. Although Troy was referring to modern-day First Ladies, the argument applies to Martha Washington, Abigail Adams, and Dolley Madison as well.

12 See Klein, "Gender and the Public/Private Distinction." Klein argues that gender dichotomy between public and private during the era has been exaggerated and that "eighteenth-century culture offered possibilities and opportunities" for women's participation in public civic culture that may have been curtailed or far more uncommon in the nineteenth (104).

13 Shields and Teute, "The Republican Court," 169, 170.

14 Ibid., 170.

15 In his 1990 essay, "The Women of Boston," Young finds active female involvement in the American Revolution among Boston women in eight areas, including involvement as spectators, as enforcers of consumer boycotts, as rioters, and so on. He also claims that the "female patriotism" exhibited by Abigail Adams and other Boston women "opened a path to female improvement" that inspired later young women in the area of female education (218). For a detailed view of how the "politics" of consumption influenced the American Revolution, see Breen, *The Marketplace of Revolution*. Breen also contends that the conversation about British imports "invited people to think about political life in more inclusive terms," including the role of women (288).

16 Arendt, "Ladies Going about for Money."

17 Zagarri, "Women and Party Conflict," 109.

18 Mercy Warren to Hannah Lincoln, September 3, 1774, Mercy Otis Warren Papers, Massachusetts Historical Society, Boston, Letterbook, 33–36, P-20 (microfilm), reel 1.

19 Gelles, *Portia*, 91. Gelles makes this salient point regarding Abigail, but by extension it applies to Martha Washington and Dolley Madison as well.

20 Shields and Teute, "The Republican Court," 170.

21 Kerber, *Towards an Intellectual History of Women*, 16–17, 61.

22 Two pioneering books by the historian Catherine Allgor are particularly noteworthy in this arena: *Parlor Politics* and *A Perfect Union*. However, understandably both volumes focus primarily on Dolley Madison and other prominent women in early Washington, DC, and not on the earlier roles of Martha Washington and Abigail Adams.

23 For example, Holton, *Abigail Adams*, xii, styles Adams a "proto feminist" and emphasizes Abigail's "revolutionary" economic role and what he considers her "own declaration of independence" within her own household. In 1996, Abigail's biographer Phyllis Lee Levin claimed that on several occasions Abigail "would champion a heartfelt feminist theme." See Levin, "Abigail (Smith) Adams," 26.

24 De Pauw, "The American Revolution and the Right of Women," 209.

25 Zagarri, "The Rights of Man and Woman," 205, 230.

26 Lynn Hunt, *Inventing Human Rights*, 39, 175.

27 For an examination of the public opportunities for women in the new capital of the United States, see Kennon, *A Republic for the Ages*, xi; and especially the following essays within it: Teute, "Roman Matron"; and Lewis, "Politics and the Ambivalence of the Private Sphere."

28 Shields and Teute, "The Court of Abigail Adams," 233.

29 See particularly Allgor's *Parlor Politics*.

30 Foster, *Sex and the Founding Fathers*, 73.

31 Norton, *Separated by Their Sex*, xii, xiv.

32 Norton, *Liberty's Daughters*, 151, 225, 227.

33 In Gelles's 1992 *Portia*, her examination of various facets of Abigail's life begins with a chapter about "The Abigail Industry." Gelles is highly critical of virtually all of Abigail's many biographers up to the time *Portia* was published, including those who portray her as the saintly or romantic Abigail. She is even harsher about those authors who introduce Freudian or feminist interpretations. According to Gelles, the latter group is especially culpable of presentism, assigning wishful modern-day motivations and outlooks that are not reflective of the mores of the time Abigail lived or of Abigail's clearly displayed appreciation for her domestic role.

34 Norton, *Separated by Their Sex*, xv.

35 The historian Karin Wulf exhibits a pessimistic view of women's political opportunities. In *Not All Wives*, she concludes that "in the new Republic membership was strictly defined by race and by gender, and a model of domestic femininity based on the experience of white, middle-class wives, but rigorously applied to all women, had become hegemonic" (207).

36 See Zagarri, *Revolutionary Backlash*, esp. 1–9.

37 Zagarri, "Women and Party Conflict," 109, 118–121.

38 Lewis, "The Republican Wife," 708.

39 Gelles, "The Marriage of Abigail and John Adams," 36.

40 George Washington to Elizabeth Parke Custis, September 14, 1794, in Hoth and Ebel, *The Papers of George Washington*, 16:682–683.

41 Conger, *The Widow's Might*.

42 Kerber, *Women of the Republic*, 9.

43 Teute, "Roman Matron," 93.

44 See Desan, *The Family on Trial*, 313.

45 Kerber, "I Have Don . . . much to Carrey on the Warr," 244.

46 Zagarri, "Morals, Manners," 192.

47 Lewis, "The Republican Wife."

48 Kerber, *Women of the Republic*, 285, 287.

49 Norton, *Separated by Their Sex*, 137.

50 Ibid., 138.

51 Akers, *Abigail Adams*, 33.

52 Thomas Jefferson to James Madison, May 25, 1788, in Boyd, *The Papers of Thomas Jefferson*, 13:202.

53 John Adams to James Sullivan, May 26, 1776, in Robert J. Taylor, *The Adams Papers*, 4:212–213.

54 John Adams to Thomas Boylston Adams, October 17, 1799, *Founders Online*.

55 Zagarri, "The Rights of Man and Woman," 214.

56 Norton made that point in her book *Liberty's Daughters*, 50. Although the radical feminist critique offered a few years earlier by Joan Hoff Wilson, "The Illusion of Change," was often shrill and overly dark and negative, it did make some important points. Hoff saw very little fundamental or lasting expansion of women's role during the American Revolution and considered any advances only temporary and only made owing to economic dislocations produced by the war. She argued strongly that Abigail Adams may have had limited interest in women's rights—in the areas of education and legal recourse from abusive husbands—but she did not incorporate even a nascent feminist ideology. According to Wilson, "Abigail Adams was not in any sense demanding legal, let alone political or individual equality with men at the beginning of the American Revolution. If anything her concept of the separateness of the two separate spheres in which men and women operated was accentuated by the war and the subsequent trials of the new republic between 1776 and 1800" (427). For a lucid and convincing analysis of the parameters of Abigail's letter, see also Gelles, *Abigail and John*, 78–80.

57 Abigail Adams to Francis Vanderkemp, February 3, 1814, in Abigail Adams, *The Letters of Mrs. Adams*, 416.

58 Holton, *Abigail Adams*, ix.

59 Abigail Adams to Mary Cranch, July 12, 1789, in Stewart Mitchell, *New Letters of Abigail Adams*, 15.

60 Teute and Shields, "Jefferson in Washington," 246.

61 Anthony, *First Ladies*, 55–56; and Allgor, *The Queen of America*, 96. As Catherine Allgor and Holly Shulman, editor of Dolley Madison's papers, have pointed out, Cutts's "memoir" of Dolley was written in a manner that reflected her desire to make Dolley's story conform to the ideal of domestic womanhood of her own era and glosses over any negative or controversial aspects of her aunt's life.

62 Brady, *Martha Washington*, 144.

63 Wood, "Pursuit of Happiness."

64 Martha Washington to John Hanbury and Company, August 20, 1757, in Fields, "*Worthy Partner*," 6.

65 Cara Anzilotti has noted this general pattern in her book, *In the Affairs of the World*, 188–193.

66 Wulf, *Not All Wives*, 4.

67 Martha Washington to Fanny Bassett Washington, February 25, 1788, in Fields, "*Worthy Partner*," 205.

68 Branson, *These Fiery Frenchified Dames*, 129.

69 In *Women and the Public Sphere*, the feminist historian Joan B. Landes maintains that there existed "politically influential women . . . in the absolutist court and salon of Old Regime France," and moreover, despite monarchical power, "women of the period participated in and influenced political events and public language" (1–2). Later Goodman expands that argument and emphasizes the important role of women in the salons in *The Republic of Letters*, 54, 91.

   However, Lilti, in "The Kingdom of Politesse," 2, 9–10, refutes the earlier scholarship. In the translated version of *The World of the Salons*, originally published in French in 2005, Lilti asserts that the French salons were not literary or intellectual venues but, "above all, the social spaces of elite leisure" (4). Neither were they "egalitarian gatherings," as they were closely tied to the court (91). Lilti also maintains that salons were not public spaces "that had public effects" (238). As Rosenfeld succinctly puts it, "Alas, it is generally agreed now that the European past that Goodman and Landes described was also largely mythical" ("'Europe,' Women, and the American Political Imaginary," 275).

70 Rosenfeld, "'Europe,' Women, and the American Political Imaginary," 274–276.

71 Dolley Payne Todd Madison to James Madison, November 1, [1805], in Shulman, *The Dolley Madison Digital Edition*.

72 See, e.g., Meachem, *Thomas Jefferson*.

73 Allgor, *Parlor Politics*.

74 *Alexandria Advertiser and Commercial Intelligencer* (Virginia), May 25, 1802.

75 Mercy Otis Warren to Abigail Adams, April 17, 1776, in Butterfield, *The Adams Papers*, 1:385–386.

76 Martha Washington to Mercy Otis Warren, December 26, 1789, in Fields, *"Worthy Partner,"* 223–224.

77 Martha Washington to Fanny Bassett Washington, October 23, 1789, in ibid., 220.

78 Martha Washington to John Adams, December 31, 1799, in ibid., 332.

79 Ellis, *First Family*, 12.

80 Gelles, *Abigail and John*, 198.

81 Abigail Adams Smith, *Journal and Correspondence of Miss Adams*, 83.

82 Mercy Warren to Abigail Adams, February 7, 1776, in Butterfield, *The Adams Papers*, 1:343–345.

83 John Adams to Abigail Adams, March 27, 1797, *Adams Family Papers: An Electronic Archive*.

84 Powell, *Bring Out Your Dead*, 233.

85 Cited in Anthony, *First Ladies*, 80–81.

86 Teute, "Roman Matron," 98. Teute also maintains that these types of social gatherings hosted by women in the early Republic "provided alternative circuits for power to circulate" and that they operated "in a public sphere of private society" (111, 119).

87 Although versions of this quote have been cited repeatedly, it may have perhaps been apocryphal. In his popular biography of Dolley Madison, *The Velvet Glove*,

241, Gerson maintains that Webster uttered these remarks to Dolley at a small dinner party at his home.

88 Allgor, *A Perfect Union*, 9.

89 Kierner, *Beyond the Household*, 212–218.

90 See Ulrich, *Good Wives*.

91 Soderlund, "Women's Authority."

92 As cited in Branson, *These Fiery Frenchified Dames*, 65–66. The purchase of the volumes was noted in George Washington's household account books.

93 For a detailed study of their lives from the perspective of medical issues, see Abrams, *Revolutionary Medicine*.

94 Alan Taylor, *American Revolutions*, 25.

CHAPTER 1. MARTHA WASHINGTON

1 Shields and Teute, "The Court of Abigail Adams," 228, 229, 232.

2 Zagarri, "Morals, Manners," 201.

3 Decatur, *Private Affairs of George Washington*, 50.

4 Kerber lists some of the more well known subscribers to Murray's books in *Towards an Intellectual History of Women*, 116.

5 For general background on Martha Washington's early life, see Brady, *Martha Washington*; and Bryan, *Martha Washington*.

6 For a detailed description of the illnesses that assailed the Washington extended family, see Abrams, *Revolutionary Medicine*.

7 Martha Custis to Robert Cary and Company, August 20, 1759, in Fields, *"Worthy Partner,"* 5.

8 Chadwick, *General and Mrs. Washington*, 8–9.

9 Martha Washington to Fanny Bassett Washington, September 15, 1794, in Fields, *"Worthy Partner,"* 274.

10 Brady, *Martha Washington*, 60.

11 George Washington to Richard Washington, September 20, 1759, in Abbot, *Papers of George Washington*, 6:359.

12 Chadwick, *General and Mrs. Washington*, 57–59.

13 Invoices to Robert Cary & Co., July 18, [1771], and July 15, 1772, in Abbot, *Papers of George Washington*, 8:510, 9:64–65.

14 Abigail Adams to her sister, June 28, 1789, in Stewart Mitchell, *New Letters of Abigail Adams*, 13.

15 George Washington to Martha Washington, June 18, 1776, in Fields, *"Worthy Partner,"* 159–160.

16 Brady, *Martha Washington*, 35.

17 Cited in Rasmussen and Tilton, *George Washington*, 297.

18 George Washington to Jack Parke Custis, June 19, 1775, in Chase, *The Papers of George Washington*, 15–16.

19 George Washington to Martha Washington, June 18, 1775, and June 23, 1775, in Fields, *"Worthy Partner,"* 159, 161.

20 As cited in Breen, *American Insurgents*, 203.

21 Fields, *"Worthy Partner,"* xxii.

22 Berkin, *Revolutionary Mothers*, 45–48; and Gundersen, *To Be Useful to the World*, 162–163.

23 Martha Wayles Skelton Jefferson to Ellen Conway Madison, August 8, 1780, in Boyd, *The Papers of Thomas Jefferson*, 3:532.

24 John Adams to Mercy Otis Warren, November 25, 1775, *Founders Online*.

25 Martha Washington to Elizabeth Ramsay, December 30, 1775, in Fields, *"Worthy Partner,"* 164.

26 Martha Washington to Mercy Otis Warren, January 8, 1776, in ibid., 166.

27 Martha Washington to Anna Maria Bassett, January 31, 1776, and Martha Washington to Mercy Otis Warren, March 7, 1778, in ibid., 167, 177.

28 Martha Washington to Anna Maria Bassett, January 31, 1776, and August 28, 1776, in ibid., 167, 172.

29 Martha Washington to Hannah Stockton Boudinot, January 15, 1784, in ibid., 193.

30 Hunter, "An Account of a Visit," 77, 81.

31 For an engaging analysis that highlights Washington's seminal role, see Ellis, *The Quartet*.

32 Martha Washington to Fanny Bassett Washington, February 25, 1788, in Fields, *"Worthy Partner,"* 205.

33 Martha Washington to John Dandridge, April 20, 1789, and Martha Washington to Mercy Otis Warren, December 26, 1789, in ibid., 213, 223.

34 Newman, "Principles or Men?" 482–483.

35 Caroli, *First Ladies*, 2.

36 Martha Washington to Fanny Bassett Washington, June 8, 1789, in Fields, *"Worthy Partner,"* 215.

37 Ibid.

38 Brady, *Martha Washington*, 170–172.

39 Parry-Giles and Blair, "The Rise of the Rhetorical First Lady," 568.

40 Among those who have maintained that Washington or Lear at least drafted many of Martha's letters during her husband's tenure in office, her biographer Helen Bryan claims that many of the oft-quoted letters are pure "spin" sentiments crafted by Lear. See Bryan, *Martha Washington*, 3. In my opinion, however amiable Martha was, she was too strong and honest a personality to allow a letter to a friend in her name to be composed without her strong input. If Lear was involved, it was likely to correct spelling and grammar and to add more sophisticated prose.

41 Martha Washington to Mercy Warren, December 26, 1789, in Fields, *"Worthy Partner,"* 223.

42 John Adams to Mercy Otis Warren, April 16, 1776, in Robert J. Taylor, *The Adams Papers*, 4:123–126.

43 Shields and Teute, "The Court of Abigail Adams," 232.

44 Ibid.

45 Newman, "Principles or Men?" 480.

46 Gordon-Reed and Onuf, *"Most Blessed,"* xix.

47 Ibid., 74–175, 186.

48 See Rosenfeld, "'Europe,' Women and the American Political Imaginary," 275.

49 Branson, *These Fiery Frenchified Dames*, 128–131.

50 Moats, *Celebrating the Republic*, 37.

51 Abigail Adams to Mary Cranch, July 27, 1790, in Stewart Mitchell, *New Letters of Abigail Adams*, 55.

52 Abigail Adams to Mary Cranch, January 5, 1790, in ibid., 35.

53 Abigail Adams to John Adam, July 16, 1775, in Butterfield, *The Adams Papers*, 1:245–251.

54 Branson, *These Fiery Frenchified Dames*, 131.

55 Abigail Adams to Mary Cranch, January 24, 1789, in Stewart Mitchell, *New Letters of Abigail Adams*, 8.

56 Abigail Adams to Mary Cranch, June 28,1789, in ibid., 13.

57 Radomsky, "The Social Life of Politics," 19–20.

58 For a detailed examination of the role of fashion in the early republic, see Brekke, "Fashioning America."

59 For a more detailed description of Washington's many illnesses, see Abrams, *Revolutionary Medicine*, 63–65.

60 Abigail Adams to Mary Cranch, July 12, 1789, in Stewart Mitchell, *New Letters of Abigail* Adams, 15.

61 Abigail Adams to Mary Cranch, August 9, 1789, in ibid., 19.

62 Decatur, *Private Affairs of George Washington*, 45.

63 Newman, "Principles or Men?" 486–489.

64 Ellet, *The Court Circles*, 19.

65 Abigail Adams to Abigail Adams Smith, February 21, 1797, *Founders Online*.

66 Diary entry, July 25, 1947, in Truman, *Harry S. Truman 1947 Diary*.

67 Martha Washington to Fanny Bassett Washington, October 23, 1789, in Fields, *"Worthy Partner,"* 220.

68 Martha Washington to Mercy Otis Warren, December 26, 1789, in ibid., 223.

69 Ibid., 224.

70 Martha Washington to Mercy Otis Warren, June 12, 1790, in Fields, *"Worthy Partner,"* 226.

71 Abigail Adams to Mary Cranch, October 11, 1789, in Stewart Mitchell, *New Letters of Abigail Adams*, 29–30.

72 Ibid., 30.

73 Martha Washington to Mrs. Abigail Smith Adams, October, 1789, and Martha Washington to Abigail Smith Adams, November 4, 1789, in Fields, *"Worthy Partner,"* 219, 221.

74 Abigail Adams to Mary Cranch, November 1, 1789, in Stewart Mitchell, *New Letters of Abigail Adams*, 32.

75 Abigail Adams to Mary Cranch, January 5, 1790, in ibid., 35.

76 Abigail Adams to Mary Cranch, April 21, 1790, in ibid., 46.

77 Martha Washington to Abigail Adams, May 12, 1790, in Hogan et al., *The Adams Papers*, 9:55.

78 Abigail Adams to Mary Cranch, July 27, 1790, in Stewart Mitchell, *New Letters of Abigail Adams*, 55.

79 Abigail Adams to Mary Cranch, June 13, 1790, in ibid., 51.

80 Decatur, *Private Affairs of George Washington*, 139–141.

81 Abigail Adams to Mary Cranch, August 29, 1790, in Stewart Mitchell, *New Letters of Abigail Adams*, 57.

82 Martha Washington to Abigail Adams, January 15, [1791], in Hogan et al., *The Adams Papers*, 9:184.

83 Martha Washington to Janet Livingston Montgomery, January 29, 1791, in Fields, *"Worthy Partner,"* 229.

84 Henrietta Liston to her uncle, February [24?], 1797, in Perkins, "A Diplomat's Wife," 607.

85 Steele, *Thomas Jefferson and American Nationhood*, 57.

86 Anne Willing Bingham to Thomas Jefferson, June 1, 1787, and Thomas Jefferson to Anne Willing Bingham, May 11, 1788, in Boyd, *The Papers of Thomas Jefferson*, 12:392–393, 13:151–152.

87 See Lilti, "The Kingdom of Politesse."

88 Teute and Shields, "Jefferson in Washington," 245–246.

89 Branson, *Those Fiery Frenchified Dames*, 133.

90 Ibid., 125.

91 Martha Washington to Abigail Adams, May 30, 1791, in Hogan et al., *The Adams Papers*, 9:214.

92 Abigail Adams to Martha Washington, June 25, 1791, in ibid., 9:218–219.

93 Martha Washington to Abigail Adams, September 4, 1791, in ibid., 9:227–228.

94 Abigail Adams to John Adams, January 16, 1795, *Adams Family Papers: An Electronic Archive*.

95 Martha Washington to Fanny Bassett Washington, September 29, 1794, in Fields, *"Worthy Partner,"* 277.

96 Newman, "Principles or Men?" 496, 499.

97 Mercy Otis Warren to a member of Congress, 1795, Mercy Otis Warren Papers, Massachusetts Historical Society, Boston, Letterbook, 1:483.

98 Decatur, *Private Affairs of George Washington*, 289.

99 Cutts, memoir 1, in Allgor, *The Queen of America*, 96, 99.

100 Anthony, *First Ladies*, 56.

101 Shields and Teute, "The Court of Abigail Adams," 233.

102 Abigail Adams to Martha Washington, June 20, 1794, in Hogan et al., *The Adams Papers*, 10:206.

103 John Adams to Abigail Adams, December 28, 1795, *Adams Family Papers: An Electronic Archive*.

104 Martha Washington to John Trumbull, January 12, 1797, in Fields, *"Worthy Partner,"* 296.

105 Henrietta Liston to her uncle, February [24?], 1797, in Perkins, "A Diplomat's Wife," 608.

106 Martha Washington to Catherine Littlefield Greene Miller, March 3, 1797, in Fields, *"Worthy Partner,"* 297.

107 Abigail Adams to Martha Washington, February 9, 1797, in Hogan et al., *The Adams Papers*, 11:552–553.

108 Letter from Abigail Adams to John Adams, January 10, 1796, *Adams Family Papers: An Electronic Archive*.

109 Abigail Adams to Mary Cranch, March 5,1798, in Stewart Mitchell, *New Letters of Abigail Adams*, 140.

110 Martha Washington to Lucy Flucker Knox, [Spring 1797?], in Fields, *"Worthy Partner,"* 303.

111 Martha Washington to Mrs. Elizabeth Powel, May 20, 1797, in ibid., 303.

112 For more detail on Washington's final illness, see Abrams, *Revolutionary Medicine*, 73–78.

113 Henrietta Liston to her uncle, February [24?], 1797, in Perkins, "A Diplomat's Wife," 628.

114 Abigail Adams to Mary Cranch, December 22, 1799, in Stewart Mitchell, *New Letters of Abigail Adams*, 222.

115 Abigail Smith Adams to Elizabeth Smith Shaw Peabody, February 3, 1800, *Founders Online*.

116 Abigail Adams to Mary Cranch, December 30,1799, in Stewart Mitchell, *New Letters of Abigail Adams*, 225.

117 Abigail Adams to Mary Cranch, January 7, 1800, in ibid., 227.

118 Martha Washington to Jonathan Trumbull, January 15, 1800, in Fields, *"Worthy Partner,"* 339.

119 John Adams to Martha Washington, December 27, 1799, in ibid., 328.

120 Cutler and Cutler, *Life, Journal and Correspondence*, 2:56–58.

CHAPTER 2. ABIGAIL AND JOHN ADAMS

1 Richard A. Ryerson, who served as the chief editor of *The John Adams Papers*, makes the persuasive point that, despite his modest beginnings, Adams became a prime example of an American aristocrat in the new republic, owing to his high

level of education and intelligence, coupled with his successful legal career and persuasive oratory and writing powers. However, according to Ryerson, Adams viewed his pursuit of political fame and power in line with his quest for the public good, as he saw himself as one who protected American citizens from "other, less scrupulous men." See Ryerson, "John Adams in Europe," 148–149.

2 The introduction in Kaminski, *The Quotable Abigail Adams*, provides a very helpful, concise summary of the life of Abigail Adams.

3 Duffy, *Epidemics in Colonial America*, 125.

4 For an insightful description of the role of wives in colonial New England, see Ulrich, *Good Wives*.

5 Indeed, Abigail's widespread reading influenced her writing, and as noted in Crane, "Abigail Adams," she sometimes incorporated almost verbatim the words of other writers into her own letters, including her famous "Remember the Ladies" missive. See also Gelles, *Abigail Adams*.

6 Charles Francis Adams, the grandson of John and Abigail Adams, provided invaluable information about Abigail and John's early life in his memoir. See Abigail Adams, *The Letters of Mrs. Adams*.

7 Ellis, *First Family*, 12.

8 Abigail Smith Adams to John Adams, August 11, 1763, in Butterfield, *The Adams Papers*, 1:6.

9 Demos, *A Little Commonwealth*, 181. See esp. chap. 5 and the conclusion.

10 Abigail Adams to Isaac Smith, Jr., April 20, 1771, in Butterfield, *The Adams Papers*, 1:76.

11 Abigail Adams, *The Letters of Mrs. Adams*, xxx.

12 Abigail Adams to Mercy Otis Warren, December 5, 1773, *Founders Online*.

13 See Barbara Clark Smith, *The Freedoms We Lost*, 106–109.

14 Butterfield, *Diary and Autobiography of John Adams*, 3:296.

15 John Adams to Isaac Smith, April 11, 1771, in Butterfield, *The Adams Papers*, 1:75.

16 Gelles, *Portia*, 34–35.

17 Abigail Adams to John Adams, October 16, 1774, in Butterfield, *The Adams Papers*, 1:172.

18 Abigail Adams to John Adams, June 16, 1775, in Hogan and Taylor, *My Dearest Friend*, 60–61.

19 John Adams to Abigail Adams, October 7, 1775, in Butterfield, *The Adams Papers*, 1:295.

20 Abigail Adams to John Adams, June 3, 1776, *Adams Family Papers: An Electronic Archive*.

21 Abigail Adams to John Thaxter, February 15, 1778, in Butterfield, *The Adams Papers*, 2:390.

22 Zagarri, "The Rights of Man and Woman," 205–212.

23 John Adams to James Warren, June 25, 1774, in Robert J. Taylor, *The Adams Papers*, 2:99–100.

24 John Adams to Abigail Adams, November 4, 1775, in Butterfield, *The Adams Papers*, 1:320.

25 Abigail Adams to John Adams, May 9, 1776, in ibid., 1:404.

26 John Adams to James Warren, September 26, 1775, in Robert J. Taylor, *The Adams Papers*, 3:168–171.

27 John Adams to Mercy Otis Warren, July 27, 1807, *Founders Online*.

28 See Hesse's book on the influence of print culture on French women, *The Other Enlightenment*, xii.

29 Gelles makes a similar point in *Abigail and John*, 52–53.

30 Abigail Adams to John Adams, March 31, 1776, in Butterfield, *The Adams Papers*, 1:369.

31 John Quincy Adams's views are captured in a version of his diary edited by Walstreicher and Mason, *John Quincy Adams and the Politics of Slavery*.

32 In his biography of Adams, Holton claimed that her letter is "the best-known protofeminist statement of the revolutionary era"; see Holton, *Abigail Adams*, 39. For an earlier radical feminist critique by the historian Joan Hoff Wilson, about the notion that Abigail Adams supported a nascent feminist ideology, see the Introduction, note 56.

33 Abigail Adams to John Adams, April 5, 1776, in Butterfield, *The Adams Papers*, 1:370.

34 Zagarri, "The Rights of Man and Woman," 205.

35 See Holton, *Abigail Adams*, 159.

36 John Adams to Abigail Adams, April 4, 1776, in Butterfield, *The Adams Papers*, 1:282–283.

37 John Adams to Mercy Warren, April 16, 1776, in *Warren-Adams Letters*, 1:221.

38 Abigail Adams to John Adams, June 17, 1782, in Butterfield and Friedlaender, *The Adams Papers*, 4:328.

39 Abigail Adams to John Adams, May 7, 1776, in ibid., 1:402.

40 Abigail Adams to John Adams, April 21, 1776, *Adams Family Papers: An Electronic Archive*.

41 John Adams to Abigail Adams, May 12, 1776, at ibid.

42 Abigail Adams to Mary Cranch, November 15, 1797, in Stewart Mitchell, *New Letters of Abigail Adams*, 112.

43 Cited in Akers, *Abigail Adams*, 116.

44 John Adams to Abigail Adams, June 26, 1776, in Butterfield, Friedlaender, and Kline, *Book of Abigail and John*, 137–138.

45 Abigail Adams to John Adams, July 13, 1776, in Hogan and Taylor, *My Dearest Friend*, 128.

46 Abigail Adams to John Adams, July 14, 1776, in ibid., 130.

47 John Adams to Abigail Adams, July 27, 1776, in Butterfield, *The Adams Papers*, 2:63.

48 Abigail Adams to John Adams, July 21, 1776, in Hogan and Taylor, *My Dearest Friend*, 132.

49 Abigail Adams to John Adams, August 1, 1776, in Butterfield, *The Adams Papers*, 2:72.

50 Abigail Adams to John Adams, August 14, 1776, in Hogan and Taylor, *My Dearest Friend*, 139.

51 Abigail Adams to John Adams, September 7, 1776, in ibid., 150–151.

52 Hartigan-O'Connor, *The Ties That Buy*, 193.

53 Abigail Adams to Cotton Tufts, April 26, 1785, *Founders Online*.

54 Thomas Jefferson to James Madison, May 25, 1788, in Boyd, *The Papers of Thomas Jefferson*, 13:202.

55 Steele, *Thomas Jefferson and American Nationhood*, 78.

56 Abigail Adams to John Adams, July 16, 1775, in Abigail Adams, *The Letters of Mrs. Adams*, 40.

57 Abigail Adams to Mercy Warren, April 8, 1776, in Butterfield, *The Adams Papers*, 1:378.

58 Mercy Warren to Abigail Adams, April 17, 1776, in ibid., 1:385–386.

59 Gelles, *Portia*, 48.

60 Abigail Adams to Elizabeth Peabody, July 19, 1799, *Founders Online*.

61 Abigail Adams to John Adams, July 14, 1776, in Butterfield, *The Adams Papers*, 2:93–94.

62 John Adams to Abigail Adams, August 25, 1776, in ibid., 2:109.

63 Seymour, *On the Management and Education of Children*.

64 Jacobs, *Dear Abigail*, 38–39.

65 Abigail Adams to John Thaxter, February 15, 1778, in Butterfield, *The Adams Papers*, 2:390–393.

66 Abigail Adams to John Adams, June 30, 1778, in Abigail Adams, *The Letters of Mrs. Adams*, 97–99.

67 John Adams to Abigail Adams, October 9, 1781, in Butterfield, Friedlaender, and Kline, *The Book of Abigail and John*, 298.

68 Abigail Adams to John Adams, July 5, 1780, in ibid., 264.

69 Abigail Adams to John Adams, June 17, 1782, *Adams Family Papers, An Electronic Archive*.

70 Abigail Adams to John Adams, February 11, 1784, in Ryerson et al., *The Adams Papers*, 5:303.

71 Abigail Adams to John Adams, May 25, 1784, in ibid., 5:331.

72 Abigail Adams to Mary Cranch, July 6, 1784, and Abigail Adams to Mary Cranch, July 20, 1784, in Abigail Adams, *The Letters of Mrs. Adams*, 157–158, 168.

73 Abigail Adams to Mercy Warren, September 5, 1784, and Abigail Adams to Mary Cranch, December 9, 1784, in ibid., 200–206, 213–214.

74 For a recent look at the way in which Jefferson constructed his worldview, see Gordon-Reed and Onuf, *"Most Blessed."*

75 Steele, *Thomas Jefferson and American Nationhood*, esp. chap. 2, "American Women," 53–90.

76 Thomas Jefferson to George Washington, December 4, 1788, in Boyd, *The Papers of Thomas Jefferson*, 14:330.

77 Abigail Adams to Mary Cranch, May 8, 1785, in Abigail Adams, *The Letters of Mrs. Adams*, 248.

78 Abigail Adams to Cotton Tufts, January 3, 1785, in Ryerson et al., *The Adams Papers*, 6:41–42.

79 Abigail Adams to Cotton Tufts, March 8, 1785, in ibid., 6:76–78.

80 Gelles suggested this important point twenty-five years ago in her chapter titled, "The Abigail Industry," in Gelles, *Portia*, 15.

81 Abigail Adams to Cotton Tufts, August 18, 1785, in Ryerson, *The Adams Family Papers*, 6:285.

82 Gelles, *Portia*, 103.

83 Abigail Adams to Elizabeth Shaw, October 12, 1787, in Hogan et al., *The Adams Papers*, 8:190–191.

84 Abigail Adams Smith, *Journal and Correspondence of Miss Adams*, 83.

85 For an informative look at how fashion influenced the Adamses and Jefferson in Europe, see Gaye Wilson, "Jefferson."

86 Abigail Adams to Mary Smith Cranch, September 5, 1784, in Ryerson et al., *The Adams Papers*, 5:443.

87 Abigail Adams to Mary Cranch, June 26, 1785, in Abigail Adams, *The Letters of Mrs. Adams*, 255–256.

88 Abigail Adams to Mary Cranch, September 30, 1785, in Ryerson et al., *The Adams Papers*, 6:392.

89 Abigail Adams to Mary Cranch, May 21, 1786, in Hogan et al., *The Adams Papers*, 7:178–179.

90 Abigail Adams to Lucy Cranch, April 26, 1787, in ibid., 8:24.

91 Abigail Adams to John Quincy Adams, November 22, 1786, in ibid., 7:395–396.

92 Abigail Adams to John Quincy Adams, March 20, 1787, in ibid., 8:12.

93 Gelles, *Abigail and John*, 198.

94 Abigail Adams to Lucy Cranch, April 26, 1787, in Hogan et al., *The Adams Papers*, 8:25.

95 Ibid. The draft of the pertinent paragraph appears as an annotation in 8:26n6.

96 Abigail Adams to Thomas Jefferson, January 29, 1787, in Hogan et al., *The Adams Papers*, 7:458.

97 Thomas Jefferson to Abigail Adams, February 22, 1787, in ibid., 7:468.

98 Abigail Adams to John Adams, March 23, 1788, *Adams Family Papers: An Electronic Archive*.

99 Abigail Adams to John Adams, November 16, 1788, at ibid.

100 See Allgor, *Parlor Politics* and *A Perfect Union*.

101 John Adams to Abigail Adams, May 24, 1789, *Adams Family Papers: An Electronic Archive*.

102 Abigail Adams to Elizabeth Shaw, September 27, 1789, in Abigail Adams, *The Letters of Mrs. Adams*, 343–345.

103 Ibid.

104 Abigail Adams to Mary Cranch, July 12, 1789, in Stewart Mitchell, *New Letters of Abigail Adams*, 15.

105 Abigail Adams to Mary Cranch, June 28, 1789, in ibid., 13.

106 Abigail Adams to Mary Cranch, July 12, 1789, and Abigail Adams to Mary Cranch, October 11, 1789, in ibid., 15, 30.

107 Abigail Adams to John Adams, October 20, 1789, *Adams Family Papers: An Electronic Archive*.

108 Abigail Adams to John Adams, December 29, 1792, at ibid.

109 Abigail Adams to Mary Cranch, August 9, 1789, in Stewart Mitchell, *New Letters of Abigail Adams*, 19.

110 Ibid., 19–20.

111 Abigail Adams to Mary Cranch, September 1, 1789, in Stewart Mitchell, *New Letters of Abigail Adams*, 26.

112 Breen, *George Washington's Journey*, 17–18.

113 Abigail Adams to Mary Cranch, October, 3, 1789, in Stewart Mitchell, *New Letters of Abigail Adams*, 59.

114 Abigail Adams to Mary Cranch, October 10, 1790, in ibid., 60.

115 For more about Abigail's health challenges and the effect of the 1793 yellow fever epidemic on America's founders, see Abrams, *Revolutionary Medicine*.

116 Abigail Adams to Abigail Adams Smith, November 21 and 28, 1790, in Abigail Adams, *The Letters of Mrs. Adams*, 348–350.

117 Abigail Adams to Mrs. Smith, December 26, 1790, in ibid., 350–351.

118 Abigail Adams to Mary Cranch, March 12, 1791, in Stewart Mitchell, *New Letters of Abigail Adams*, 71.

119 Abigail Adams to Mary Cranch, December 18, 1791, in ibid., 75.

120 Abigail Adams to Abigail Adams Smith, January 8, 1791, in Abigail Adams, *The Letters of Mrs. Adams*, 352–353.

121 Branson, *These Fiery Frenchified Dames*, 108–109.

122 John Adams to Abigail Adams, December 29 1792, *Adams Family Papers: An Electronic Archive*.

123 John Adams to Abigail Adams, December 30, 1793, at ibid.

124 Abigail Adams to Mary Cranch, April 20, 1792, in Stewart Mitchell, *New Letters of Abigail Adams*, 83.

125 John Adams to Abigail Adams, December 19, 1793, *Adams Family Papers: An Electronic Archive*.

126 John Adams to Abigail Adams, January 20, 1796, at ibid.

127 Abigail Adams to Abigail Adams Smith, February 11, 1793, in Abigail Adams, *Letters of Mrs. Adams*, 361.

128 Abigail Adams to John Adams, December 31, 1793, *Adams Family Papers: An Electronic Archive*.

129 Abigail Adams to George Cabot, Post 17, January 1794, *Founders Online*.

130 Abigail Adams to John Adams, February 26, 1796, *Adams Family Papers: An Electronic Archive.*

131 Decatur, *Private Affairs of George Washington*, 96.

132 See Holton, *Abigail Adams.*

CHAPTER 3. ABIGAIL ADAMS

1 Abigail Adams to John Adams, February 8, 1797, *Adams Family Papers: An Electronic Archive.*

2 Abigail Adams to John Adams, February 19, 1797, at ibid.

3 John Adams to Abigail Adams, March 22, 1797, at ibid.

4 John Adams to Abigail Adams, December 30, 1796, at ibid.

5 Abigail Adams to Thomas B. Adams, November 8, 1796, in Abigail Adams, *The Letters of Mrs. Adams*, 371–372.

6 Abigail Adams to Abigail Adams Smith, February 10, 1793, in Hogan et al., *The Adams Papers*, 9:397–401.

7 Abigail Adams to John Adams, November 27, 1796, *Adams Family Papers: An Electronic Archive.*

8 Abigail Adams to John Adams, January 29, 1797, at ibid.

9 Abigail Adams to Mary Cranch, May 16, 1797, in Stewart Mitchell, *New Letters of Abigail Adams*, 90.

10 Abigail Adams to Mary Cranch, March 14, 1798, in ibid., 145.

11 Abigail Adams to John Adams, May 22, 1800, *Adams Family Papers: An Electronic Archive.*

12 Abigail Adams to John Adams, January 15, 1797, at ibid.

13 Abigail Adams to Elbridge Gerry, December 31, 1796, in Hogan et al., *The Adams Papers*, 11:475–477.

14 Abigail Adams to Mary Cranch, May 30, 1790, in Hogan et al., *The Adams Papers*, 9:62.

15 Abigail Adams to Mary Cranch, April 30, 1797, in Stewart Mitchell, *New Letters of Abigail Adams*, 87.

16 See Ryerson, "John Adams in Europe," 132–133.

17 *Aurora* (Philadelphia), November 11, 1797.

18 Moats, *Celebrating the Republic*, 60–61.

19 Shields and Teute, "The Republican Court," 180.

20 Abigail Adams to Mary Cranch, May 16, 1797, in Stewart Mitchell, *New Letters of Abigail Adams*, 90–91.

21 Ibid., 90.

22 Shields and Teute, "The Court of Abigail Adams," 228, 232.

23 Abigail Adams to Mary Cranch, May 24, 1797, in Stewart Mitchell, *New Letters of Abigail Adams*, 91.

24 Abigail Adams to Mary Cranch, June 23, 1797, and July 6, 1797, in ibid., 98–99, 100.

25 Shields and Teute, "The Court of Abigail Adams," 228.

26 Ellet, *The Court Circles*, 47–48.

27 "Signora Catoni" [Sarah McKean] to Dolley Madison, August 3, 1797, *Founders Online*.

28 Ibid.

29 Abigail Adams to Mary Cranch, February 28, 1798, in Stewart Mitchell, *New Letters of Abigail Adams*, 137.

30 Abigail Adams to Mary Cranch, April 22, 1798, in ibid., 162.

31 Abigail Adams to Mary Cranch March 13, 1798, in ibid., 143–144.

32 Abigail Adams to Mary Cranch, April 7, 1798, in ibid., 155.

33 Abigail Adams to Mary Cranch, April 13, 1798, in ibid., 156.

34 Abigail Adams to Mercy Warren, June 17, 1798, in *Warren-Adams Letters*, 339–340.

35 Abigail Adams to Mary Cranch, July 3, 1798, in Stewart Mitchell, *New Letters of Abigail Adams*, 199.

36 Abigail Adams to Mary Cranch, December 12, 1797, in ibid., 117.

37 Abigail Adams to Mary Cranch, March 13, 1798, in ibid., 144.

38 Abigail Adams to Mary Cranch, May 21, 1798, in ibid., 177.

39 Abigail Adams to Mary Cranch, June 25, 1798, in ibid., 196.

40 Abigail Adams to John Adams, February 27–28, 1799, *Adams Family Papers: An Electronic Archive*.

41 Abigail Adams to John Adams, March 9, 1799, at ibid.

42 Abigail Adams to Mary Cranch, February 1–5, 1798, in Stewart Mitchell, *New Letters of Abigail Adams*, 127.

43 Abigail Adams to Mary Cranch, July 12, 1789, in ibid., 15.

44 Abigail Adams to Mary Cranch, June 8, 1797, in ibid., 96–97.

45 Abigail Adams to Mary Cranch, June 8, 1798, in ibid., 189.

46 Abigail Adams to Mary Cranch, August 9, 1789, in ibid., 20–21.

47 Abigail Adams to Mary Cranch, May 24, 1797, in ibid., 92.

48 Abigail Adams to Mary Cranch, June 8, [1797], in ibid., 97.

49 Henrietta Liston to her uncle, July 14, 1797, in Perkins, "A Diplomat's Wife," 613.

50 Henrietta Liston to her uncle, January 15, 1797, in ibid., 608.

51 Abigail Adams to Mary Cranch, March 20, 1798, and April 28, 1798, in Stewart Mitchell, *New Letters of Abigail Adams*, 146–147, 167.

52 Abigail Adams to Mary Cranch, March 20, 1798, in ibid., 147.

53 Abigail Adams to Mary Cranch, March 27, 1798, in ibid., 148.

54 Abigail Adams to Mary Cranch, April 26, 1798, and May 10, 1798, in ibid., 165, 171.

55 Abigail Adams to Mary Cranch, May 26, 1798, in ibid., 179.

56 Cited in Henry Adams, *The Life of Albert Gallatin*, 185.

57 Abigail Adams to John Adams, December 9, 1798, *Adams Family Papers: An Electronic Archive*.

58 John Adams to Abigail Adams, February 25, 1799, at ibid.

59 Abigail Adams to Elizabeth Smith Shaw Peabody, July 19, 1799, *Founders Online*.

60 Abigail Adams to Mary Cranch, November 15, 1799, in Stewart Mitchell, *New Letters of Abigail Adams*, 214.

61 Abigail Adams to Mary Cranch, December 11, 1799, and December 30, 1799, in ibid., 221, 224–225.

62 Abigail Adams to Mary Cranch, January 28, 1800, in Stewart Mitchell, *New Letters of Mrs. Adams*, 228–229.

63 Abigail Adams to Mary Cranch, January 30, 1800, in ibid., 231.

64 Abigail Adams to Mary Cranch, March 5, 1800, in ibid., 237.

65 Abigail Adams to Mary Cranch, April 26, 1800, in ibid., 247–249.

66 John Adams to Abigail Adams, June 13, 1800, *Adams Family Papers: An Electronic Archive*.

67 Abigail Adams to Mary Cranch, November 10, 1800, in Stewart Mitchell, *New Letters of Mrs. Adams*, 255.

68 John Adams to Thomas Jefferson, March 24, 1801, in Cappon, *The Adams-Jefferson Letters*, 264.

69 Abigail Adams to Mary Cranch, November 21, 1800, in Stewart Mitchell, *New Letters of Abigail Adams*, 259.

70 See Lusane, *The Black History of the White House*.

71 John Adams to Abigail Adams, November 1, 1800, *Adams Family Papers: An Electronic Archive*.

72 Abigail Adams to Mary Cranch, November 21, 1800, in Stewart Mitchell, *New Letters of Mrs. Adams*, 257–259.

73 Abigail Adams to Abigail Adams Smith, November 27, 1800, in Abigail Adams, *The Letters of Mrs. Adams*, 384.

74 Abigail Adams to Mary Cranch, December 1, 1800, in Stewart Mitchell, *New Letters of Mrs. Adams*, 261.

75 Abigail Adams to Thomas Boylston Adams, November, 13, 1800, in Abigail Adams, *The Letters of Mrs. Adams*, 380–381.

76 Abigail Adams to Mary Cranch, January 15, 1801, in Stewart Mitchell, *New Letters of Mrs. Adams*, 263.

77 Akers, *Abigail Adams*, 19.

78 Steele, *Thomas Jefferson and American Nationhood*, 6.

79 Abigail Adams to John Adams, January 29, 1797, *Adams Family Papers: An Electronic Archive*.

80 Abigail Adams to Abigail Adams Smith, March 18, 1808, in Forbes, "Abigail Adams, Commentator," 128.

81 Ibid.

82 Ibid.

83 Abigail Adams to Abigail Adams Smith, May 20, 1808, in Forbes, "Abigail Adams, Commentator," 139.

84 Abigail Adams to Abigail Adams Smith, August 29, 1808, in ibid., 144.

85 Abigail Adams to James Madison, August 1, 1810, in Stagg, *The Papers of James Madison*, 2:455–456.

86 James Madison to Abigail Adams, August 15, 1810, in ibid., 2:485.

87 Abigail Adams to Abigail Adams Smith, October 3, 1808, in Forbes, "Abigail Adams, Commentator," 146.

88 Abigail Adams to Abigail Adams Smith, March 27, 1808, in ibid., 134.

89 Abigail Adams to Catherine Johnson, May 9, 1810, and May 30, 1810, *Founders Online*.

90 Abigail Adams to Francois Adriaan van der Kemp, February 23, 1814, at ibid.

91 Abigail Adams to Elizabeth Peabody Shaw, May 12, 1814, at ibid.

92 Abigail Adams to Louisa Catherine Adams, January 24, 1818, at ibid.

93 Breen, *George Washington's Journey*, 17.

CHAPTER 4. DOLLEY MADISON

1 For a fine brief overview of the life of Dolley Madison, see the introductions to each section of the letters in Mattern and Shulman, *Selected Letters*.

2 Dolley Payne Madison to Margaret Bayard Smith, August 21, 1834, in ibid., 306.

3 See Powell, *Bring Out Your Dead*, 231–234, for a detailed account of John Todd's experiences and death during the epidemic. Also see Abrams, *Revolutionary Medicine*, 10–12, for a look at Dolley's tragic encounter with the epidemic.

4 Dolley Payne Madison to James Todd, October 1793, in Mattern and Shulman, *Selected Letters*, 24–25.

5 Anthony Morris to Anna Payne, June 26, 1837, in Peter, "Unpublished Letters," 217–220.

6 Elizabeth Collins Lee to Zaccheus Collins Lee, [1849], in Mattern and Shulman, *Selected Letters*, 390–391.

7 Cited in Anthony, *First Ladies*, 83.

8 For a detailed account of some of Dolley's troubled relations with the Madison family and her Montpelier neighbors, see Shulman, "History, Memory," 56–59.

9 John Adams to Abigail Adams, February 27, 1796, *Adams Family Papers: An Electronic Archive*.

10 Ibid.

11 Zagarri, "Women and Party Conflict," 121.

12 Shulman, "Dolley (Payne Todd) Madison," 50, 54.

13 Abigail Adams to Mary Cranch, November 15, 1799, in Stewart Mitchell, *New Letters of Abigail Adams*, 214.

14 Abigail Smith Adams to Dolley Payne Todd Madison, May 14, 1815, in Shulman, *The Dolley Madison Digital Edition*.

15 Dolley Payne Todd Madison to Abigail Smith Adams, October 12, 1816, in ibid.

16 Abigail Smith Adams to Dolley Payne Todd Madision, October 24, 1816, in ibid.

17 John Adams to Abigail Adams, January 14, 1797, *Adams Family Papers: An Electronic Archive.*

18 See Teute and Shields, "Jefferson in Washington" and "The Confederation Court."

19 Thomas Jefferson to George Washington, December 4, 1788, in Boyd, *The Papers of Thomas Jefferson,* 14:330.

20 See Haynes, "Letters of Samuel Taggart."

21 Newman, "Principles or Men?" 503–507.

22 For a detailed discussion of Jefferson's dining habits, see Crews, "Thomas Jefferson."

23 Scofield, "Assumptions of Authority," 94.

24 Allgor, *A Perfect Union,* 50–55, 62, 73.

25 Margaret Bayard Smith, "Mrs Madison," 4.

26 Zaggari, "Women and Party Conflict," 119–123.

27 Mayo, "Party Politics," 580.

28 Shulman, "Dolley (Payne Todd) Madison," 52.

29 Eliza Collins Lee to Dolley Payne Madison, March 2, 1809, in Mattern and Shulman, *Selected Letters,* 107.

30 John Quincy Adams, March 13, 1806, in *Memoirs of John Quincy Adams,* 420.

31 Samuel Latham Mitchell to Catherine Akerly Cocks Mitchell, November 23, 1808, in Samuel Latham Mitchell, "Dr. Mitchell's Letters," 752.

32 Cited in Anthony, *First Ladies,* 80–81.

33 Samuel Latham Mitchell to Catherine Akerly Cocks Mitchell, January 3, 1802, in Samuel Latham Mitchell, "Dr. Mitchell's Letters," 743.

34 Samuel Latham Mitchell to Catherine Akerly Cocks Mitchell, January 25, 1808, in ibid., 752.

35 Abigail Adams to Abigail Adams Smith, November 3, 1808, in Forbes, "Abigail Adams, Commentator," 149.

36 Abigail Adams to Abigail Adams Smith, November 27, 1800, in Abigail Adams, *The Letters of Mrs. Adams,* 384.

37 *National Intelligencer* (March 4, 1809).

38 Ames, "The National Intelligencer." 71.

39 Margaret Bayard Smith to Susan Bayard Smith, March 1809, in Margaret Bayard Smith, *The First Forty Years,* 62.

40 Allgor, *A Perfect Union,* 144.

41 See the introduction to Mattern and Shulman, *Selected Letters,* 6.

42 Margaret Bayard Smith to Mrs. Kirkpatrick, March 13, 1814, in Margaret Bayard Smith, *The First Forty Years,* 96.

43 Anthony Morris to Anna Payne, June 26, 1837, in Peter, "Unpublished Letters," 218.

44 Scofield, "Assumptions of Authority," 108–109.

45 Benjamin Henry Latrobe to Dolley Payne Madison, March 22, 1809, in Mattern and Shulman, *Selected Letters,* 111.

46 Margaret Bayard Smith to Susan Bayard Smith, March 1809, in Margaret Bayard Smith, *The First Forty Years*, 62.

47 Margaret Bayard Smith, "Mrs Madison," 21.

48 Margaret Bayard Smith to Mrs. Kirkpatrick, March 13, 1814, in Margaret Bayard Smith, *The First Forty Years*, 97.

49 Brandt, *The Fourth President*, 407.

50 Galliard Hunt, "Mrs. Madison's First Drawing Room," 145.

51 Benjamin Henry Latrobe to George Harrison, June 20, 1809, in Van Horne, *Correspondence*, 731.

52 Mary Boardman Crowninshield to her mother, January 2, 1816, in Crowninshield, *Letters*, 35.

53 Benjamin Henry Latrobe to George Harrison, June 20, 1809, in Van Horne, *Correspondence*, 731.

54 Margaret Bayard Smith to Mrs. Kirkpatrick, March 13, 1814, in Margaret Bayard Smith, *The First Forty Years*, 97.

55 Shulman, "Dolley (Payne Todd) Madison," 52.

56 Allgor, *A Perfect Union*, 198–200.

57 For example, in regard to Dolley's influence in retaining Washington as the seat of government after the 1814 destruction of the capital, Allgor may have overstated that First Lady's influence. Scofield, "Yea or Nay," has recently offered a convincing argument based on historical evidence that counters Allgor's assertion. Scofield maintains that "neither community spirit nor Mrs. Madison's influential drawing rooms and persuasive conferences" determined the fate of the capital (454). According to Scofield, Washington was still a frontier outpost at the time, considered neither a "center of power" or a "viable city" by most contemporary politicians. Instead, according to Scofield, the vote to retain Washington as the capital prevailed because remaining in Washington "became a point of honor" connected to national pride, and the vote fundamentally "represented southern sectional interests" and issues surrounding party loyalty (465–466).

58 Allgor, *A Perfect Union*, 6.

59 *Ladies Magazine and Literary Gazette* 4 (December 1831): 530.

60 Hugh Howard, *Mr. and Mrs. Madison's War*, viii.

61 Dolley Payne Todd Madison to Anna Payne Cutts, December 22, [1811], in Shulman, *The Dolley Madison Digital Edition*.

62 Dolley Madison to Samuel P. Todd, March 16, 1809, and March 31, 1809, in Mattern and Shulman, *Selected Letters*, 110–112.

63 Allgor, *A Perfect Union*, 222–224.

64 Dolley Payne Madison to Ruth Barlow, November 15, 1811, in Mattern and Shulman, *Selected Letters*, 151.

65 Ruth Barlow to Dolley Payne Madison, March 4, 1812, in ibid., 156.

66 Chadwick, *James and Dolley Madison*, 176.

67 James Madison to Dolley Payne Madison, August 7, 1809, and August 9, 1809, in Mattern and Shulman, *Selected Letters*, 121, 122.

68 Parry-Giles and Blair, "The Rise of the Rhetorical First Lady," 574.

69 Dolley Payne Madison to Ann Cutts, c. March 27, 1812, in Mattern and Shulman, *Selected Letters*, 158.

70 Dolley Payne Madison to Anna Cutts, May 1812, in ibid., 165.

71 Dolley Payne Madison to Edward Coles, May 13, 1813, in ibid., 176.

72 Dolley Payne Madison to Martha Jefferson Randolph, January 9, [18]14, in ibid., 182.

73 Cited in Clark, *Life and Letters*, 265–266.

74 Dolley Payne Madison to Phobe P. Morris, October 17, 1812, in Mattern and Shulman, *Selected Letters*, 173.

75 James G. Blaine to James A. Garfield, December 15, 1880, in Hamilton, *Biography of James G. Blaine*, 492.

76 *Federal Republican*, August 13, 1813.

77 Dolley Payne Madison to Edward Coles, July 2, 1813, in Mattern and Shulman, *Selected Letters*, 177.

78 Thomas Jefferson to James Madison, July 13, 1813, in James Morton Smith, *The Republic of Letters*, 3:1725.

79 Quoted in Arnett, *Mrs. James Madison*, 214.

80 Allgor, *A Perfect Union*, 275.

81 Ibid., 7.

82 Dolley Payne Madison to Edward Coles, May 13 [18]13, in Mattern and Shulman, *Selected Letters*, 176.

83 Dolley Payne Madison to Hanna Gallatin, July 28, [18]14, in ibid., 189.

84 James Madison to Dolley Payne Madison, August 23, 1814, in ibid., 192.

85 Dolley Madison to Lucy Payne Washington Todd, August 23, 1814, in ibid., 193.

86 Quoted in Peter, "Unpublished Letters," 216.

87 Eliza Collins Lee to Dolley Payne Madison, March 4, 1817, in Mattern and Shulman, *Selected Letters*, 214.

88 Ibid., 215.

89 Eliza Collins Lee to Dolley Payne Madison, March 30, 1819, in Mattern and Shulman, *Selected Letters*, 235.

90 See the section "A Well-Deserved Retirement," in ibid., 220.

91 Dolley Payne Madison to Mary E. P. Allen, February 25, 1834, in Mattern and Shulman, *Selected Letters*, 304.

92 Arnett, *Mrs. James Madison*, 317.

93 Dolley Payne Madison to Dolley P. Madison Cutts, May 11, 1835, in Mattern and Shulman, *Selected Letters*, 311.

94 Anna Payne to Frances D. Lear, July, 16, 1836, quoted in ibid., 326.

95 For a granular review of Madison's notes on the 1787 Constitutional Convention, see Bilder, *Madison's Hand*.

96 Shulman, "History, Memory," 59–68.

97 Dolley Madison to Mary E. E. Cutts, September 16, 1831, in Mattern and Shulman, *Selected Letters*, 293.

98 Dolley Payne Madison to the Committee of Cincinnati Citizens, November 17, 1838, in Shulman, *The Dolley Madison Digital Edition.*

99 Dolley Payne Madison to Richard D. Cutts, February 27, 1841, in Mattern and Shulman, *Selected Letters*, 358.

100 Cutts, *Memoirs and Letters*, 209.

101 "Mrs. Madison," *Port Folio* 5 (February 1818): 91–92.

102 Allgor, *A Perfect Union*, 253, 254, 279, 344.

103 *Daily National Intelligencer*, July 14, 1849.

104 Shulman, "History, Memory," 69.

105 John Adams to Thomas Jefferson, February 2, 1817, in Cappon, *The Adams-Jefferson Letters*, 508.

106 Ibid.

CONCLUSION

1 Suzanne Desan has examined in great detail the intersection between family and the state in revolutionary France and how the revolutionaries viewed the family as "the elemental building block of society." See Desan, *The Family on Trial*, 3–4.

2 See Forbes, "Abigail Adams, Commentator."

3 Radomsky, "The Social Life of Politics," ix.

4 Rosenfeld, "'Europe,' Women, and the American Political Imaginary," 277.

5 Zagarri, "Women and Party Conflict," 108.

6 Watson and Eksterowicz, *The Presidential Companion*, xv.

7 Mayo, "Party Politics," 577.

8 Wekkin, "Role Constraints ," 603.

9 Ditz, "Masculine Republics," 264–265.

10 Moats, *Celebrating the Republic*, 4–5.

11 Allgor, *Parlor Politics*, 18.

12 Zagarri, "Morals, Manners," 194.

13 Ibid., 205.

14 Tilton, "An Oration," 372.

15 Zagarri, "Morals, Manners," 207, 210.

16 Berkin, *Revolutionary Mothers*, x.

17 Zagarri, "Women and Party Conflict," 123.

18 Hartigan-O'Connor, *The Ties That Buy*, 195.

19 Shields and Teute, "The Republican Court," 182, 183.

20 Rosenfeld, "'Europe,' Women, and the American Political Imaginary," 277.

21 Cited in Clark, *Life and Letters*, 261.

BIBLIOGRAPHY

PRIMARY SOURCES

Abbot, W. W., ed. *Papers of George Washington: Colonial Series*. Vols. 6, 8, 9. Charlottesville: University Press of Virginia, 1988–1994.

Adams, Abigail. *The Letters of Mrs. Adams, the Wife of John Adams: With an Introduction by Her Grandson Charles Francis Adams*. 4th ed. Boston: Wilkins, Carter, 1848.

Adams, John. *A Defense of the Constitutions of Government of the United States of America*. London: Printed for C. Dilly, in the Poultry, 1787.

Adams, John. "Thoughts on Government: Applicable to the Present State of the American Colonies in a Letter from a Gentleman to His Friend." Philadelphia: Printed by John Dunlap, 1776.

Adams, John Quincy. *Memoirs of John Quincy Adams: Comprising Portions of His Diary from 1795 to 1848*. Vol. 1. Edited by Charles Francis Adams. Philadelphia: J. B. Lippincott, 1874.

Adams Family Papers: An Electronic Archive. Boston: Massachusetts Historical Society, 2017. www.masshist.org.

American Memory. Washington, DC: Library of Congress. www.loc.gov.

Boyd, Julian P., ed. *The Papers of Thomas Jefferson*. Vols. 3, 12–14. Princeton, NJ: Princeton University Press, 1951–1958.

Butterfield, Lyman H., ed. *The Adams Papers*. Series 2: *Adams Family Correspondence*. Vols. 1–2. Cambridge, MA: Harvard University Press, 1963.

Butterfield, Lyman H., ed. *Diary and Autobiography of John Adams*. 4 vols. Cambridge, MA: Harvard University Press, 1961.

Butterfield, Lyman H., and Marc Friedlaender, eds., *The Adams Papers*. Series 2: *Adams Family Correspondence*. Vol 4. Cambridge, MA: Harvard University Press, 1973.

Butterfield, Lyman H., Marc Friedlaender, and Mary-Jo Kline, eds. *Book of Abigail and John: Selected Letters of the Adams Family, 1762–1784*. Cambridge, MA: Harvard University Press, 1975.

Cappon, Lester J. *The Adams-Jefferson Letters*. New York: Simon & Schuster, 1971.

Chase, Philander D., ed. *The Papers of George Washington: Revolutionary War Series*. Vol. 1: *16 June 1775–15 September 1775*. Charlottesville: University Press of Virginia, 1985.

Crackel, Theodore J., et al., eds. *Papers of George Washington Digital Edition*. Charlottesville: University of Virginia Press, Rotunda, 2007–. www.upress.virginia.edu.

Crowninshield, Francis Boardman, ed. *Letters of Mary Boardman Crowninshield,1815–1816*. Cambridge, MA: Riverside Press, 1905.

Cutler, William Parker, and Julia Perkins Cutler, eds. *Life, Journal and Correspondence of Rev. Manasseh Cutler, LLD*. Cincinnati, OH: Robert Clarke, 1880.

The Earl Marshal. "The Form of Proceeding to the Royal Coronation of Their Most Excellent Majesties King George III and Queen Charlotte." London: Printed by William Bowyer, 1761.

Fields, Joseph, E., comp., *"Worthy Partner": The Papers of Martha Washington*. Westport, CT: Greenwood Press, 1994.

Forbes, Allyn B., ed. "Abigail Adams, Commentator." *Proceedings of the Massachusetts Historical Society*, 3rd ser., 66 (October 1936–May 1941): 126–153. A number of important letters written by Abigail Adams to her daughter and other relatives that are held at the Massachusetts Historical Society are transcribed here.

Founders Online. Washington, DC: National Archives. www.archives.gov.

Haynes, George H., ed., "Letters of Samuel Taggart, Representative in Congress, 1803–1814: Part I, 1803–1807." *Proceedings of the American Antiquarian Society* 33 (April 1923): 113–226.

Hogan, Margaret, and C. James Taylor, eds. *My Dearest Friend: Letters of Abigail and John Adams*. Cambridge, MA: Harvard University Press, 2007.

Hogan, Margaret, et al., eds. *The Adams Papers*. Series 2: *Adams Family Correspondence*. Vols. 7–11. Cambridge, MA: Harvard University Press, 2005–2013.

Hoth, David R., and Carol S. Ebel, eds. *The Papers of George Washington: Presidential Series*. Vol. 16. Charlottesville: University of Virginia Press, 2011.

Mattern, David B., and Holly C. Shulman, eds. *Selected Letters of Dolley Payne Madison*. Charlottesville: University of Virginia Press, 2003.

Mitchell, Samuel Latham. "Dr. Mitchell's Letters from Washington." *Harper's New Monthly Magazine* 58 (1879) : 740–755.

Mitchell, Stewart, ed., *New Letters of Abigail Adams, 1788–1801*. Boston: Houghton Mifflin, 1947.

Oberg, Barbara B., and J. Jefferson Looney, eds. *Papers of Thomas Jefferson Digital Edition*. www.upress.virginia.edu.

Peter, Grace Dunlop. "Unpublished Letters of Dolly Madison to Anthony Morris relating to the Nourse Family of the Highlands." *Records of the Columbia Historical Society, Washington, D.C.* 44/45 (1942/1943): 215–239.

Ryerson, Alan, et al., eds. *The Adams Papers*. Series 2: *Adams Family Correspondence*. Vols. 5, 6. Cambridge, MA: Harvard University Press, 1993.

Seymour, Hon. Juliana-Susannah [pseud.]. *On the Management and Education of Children: A Series of Letters Written to a Niece*. London: n.p., 1754. Reprinted as John Hill, *On the Management and Education of Children*. New York: Garland Publishing, 1985.

Shulman, Holly C., ed. *The Dolley Madison Digital Edition*. Charlottesville: University of Virginia Press, Rotunda, 2004–. www.upress.virginia.edu.

Smith, Abigail Adams. *Journal and Correspondence of Miss Adams, Daughter of John Adams, Second President of the United States: Written in France and England in 1785*. New York: Wiley, 1841.

Smith, James Morton, ed. *The Republic of Letters: The Correspondence between Thomas Jefferson and James Madison, 1776–1826*. Vol. 3. New York: W. W. Norton, 1995.

Smith, Margaret Bayard. *The First Forty Years of Washington Society, Portrayed by the Family Letters of Mrs. Samuel Harrison Smith (Margaret Bayard) from the Collection of her Grandson, J. Henley Smith.* New York: Scribner's, 1906.

Smith, Margaret Bayard. "Mrs Madison." In *The National Portrait Gallery of Distinguished Americans,* edited by James B. Longacre and James Herring. Vol. 3. New York: Hermon Bancroft, 1836.

Stagg, J. C. A., ed. *The Papers of James Madison: Presidential Series.* Vol. 2. Charlottesville: University Press of Virginia, 1992.

Taylor, Robert J., ed. *The Adams Papers.* Series 3: *Papers of John Adams.* Vols. 2–4. Cambridge, MA: Harvard University Press, 1977–1979.

Tilton, James, M.D. "An Oration, Pronounced on the 5th July, 1790." *Universal Asylum and Columbian Magazine* 5 (December 1790): 369–372.

Van Horne, John C., ed. *Correspondence and Miscellaneous Papers of Benjamin Henry Latrobe.* Vol. 2: *1805–1810.* New Haven, CT: Yale University Press, 1986).

Warren-Adams Letters: Being Chiefly a Correspondence among John Adams, Samuel Adams, and James Warren . . . 1743–1814. [Boston]: Massachusetts Historical Society, 1917–1925.

Wollstonecraft, Mary. *A Vindication of the Rights of Woman: With Strictures on Political and Moral Subjects.* Boston: Thomas & Andrews, 1792.

NEWSPAPERS

Alexandria Advertiser and Commercial Intelligencer (Virginia).

Aurora (Philadelphia), November 11, 1797.

Federal Republican.

Gazette (New York).

Ladies Magazine and Literary Gazette.

Port Folio.

BOOKS AND DISSERTATIONS

Abrams, Jeanne E. *Revolutionary Medicine: The Founding Fathers and Mothers in Sickness and in Health.* New York: New York University Press, 2013.

Adams, Henry. *The Life of Albert Gallatin.* Philadelphia: J. B. Lippincott, 1879.

Akers, Charles W. *Abigail Adams: An American Woman.* Boston: Little, Brown, 1980.

Allgor, Catherine. *Parlor Politics: In Which the Ladies of Washington Help Build a City and a Government.* Charlottesville: University Press of Virginia, 2000.

Allgor, Catherine. *A Perfect Union: Dolley Madison and the Creation of the American Nation.* New York: Henry Holt, 2008.

Allgor, Catherine, ed. *The Queen of America: Mary Cutts's Life of Dolley Madison.* Charlottesville: University of Virginia Press, 2012.

Anthony, Carl Sferrazza. *First Ladies: The Saga of the Presidents' Wives and Their Power, 1789–1961.* New York: William Morrow, 1990.

Arnett, Ethel Stephens. *Mrs. James Madison: The Incomparable Dolley.* Greensboro, NC: Piedmont Press, 1972.

Anzilotti, Cara. *In the Affairs of the World: Women, Patriarchy, and Power in Colonial South Carolina.* Westport, CT: Greenwood Press, 2002.

Berkin, Carol. *Revolutionary Mothers: Women in the Struggle for America's Independence.* New York: Alfred A. Knopf, 2005.

Bilder, Mary Sarah. *Madison's Hand: Revising the Constitutional Convention.* Cambridge, MA: Harvard University Press, 2015.

Brady, Patricia. *Martha Washington: An American Life.* New York: Viking, 2005.

Brandt, Irving. *The Fourth President: A Life of James Madison.* Indianapolis, IN: Bobbs-Merrill, 1970).

Branson, Susan. *These Fiery Frenchified Dames: Women and Political Culture in Early National Philadelphia.* Philadelphia: University of Pennsylvania Press, 2001.

Breen, T. H. *American Insurgents, America Patriots: The Revolution of the People.* New York: Hill & Wang, 2010.

Breen, T. H. *George Washington's Journey: The President Forges a New Nation.* New York: Simon & Schuster, 2016.

Breen, T. H. *The Marketplace of Revolution: How Consumer Politics Shaped American Independence.* New York: Oxford University Press, 2004.

Brekke, Linzy A. "Fashioning America: Clothing, Consumerism, and the Politics of Appearance in the Early Republic." Ph.D. dissertation, Harvard University, 2007.

Bryan, Helen. *Martha Washington: First Lady of Liberty.* New York: John Wiley & Sons, 2002.

Caroli, Betty Boyd. *First Ladies.* New York: Oxford University Press, 2010.

Chadwick, Bruce. *General and Mrs. Washington: The Untold Story of a Marriage and a Revolution.* Naperville, IL: Sourcebook, 2007.

Chadwick, Bruce. *James and Dolley Madison: America's First Power Couple.* Amherst, NY: Prometheus Books, 2014.

Clark, Allen C. *Life and Letters of Dolley Madison.* Washington, DC: Press of W. F. Roberts Co., 1914.

Conger, Vivian Bruce. *The Widow's Might: Widowhood and Gender in Early British America.* New York: New York University Press, 2009.

Cutts, Lucia B. *Memoirs and Letters of Dolley Madison.* Port Washington, NY: Kennikat Press, 1971. Originally published 1886.

Decatur, Stephen, Jr. *Private Affairs of George Washington: From the Records and Accounts of Tobias Lear, Esquire, His Secretary.* New York: De Capo Press, 1969. Originally published 1933.

Demos, John. *A Little Commonwealth: Family Life in Plymouth Colony.* 2nd ed. New York: Oxford University Press, 2000.

Desan, Suzanne. *The Family on Trial in Revolutionary France.* Berkeley: University of California Press, 2004.

Duffy, John. *Epidemics in Colonial America.* Baton Rouge: Louisiana State University Press, 1951.

Elias, Norbert. *The Court Society*. Translated by Edmund Jephcott. New York: Pantheon Books, 1983.

Ellet, Elizabeth. *The Court Circles of the Republic*. Hartford, CT: Hartford Publishing Co., 1869.

Ellis, Joseph. *First Family: Abigail and John*. New York: Knopf, 2010.

Ellis, Joseph. *Founding Brothers: The Revolutionary Generation*. New York: Vintage, 2001.

Ellis, Joseph J. *The Quartet: Orchestrating the Second American Revolution, 1783–1789*. New York: Alfred A Knopf, 2015.

Foster, Thomas A. *Sex and the Founding Fathers: The American Quest for a Reliable Past*. Philadelphia: Temple University Press, 2015.

Fraser, Flora. *The Washingtons: George and Martha: "Join'd by Friendship, Crown'd by Love."* New York: Alfred A. Knopf, 2015.

Gelles, Edith B. *Abigail Adams: A Writing Life*. New York: Routledge, 2002.

Gelles, Edith B. *Abigail and John: Portrait of a Marriage*. New York: William Morrow, 2009.

Gelles, Edith B. *Portia: The World of Abigail Adams*. Bloomington: Indiana University Press, 1992.

Gerson, Noel B. *The Velvet Glove*. Nashville, TN: Thomas Nelson, 1975.

Goodman, Dena. *The Republic of Letters: A Cultural History of the French Enlightenment*. Ithaca, NY: Cornell University Press, 1994.

Gordon-Reed, Annette, and Peter S. Onuf. *"Most Blessed of the Patriarchs": Thomas Jefferson and the Empire of the Imagination*. New York: W. W. Norton, 2016.

Gould, Lewis L., ed. *American First Ladies: Their Lives and Their Legacy*. New York: Garland Press, 1996.

Gunderson, Joan R. *To Be Useful to the World: Women in Revolutionary America, 1740–1790*. New York: Twayne Publishers, 1996.

Hamilton, Gail. *Biography of James G. Blaine*. Norwich, CT: H. Bill Publishing, 1895.

Hartigan-O'Connor, Ellen. *The Ties That Buy: Women and Commerce in Revolutionary America*. Philadelphia: University of Pennsylvania Press, 2009.

Hedley, Olwen. *Queen Charlotte*. London: John Murray, 1975.

Hendricks, Nancy. *America's First Ladies*. Santa Barbara, CA: ABC-Clio, 2015.

Hesse, Carla. *The Other Enlightenment: How French Women Became Modern*. Princeton, NJ: Princeton University Press, 2001.

Holton, Woody. *Abigail Adams*. New York: Free Press, 2009.

Howard, Hugh. *Mr. and Mrs. Madison's War*. New York: Bloomsbury Press, 2012.

Hunt, Lynn. *Inventing Human Rights: A History*. New York: W. W. Norton, 2007.

Jacobs, Diane. *Dear Abigail: The Intimate Lives and Revolutionary Ideas of Abigail Adams and Her Two Sisters*. New York: Ballantine Books, 2014.

Kaminski, John P. *The Quotable Abigail Adams*. Cambridge, MA: Harvard University Press, 2009.

Kennon, Donald R., ed. *A Republic for the Ages: The United States and the Political Culture of the Early Republic*. Charlottesville: University Press of Virginia, 1999.

Kerber, Linda K. *Towards an Intellectual History of Women*. Chapel Hill: University of North Carolina Press, 1997.

Kerber, Linda K. *Women of the Republic: Intellect and Ideology in Revolutionary America*. Chapel Hill: University of North Carolina Press, 1980.

Kierner, Cynthia A. *Beyond the Household: Women's Place in the Early South*. Ithaca, NY: Cornell University Press, 1998.

Landes, Joan B. *Women and the Public Sphere in the Age of the French Revolution*. Ithaca, NY: Cornell University Press, 1988.

Lilti, Antoine. *The World of the Salons: Sociability and Worldliness in Eighteenth-Century Paris*. Translated by Lydia G. Cochrane. New York: Oxford University Press, [2015].

Lusane, Clarence. *The Black History of the White House*. New York: City Lights Open Press, 2011.

Meachem, Jon. *Thomas Jefferson: The Art of Power*. New York: Random House, 2012.

Moats, Sandra. *Celebrating the Republic: Presidential Ceremony and Popular Sovereignty, from Washington to Monroe*. DeKalb: Northern Illinois University Press, 2010.

Norton, Mary Beth. *Liberty's Daughters: The Revolutionary Experience of American Women, 1750–1800*. Boston: Little, Brown, 1980.

Norton, Mary Beth. *Separated by Their Sex: Women in Public and Private in the Colonial Atlantic World*. Ithaca, NY: Cornell University Press, 2011.

Powell, John Harvey. *Bring Out Your Dead: The Great Plague of Yellow Fever in Philadelphia in 1793*. New York, Arno Press, 1970. Originally published 1949.

Radomsky, Susan. "The Social Life of Politics: Washington's Official Society and the Emergence of a National Political Elite." Ph.D. dissertation, University of Chicago, 2006.

Rasmussen, William M. S., and Robert S. Tilton. *George Washington: The Man behind the Myth*. Charlottesville: University of Virginia Press, 1999.

Roberts, Cokie. *Ladies of Liberty*. New York: William Morrow, 2008.

Sadosky, Leonard J., Peter Nicolaisen, Peter S. Onuf, and Andrew J. O'Shaughnessy, eds. *Old World, New World: America and Europe in the Age of Jefferson*. Charlottesville: University of Virginia Press, 2010.

Scofield, Merry Ellen. "Assumptions of Authority: Social Washington's Evolution from Republican Court to Self-Rule, 1801–1831." Ph.D. dissertation, Wayne State University, 2014.

Smith, Barbara Clark. *The Freedoms We Lost: Consent and Resistance in Revolutionary America*. New York: Free Press, 2010.

Steele, Brian. *Thomas Jefferson and American Nationhood*. New York: Cambridge University Press, 2012.

Taylor, Alan, *American Revolutions: A Continental History, 1750–1804*. New York: W. W. Norton, 2016.

Truman, Harry S. *Harry S. Truman 1947 Diary*. Independence, MO: Harry S. Truman Library and Museum, 2003. www.trumanlibrary.org.

Ulrich, Laurel Thatcher. *Good Wives: Image and Reality in the Lives of Women in North-ern New England*. New York: Oxford University Press, 1983.

Walstreicher, David, and Matthew Mason, eds. *John Quincy Adams and the Politics of Slavery*. New York: Oxford University Press, 2016.

Watson, Robert P., ed. *American First Ladies*. Pasadena, CA: Salem Press, 2002.

Watson, Robert P., and Anthony J. Eksterowicz, eds. *The Presidential Companion: Readings on the First Ladies*. Columbia: University of South Carolina Press, 2003.

Wulf, Karin. *Not All Wives: Women of Colonial Philadelphia*. Ithaca, NY: Cornell University Press, 2000.

Young, Alfred, ed. *The American Revolution: Explorations in the History of Radicalism*. DeKalb: Northern Illinois University Press, 1976.

Zagarri, Rosemarie. *Revolutionary Backlash: Women and Politics in the Early Republic*. Philadelphia: University of Pennsylvania Press, 2007.

ARTICLES

Ames, William. "The National Intelligencer: Washington's Leading Political News-paper." *Records of the Columbia Historical Society, Washington, D.C.* 66 (1966/1968): 71–73.

Arendt, Emily J. "'Ladies Going about for Money': Female Voluntary Associations and Civic Consciousness in the American Revolution." *Journal of the Early Republic* 34 (Summer 2014): 157–186.

Crane, Elaine Forman. "Abigail Adams, Gender Politics, and 'The History of Em-ily Montague': A Postscript." *William and Mary Quarterly* 64 (October 2007): 839–844.

Crews, Ed. "Thomas Jefferson: Culinary Revolutionary." *Colonial Williamsburg Journal*, Summer 2013. www.history.org.

De Pauw, Linda Grant. "The American Revolution and the Right of Women: The Feminist Theory of Abigail Adams." In *Legacies of the American Revolution*, edited by Larry R. Gerlach, James A. Dolph, and Michael L. Nicholls, 199–219. Provo: Utah State University Press, 1978.

Ditz, Toby L. "Masculine Republics and 'Female Politicians' in the Age of Revolution." *Journal of the Early Republic* 35 (Summer 2015): 263–269.

Gelles, Edith B. "The Marriage of Abigail and John Adams." In *Inside the American Couple*, edited by Marilyn Yalom and Laura Carstensen, 32–49. Berkeley: University of California Press, 2002.

Hunt, Galliard. "Mrs. Madison's First Drawing Room." *Harper's Monthly Magazine* 121 (June 1, 1910): 141–148.

Hunter, John. "An Account of a Visit Made to Washington at Mount Vernon, by an English Gentleman, in 1785: From the Diary of John Hunter." *Pennsylvania Maga-zine of History and Biography* 17 (1893): 76–82.

Kerber, Linda K. "'I Have Don . . . much to Carrey on the Warr': Women and the Shaping of Republican Ideology after the American Revolution." In *Women and*

Politics in the Age of the Democratic Revolution, edited by Harriet B. Applewhite and Darline G. Levy, 227–257. Ann Arbor: University of Michigan Press, 1990.

Klein, Lawrence E. "Gender and the Public/Private Distinction in the Eighteenth Century." *Eighteenth-Century Studies* 29 (Fall 1995): 93–105.

Levin, Phyllis Lee. "Abigail (Smith) Adams." In *American First Ladies, Their Lives and Their Legacy*, edited by Lewis L. Gould, 16–44. New York: Garland Press, 1996.

Lewis, Jan. "Politics and the Ambivalence of the Private Sphere: Women in Early Washington, D.C." In *A Republic for the Ages: The United States and the Political Culture of the Early Republic*, edited by Donald R. Kennon, 122–151. Charlottesville: University Press of Virginia, 1999.

Lewis, Jan. "The Republican Wife: Virtue and Seduction in the Early Republic." *William and Mary Quarterly* 44 (October 1987): 689–721.

Lilti, Antoine. "The Kingdom of Politesse: Salons and the Republic of Letters in Eighteenth-Century Paris." *Republics of Letters: A Journal for the Study of Knowledge, Politics, and the Arts* 1 (May 1, 2009): 1–11.

Mayo, Edith P. "Party Politics: The Political Impact of the First Ladies' Social Role." *Social Science Journal* 37, no. 4 (2000): 577–590.

Newman, Simon, P. "Principles or Men? George Washington and the Political Culture of National Leadership, 1776–1801." *Journal of the Early Republic* 12 (Winter 1992): 477–507.

O'Connor, Karen, Bernadette Nye, and Laura Van Assendelft. "Wives in the White House: The Political Influence of First Ladies." *Presidential Studies Quarterly* 26, no. 3 (Summer 1996): 835–853.

Parry-Giles, Shawn J., and Diane M. Blair. "The Rise of the Rhetorical First Lady: Politics, Gender Ideology, and Women's Voice." *Rhetoric and Public Affairs* 5 (Winter 2002): 565–599.

Perkins, Bradford. "A Diplomat's Wife in Philadelphia: Letters of Henrietta Liston, 1796–1800." *William and Mary Quarterly* 11 (October 1954): 592–632.

Rosenfeld, Sophia. "'Europe,' Women, and the American Political Imaginary: The 1790s and the 1990s." *Journal of the Early Republic* 35 (Summer 2015): 272–277.

Ryerson, Richard A. "John Adams in Europe: A Provincial Cosmopolitan Confronts the Metropolitan World, 1778–1788." In *Old World, New World: America and Europe in the Age of Jefferson*, edited by Leonard J. Sadosky, Peter Nicolaisen, Peter S. Onuf, and Andrew J. O'Shaughnessy, 131–154. Charlottesville: University of Virginia Press, 2010.

Scofield, Merry Ellen. "Yea or Nay to Removing the Seat of Government: Dolley Madison and the Realities of 1814 Politics." *Historian* 74 (Fall 2012): 449–466.

Shields, David S., and Fredrika J. Teute. "The Court of Abigail Adams." *Journal of the Early Republic* 35 (Summer 2015): 227–235.

Shields, David S., and Fredrika J. Teute. "The Republican Court and the Historiography of a Women's Domain in the Public Sphere." *Journal of the Early Republic* 35 (Summer 2015): 169–183.

Shulman, Holly Cowan. "Dolley (Payne Todd) Madison." In *American First Ladies: Their Lives and Their Legacy*, edited by Lewis L. Gould, 45–68. New York: Garland Press, 1996.

Shulman, Holly C. "History, Memory, and Dolley Madison: Notes from a Documentary Editor." In *The Queen of America: Mary Cutts's Life of Dolley Madison*, edited by Catherine Allgor, 42–69. Charlottesville: University of Virginia Press, 2012.

Soderlund, Jean R. "Women's Authority in Pennsylvania and New Jersey Quaker Meetings, 1680–1760." *William and Mary Quarterly* 44 (October 1987): 722–749.

Teute, Fredrika J. "Roman Matron on the Banks of Tiber Creek: Margaret Bayard Smith and the Politicization of Spheres in the Nation's Capital." In *A Republic for the Ages: The United States Capitol and the Political Culture of the Early Republic*, edited by Donald R. Kennon, 89–121. Charlottesville: University Press of Virginia, 1999.

Teute, Fredrika J., and David S. Shields. "The Confederation Court." *Journal of the Early Republic* 35 (Summer 2015): 215–226.

Teute, Fredrika J., and David S. Shields. "Jefferson in Washington: Domesticating Manners in the Republican Court." *Journal of the Early Republic* 35 (Summer 2015): 237–259.

Troy, Gil. "Mr. and Mrs. President? The Rise and Fall of the Co-presidency." *Social Science Journal* 37 (2000): 591–600.

Wekkin, Gary D. "Role Constraints and First Ladies." *Social Science Journal* 37 (2000): 601–610.

Wilson, Gaye. "Jefferson and the Creation of an American Image Abroad." In *Old World, New World: America and Europe in the Age of Jefferson*, edited by Leonard J. Sadosky, Peter Nicolaisen, Peter S. Onuf, and Andrew J. O'Shaughnessy, 155–178. Charlottesville: University of Virginia Press, 2010.

Wilson, Joan Hoff. "The Illusion of Change: Women and the American Revolution." In *The American Revolution: Explorations in the History of Radicalism*, edited by Alfred F. Young, 384–445. DeKalb: Northern Illinois University Press, 1976.

Wood, Gordon S. "Pursuit of Happiness." *New Republic*, April 8, 2004. https://newrepublic.com.

Young, Alfred F. "The Women of Boston: 'Persons of Consequence' in the Making of the Revolution, 1765–76." In *Women and Politics in the Age of the Democratic Revolution*, edited by Harriet B. Applewhite and Darline G. Levy, 181–226. Ann Arbor: University of Michigan Press, 1990.

Zagarri, Rosemarie. "Morals, Manners, and the Republican Mother." *American Quarterly* 44 (June 1992): 102–215.

Zagarri, Rosemarie. "The Rights of Man and Woman in Post-Revolutionary America." *William and Mary Quarterly* 55 (April 1998): 203–230.

Zagarri, Rosemarie. "Women and Party Conflict in the Early Republic." In *Beyond the Founders: New Approaches to the Political History of the Early American Republic*, edited by Jeffrey L. Pasley, Robert W. Robertson, and David Waldstreicher, 107–128 Chapel Hill: University of North Carolina Press, 2004.

INDEX

ABOUT THE AUTHOR

Jeanne E. Abrams is Professor at the University Libraries and the Center for Judaic Studies at the University of Denver. She received her Ph.D. in American history from the University of Colorado at Boulder with a specialization in archival management. She is the author of *Jewish Women Pioneering the Frontier Trail: A History in the American West* (New York University Press, 2006), *Dr. Charles David Spivak: A Jewish Immigrant and the American Tuberculosis Crusade,* and *Revolutionary Medicine: The Founding Fathers and Mothers in Sickness and in Health* (New York University Press, 2013), as well as numerous articles in the fields of American, Jewish, and medical history that have appeared in scholarly journals and popular magazines. *Revolutionary Medicine* was reviewed widely in scholarly journals and the popular media, including the *Wall Street Journal,* and was named one of the *Top Books for Docs* by *Medscape.*